KU-541-564

The Dobies Book of Greenhouses

Frontispiece (Overleaf): Glass to ground, span-roofed cedar greenhouse

The Dobies
Book of Greenhouses

ARTHUR HELLYER
MBE FLS VMH AHRHS

Drawings by Debbie Kartun

Published in collaboration with Samuel Dobie & Son Limited

HEINEMANN:LONDON

By Arthur Hellyer

Carters Book for Gardeners
The Shell Guide to Gardens
The Amateur Gardener
Amateur Gardening Pocket Guide
Practical Gardening for Amateurs
Practical Gardening Illustrated
The Collingridge Encyclopaedia of Gardening
The Encyclopaedia of Garden Work and Terms
Picture Dictionary of Popular Flowering Plants
All Colour Gardening Book
All Colour Book of Indoor and Greenhouse Plants

Shrubs in Colour
Flowers in Colour
Garden Plants in Colour
Your New Garden
Your Garden Week by Week
Your Lawn
Starting with Roses
Chrysanthemums for Everyone
Garden Pests and Diseases
Gardens to Visit in Britain
Gardens of Genius

William Heinemann Ltd
10 Upper Grosvenor Street, London W1X 9PA

LONDON   MELBOURNE   TORONTO
JOHANNESBURG   AUCKLAND

© Samuel Dobie & Son Limited 1981
First published 1981
SBN 434 32626 7

Cedar glasshouse illustrations kindly loaned by Alton Glasshouses Ltd
Aluminium greenhouse illustrations loaned by Marley Greenhouses
Illustrations of pests and diseases kindly supplied by
Fisons Agro-Chemical Ltd, Murphy Chemical Ltd, and Pan-Britannica Industries Ltd

Printed by Caledonian Graphics Cumbernauld · Leeds · London

Contents

List of Tables

At work in a greenhouse, one is virtually independent of all weather.

Foreword

A garden without a greenhouse is as incomplete as a tale without a beginning. More and more people are coming to realize and appreciate the limitations imposed on their gardening by not having a place where they can start tender plants into growth, and where the very tender ones can flourish free from the harsh realities of our climate.

Seeds of half-hardy annuals such as petunias and lobelias may be sown in the greenhouse to produce plants for bedding out when the last of the frost has gone. A wide variety of pot plants can be grown from seed to flowering, for a fraction of the cost of bought plants. By carefully selecting the kinds and varieties, a steady succession of beautiful flowering and foliage plants can be available for the house all the year round: fuchsias, coleus and geraniums for the summer, for instance; and things like cyclamens and cinerarias to brighten the winter window sills.

Then there are the vegetables that need the comforting warmth of a greenhouse to get them going, or those that only yield well when grown all their lives under glass. Celery, sweet corn and courgette marrows are some vegetables that it pays to sow early in warmth for planting out later. Others, such as tomatoes, cucumbers and peppers will be heavily laden with fresh, delicious crops as rewards for the care and protection the gardener and his greenhouse afford them.

The author, Arthur Hellyer, has spent a lifetime growing all kinds of plants indoors and out. In this book he chronicles his many years of experience and expertise in the greenhouse – and all who read and follow his invaluable advice are assured of success.

S<small>AMUEL</small> D<small>OBIE</small> & S<small>ON</small>

Introduction

Gardeners, like farmers, are noted for blaming everything on the weather and there is no doubt that sometimes it can make things very difficult. But with a greenhouse one can become virtually independent of all weather, creating and controlling a climate of one's own to suit the plants and crops of one's choice. At a stroke, gardening horizons are immeasurably extended. Gone are the restrictions of temperature, water supply and humidity and there is hardly anything that cannot be grown within the limitations imposed by greenhouse size, provided one is prepared to take the necessary care and provide the required temperatures. There is no beauty from the tropics that cannot be enjoyed, no rarity that cannot be displayed to gardening friends, no tender crop that cannot be cultivated once the requirements of each have been fully understood.

There are also economic advantages to be gained from a greenhouse. Seeds can be germinated earlier and with greater certainty than would be possible outdoors, and cuttings of many plants can be rooted. Instead of having to buy plants one can raise them at home and even have some surplus to sell or give away to one's friends. By these means a greenhouse can actually become an economy, saving its owner money and paying for its cost in a few years.

For those who are gardening enthusiasts, it provides a means of continuing their hobby even when the weather is too bad to work outdoors – or, if the greenhouse is lighted, after dark. My own experience is that, having once acquired a greenhouse, one soon begins to wonder how one ever managed to garden without it.

English gardeners first felt the need for some kind of structure to protect plants when oranges first appeared in the country at the close of the sixteenth century. To begin with they used quite crude structures which John Evelyn described as tabernacles of boards but soon they became far more elaborate and the 'orangery', as it came to be known, began to occupy a prominent position as one of the highly decorative buildings in the garden.

Yet even at this stage there was no close resemblance to what we now know as a greenhouse since orangeries were largely built of stone or brick, with glass, as a rule, confined to the front or possibly to front and two ends. The roof would be solid and there would either be no heating at all or perhaps an open stove. As structures became more sophisticated in response to gardeners' demands for more efficient plant houses, flues were constructed in the back walls and these spread the heat more evenly and protected the plants from the ill effects of fumes.

Increasingly elaborate orangeries persisted until the early years of the nineteenth century by which time they were being used for many other plants besides oranges. It was the arrival of large numbers of beautiful but rather tender plants from South Africa – including the tender heathers or heaths, which became highly fashionable for a time – that really set gardeners searching for more efficient structures considered as homes for plants. More glass was used around the sides and over the roof and very beautiful conservatories were built such as that which still functions at Syon House, Brentford (*see* p. 144).

Masonry gave way to cast iron or wood; glazing bars became more slender and panes of glass larger and more numerous so that there was far more light within the structures than ever before. Heating was also improved by circulating warm water in cast-iron pipes connected with boilers which could be a considerable distance away. Incidentally the name 'greenhouse' dates right back to the earliest days when the prime function of a plant house was to protect the 'greens', i.e. the evergreen plants of which we have so few in the British Isles but which form so large a part of the vegetation in many warmer countries.

As structures which combined both utility and beauty, greenhouses had reached their peak by the mid-nineteenth century; and it is not surprising that glasshouses in the Victorian manner are back in fashion again, though mainly with the rich since they are expensive buildings to construct. The two contrasted developments most typical of our own times have been, on the one hand, vast and often ingeniously automated structures for large-scale commercial crop production and, at the other extreme, a proliferation of tiny greenhouses for amateurs which rapidly became so popular that soon there were almost more gardens with than without a greenhouse of some kind. For generations this was so peculiar to Britain that visitors from overseas often remarked that the feature which struck them most as they journeyed from the port of arrival to their destination was the number of greenhouses in the small back gardens which they could see from the train windows. Now the hobby is catching on more widely; English manufacturers are exporting small greenhouses to many countries and rival manufacturers from as far afield as North America are actually invading a market which for long seemed entirely our own. The do-it-yourself greenhouse kit can be purchased from almost any multiple stores, including Woolworths and Tesco, and the day does not seem far distant when almost every garden will have at least one greenhouse.

ARTHUR HELLYER

The orangery at Blickling Hall, Aylsham, Norfolk, built in 1781.

I Structure

What kind of Greenhouse?

There are so many designs of greenhouse and so many materials from which they can be made that selection can be very puzzling. Some matters may be resolved on purely personal grounds but two practical considerations should be kept firmly in mind. One is the place where the greenhouse must stand, the other the purpose for which it is required. The one may well have a bearing on the other for if the greenhouse must be placed, let us suppose, in a shady place it would be foolish to acquire it with the intention of growing sun-loving plants. The questions of site and orientation are dealt with below, and it will be wise to consider them before making a final decision about design and material, but here are some of the basic facts relating to both.

The most traditional design, and still probably the most popular, is the span-roofed greenhouse. This is shaped like a simple house that a child might draw with vertical (or nearly vertical) sides bearing a hipped (inverted V) roof. It has the twin merits of strength and simplicity and is an excellent choice if the house is to be entirely free standing. It is also available in a great range of sizes, from a tiny house measuring about $2 \times 1\frac{1}{2}$ m to grand constructions suitable for commercial production on the largest scale. This type of house can be glazed to ground level (see Frontispiece) or have solid walls of wood, brick, stone or concrete about waist height (see p. 2). Full glazing is best if many crops or plants are to be grown from ground level but greenhouses intended primarily for small pot plants and trays filled with seedlings or cuttings, all to be stood on staging, may just as well have low walls as these retain heat better than glass.

Perhaps the principal drawback of the span-roofed greenhouse is that it is not particularly interesting to look at. In a tiny garden that can matter, for it is difficult to conceal a greenhouse without limiting its usefulness and it can easily become the dominant garden structure. Many garden owners may find the solution to this is the so-called circular greenhouse which is very rarely strictly circular but has six, eight or even more sides supporting a more or less cone-shaped roof (see opposite). Some manufacturers are calling this a gazebo house, gazebo being an old architectural term for a little ornamental two-storeyed pavilion in the garden, and there is no doubt that well designed circular greenhouses can be distinctly decorative. However, they are not greatly adaptable as to size and are chiefly serviceable where there is only room for a small greenhouse.

The lean-to greenhouse is like one half of a span-roofed house and is designed to stand against a wall or building (see p. 5). It is the best type to use as a conservatory with direct access to the dwelling house though sometimes conservatories are designed with greater elaboration, or even

Opposite: 'Circular' greenhouse – octagonal, gazebo-shaped

Half-glass cedar greenhouse

ornamentation, to make them more decorative. The lean-to is economical to use since walls lose less heat than glass and, if the structure is placed against a building that is in constant use, it will derive a good deal of warmth from it. Like span-roofed greenhouses, lean-tos can be glazed to ground level or can have solid walls of wood, brick, stone or concrete to staging height.

What are often described as mini-greenhouses are really small lean-to structures designed to be hung on or stood against a wall. They are so narrow that it would be impossible to get inside them and

Glass to ground, span-roofed aluminium greenhouse – unequal span

they are usually fitted with sliding glazed panels in front so that plants growing in them can be tended from outside. In some circumstances it may be possible to fit them across windows so that they can also be tended from indoors. They are very economical to heat as absolutely all the space inside them is available for plants.

In addition to these basic types there are variations on them such as unequal-span houses and dome-shaped houses. Various advantages are claimed for them and some may be justified in certain circumstances but in general they do not seem likely ever to become popular or as generally serviceable as those already described. Portable greenhouses covered with polythene are frequently made tunnel-shaped and this is a very functional design for this flexible material.

Greenhouses may be framed with wood or metal and there is something to be said for and against each. Deal is probably still the cheapest material in first cost but can be the most costly in upkeep since it must be painted or treated with a safe wood preservative from time to time to prevent it from rotting. Creosote must not be used as the fumes given off in warm weather are poisonous to plants. Western red cedar costs a lot more but is much more lasting and rot resistant, and does not need painting. It is not a very strong wood and so is not recommended for large greenhouses; for them teak or some other hard wood must be used and that raises the price quite a lot.

Steel is strong and so the glazing bars can be narrow, which means that more light is admitted to the house, but it rusts badly and can be troublesome and costly to maintain. Aluminium alloys are light, fairly strong and immensely durable and they require virtually no maintenance. Many small houses made of them are sold in kit form, which means that transport costs are reduced to a minimum; indeed most of the smaller models can be brought home on the roof rack of a car. Despite the claims of the instruction books produced by the makers, most are a little fiddling to erect and a couple of days should be allowed for this, preferably with someone to hold pieces in place while nuts and bolts are fitted and tightened.

Glass is still the most favoured protective material for greenhouses, and for permanent structures it seems unlikely to be seriously challenged. But for light, easily portable greenhouses 600 gauge polythene sheeting has many advantages. It is usually stretched over a rigid metal frame, a series of tubular metal hoops in the simplest models much favoured by market gardeners. Small models can be obtained and also shapes more like those of the conventional glazed greenhouses. The polythene cover is unlikely to last more than two years but is readily and fairly cheaply replaced. The advantages of polythene houses are cheapness and ready portability but they may not retain heat so well as glass-covered houses, particularly during the radiation frosts (due to loss of soil warmth to a clear sky during windless still nights) which can be so damaging in spring. A minor drawback is that polythene transmits more ultraviolet light than horticultural glass, which is not good for some plants, but specially treated polythene can be obtained to cut out the ultraviolet. On the credit side the supports for the polythene can be widely spaced so that they cast little shade.

With glass-covered greenhouses the spacing of the glazing bars can also have a minor effect on the amount of light inside the greenhouse, which is usually unimportant in summer but can make a significant difference in winter. Widely spaced glazing bars mean large panes of glass which are relatively costly to replace when they get broken but probably on balance the advantage lies with fairly large panes and this is the direction in which manufacturers seem to be moving at the moment.

'Conservatory' is an old term rather loosely used nowadays but I take it to be any glazed structure for plants with direct access to the dwelling house. In this sense a lean-to greenhouse placed across French windows becomes a conservatory and some of the glazed 'house extensions' could justify the name. If they receive adequate light they can provide a very useful and often extremely economical method of creating a controlled climate for plants. Other alternatives to a conventional greenhouse are glazed verandahs, garden rooms and glazed loggias. In all cases what really determines their usefulness is the amount of light they admit. Since the human eye adjusts very rapidly to variations in light intensity it can be a poor guide as to the true light level, so when in doubt test with a light meter such as those used for photography, first taking a reading in the open and then another inside the structure. In a well designed, properly sited, free-standing greenhouse the difference is likely to be in the order of 5 per cent; if it is 10 per cent or more the range of plants that can be cultivated will be progressively restricted.

Large greenhouses and conservatories require proper foundations and, since the size of these will be related to the weight of the structure, this is a matter which should be discussed with the builder or

Lean-to or mini-greenhouse, adjacent to house

manufacturer. If the building is to be permanent it will almost certainly be controlled by local building regulations and the appropriate authority should be informed. Portable houses are usually sufficiently light to be supported on a row of bricks or concrete blocks or on the special foundation blocks which many manufacturers are able to supply.

What the floor should be made of depends a good deal on what the greenhouse is to be used for. Clearly if crops or plants are to be grown in beds of soil the floor must be of soil, though it may be convenient to lay a paved path through the centre or in some other convenient place so that plants can be tended in comfort. Conservatories are often paved more extensively so that chairs, and possibly a table, can be placed in them.

But even when all plants are to be grown in pots or other containers there is some advantage in having much of the floor area either soil or covered with gravel or stone chippings, any of which can be kept moist and will then give off much useful water vapour to the air.

Staging is convenient if many seedlings, cuttings and fairly small plants are to be grown. It is usually about 60 cm high and can be of any desired width, but if it is very wide it may be difficult to water and tend plants at the back of the staging. It can also be either open slat or solid and may be supported on metal or wood frames. Slat staging allows free circulation of air around the pots and plants but this is not always so desirable as it might appear. Solid staging can be covered with sand, gravel, stone chippings or special plastic mats all of which can be kept moist so that they give off water vapour exactly as a soil floor. Plants often seem to grow better on solid staging and it can also be used for capillary watering (*see* pp. 23–4).

Siting the Greenhouse

It is possible to grow plants in a greenhouse that gets no direct sunshine but inevitably the choice is very restricted and confined mainly to ferns and other shade-loving foliage plants. The greatest value is to be obtained by placing the greenhouse where it will get as much light as possible, for it is easy to provide shade but very difficult to produce an adequate substitute for sunshine. Moreover sunshine means warmth, and even on bitterly cold but bright days the temperature inside a greenhouse that catches all the sunshine can be pleasantly warm without any additional heat. So for reasons of economy as well as of plant health it is desirable to site the greenhouse where it can get sunshine for as many hours each day as possible.

In small gardens there may not be a great deal of choice where the greenhouse can go. It will probably have to be at one or other end of the garden, either near the house or as far as possible from it. If the garden front of the house faces north that automatically indicates the more distant position as preferable since even if in this situation the greenhouse is still shaded by the building in winter it is likely to get some direct sunshine as the sun mounts higher in the sky. But if the garden front has a southerly aspect there could well be advantages in placing the greenhouse near the house or even buying a lean-to greenhouse or conservatory and setting it against the house wall. It will derive shelter, and even some warmth, from the building and when the sun shines the wall, if painted white, will reflect light and warmth. It will almost certainly be cheaper to run electricity and/or gas (if available) and water into the greenhouse if it is close to the home and it may even be possible to connect to the domestic heating system which is almost always the most economical and easily controllable method of warming a greenhouse.

One drawback of the lean-to type of house is that the light comes mainly on one side and plants

A successful greenhouse – an almost infinite variety of plants can be grown.

tend to grow towards it. Exactly the same thing happens when plants are grown on a window ledge and they quickly become lopsided unless each pot is turned a little every day or so in order to even out the amount of illumination each part of the plant gets.

A free-standing house will get quite a lot of illumination even from the northern sky and this tends to keep growth balanced. If a span-roofed house is placed so that its long axis runs more or less east and west it is possible that plants growing on the south side of the greenhouse will shade those on the north side but this seems more a theoretical than a practical drawback. There is, in any case, a drawback in the alternative north/south orientated house, for though it may seem to be an advantage that one side gets the morning sun and the other the afternoon sun (which should even things out) in fact the sunshine, particularly in winter when the sun is low in the sky, strikes the sloping roof at an oblique angle and some of it is uselessly reflected back to the sky. So what one gains on the swings one may well lose on the roundabouts. In fact in small gardens there is probably not much choice about the orientation of span-roofed greenhouses which must be placed according to the character of the site but if there are alternatives the balance of advantage is probably slightly in favour of an east/west orientation.

What is far more important is that the greenhouse should be as far removed as possible from any tree or other large objects which would deprive it of light and, most important of all, that tree branches should not extend over it. In comparing one possible site with another the light meter test is a good one since the human eye can be so readily deceived. Direct the meter at the ground where the house might stand rather than at the sky above it. On a bright fairly sunny day a reading of 11 to 12 on a Weston meter is good. This can be translated into terms applicable to most meters, even those built into TLM cameras, by saying that this light intensity would give an exposure time of $\frac{1}{50}$ second and stop f8 for a film of emulsion speed 64 ASA (19 DIN).

Also of importance in considering where the greenhouse should go are ease of access and the availability of any services that are required. It is convenient to be able to get to the greenhouse dry-shod even when the ground is very wet and it is also convenient to be able to barrow sacks of compost to it. If artificial heating is to be installed one must consider how it is to be applied and in what way. That may be influenced by siting. Electric cables can be expensive to install over long distances, especially if they are underground, and above ground they can be unsightly or unsafe. So on this score there is everything to be said for having the greenhouse close to the domestic mains supply. Much the same applies to North Sea gas but of course not to bottled gas, though the cylinders are fairly heavy so it is wise to have smooth paving on which to move them. If solid fuel heating is contemplated there must be a storage place for it that is both reasonably near the greenhouse and readily accessible from the road.

It may well be that it is impossible to meet all these requirements, and that some compromise will have to be made. In deciding any order of priorities I would place good light at the top of the list.

Is Heating Necessary?

A greenhouse, like a solar cell, is a device for catching and making use of the heat of the sun. When the sun is shining on it the air inside heats up rapidly and, because it is trapped, it can become very much warmer than the freely moving air outside. Even without sunshine some sun heat can be trapped and stored by day. At night the reverse process operates and heat is lost by conduction and by radiation, most rapidly when the sky is clear or the air is cold and moving fast. So without internal heating of some kind the temperature in a greenhouse will be in a constant state of flux, relatively high by day if the weather is bright (though this can be checked by ventilation) and probably falling most of the night until it reaches its lowest point about dawn. If a good deal of warmth has been trapped by day, sufficient may be stored to prevent the temperature falling to the outside level at night but one cannot guarantee this. Much less can one say to what level the temperature will fall after a dull day during which little or no heat has been trapped. If such weather persists for several days the air inside the greenhouse will eventually become as cold as that outside. At this stage the only climatic advantages to the plants inside the greenhouse will be protection from wind and rain. Both can be important but they are not sufficient to guarantee the survival of really tender plants, except perhaps in the warmer parts of the British Isles or during exceptionally mild winters. In most places a time is likely to come when frost will penetrate an unheated greenhouse and that can be fatal to many tender plants.

Another limitation of the unheated greenhouse is that it will probably be impossible to germinate seeds or start dormant plants into growth as early as if some extra heat is available. Even seeds of quite hardy vegetables require temperatures of 10–13 °C for reliable germination and that level is unlikely to be maintained before March in many parts of Britain without at least a little assistance from internal heating.

So there are many advantages to be gained from installing some form of heating. Against them must be weighed the cost of installing and running any kind of heating apparatus but the balance must nearly always be in favour of heating and the only serious argument concerns how much.

In considering this one must first of all determine the minimum temperature requirements of the plants one proposes to grow. It is important to realize that every rise in temperature involves a considerable rise in running costs. It is not simply that more heat will be required to obtain the higher temperature but that it will be required more frequently and for longer periods. To raise the minimum winter temperature of a greenhouse from 7 to 10 °C, a mere 3 °C, can double the fuel bill. To put it up from 7 to 13 °C could multiply the heating costs five times, and so it goes on. When these facts have been appreciated it may well be that some changes will be made in the list of plants to be grown. In a large collection of exotic plants it is usually possible to divide the plants into several groups according to their temperature requirements, and divide the house into sections to suit each group or to have several greenhouses each with its own temperature range. If there is only to be one fairly small house division may not be practicable and the plant with the highest temperature requirement will set the standard for all the rest. It could well be that two or three omissions from a proposed list of greenhouse plants could alter considerably the amount of extra warmth that will need to be provided.

The possible variations are infinite but for practical purposes it is convenient to consider them as four temperature regimes which can be called cold, cool, intermediate and warm. Cold means without any form of heating other than that provided by the sun, and its limitations have already been described.

Cool is taken, in this book, to be a structure in which the temperature is never allowed to fall below 7 °C. Most of the time from October to April the temperature will be around 10–13 °C and from May to September it will rise to 18 °C or even more, but only with sun heat. This is a very economical regime to maintain since internal heating is only likely to be required intermittently from about November to March. It is possible to grow a great many exotic plants in such a greenhouse but many of them would be happier in slightly higher winter temperatures and this would also make it possible to sow seeds of half hardy plants earlier.

The intermediate regime fulfils these requirements and is the most widely serviceable range if one can afford it. The minimum winter temperature is 13 °C with the average about 16 °C from October to April, rising several more degrees in summer. These temperatures can usually be maintained by sun heat alone from about May to September but more heat will be required more frequently from October to April than in a cool greenhouse.

A warm greenhouse is one in which the winter temperature never falls below 18 °C and the summer minimum is 21 °C. Even in summer sun heat may not always be adequate and in winter heat will be necessary most of the time for some tropical plants.

Most plants will survive in temperatures considerably less than those that are ideal for them

A greenhouse is of use both for germinating seedlings to plant out later and for growing plants which need constant protection.

provided they never actually freeze. It is the formation of ice in the plant cells, or in the spaces between them, that can prove fatal to a great many plants from warm climates and if this damage can be avoided it is sometimes possible to get away with temperatures far lower than those which expert gardeners prefer to maintain. But the more the temperature falls below the optimum level the more difficult it will be to keep plants healthy and in good condition.

If it is decided to heat the greenhouse the next question must be by what means. There are six main possibilities: paraffin stoves; oil-burning boilers; oil-burning stoves distributing heated air; gas; electricity; and various solid fuel boilers.

Paraffin stoves are the cheapest to install but not necessarily the cheapest to run. They have the advantage of ready portability and are most useful where heating is only required to exclude frost. Their drawback is a tendency to produce fumes which are damaging, or even fatal, to some plants. This risk can be reduced by keeping burners and air intakes clean, not using the stoves at quite full capacity, fitting them with horizontal flues, and screening them from draughts.

Oil-fuelled boilers are efficient and can be made entirely automatic with thermostatic control. Hot water pipes secure an even distribution of heat at a level that is not damaging to the atmosphere and a properly installed flue should minimize the risk of harmful fumes entering the house. However, they are relatively expensive to install and run.

Oil-fired air heaters are much used by commercial growers but are seldom seen in small greenhouses. Usually the warm air is blown in through perforated polythene ducts which distribute it evenly. Size for size they are less costly to install than oil-fuelled boilers but they are not any cheaper to run. They can be (and in most cases should be) thermostatically controlled.

Coal gas is not a good fuel for greenhouse heating because of the harmful fumes produced in combustion but natural gas is a totally different matter. If the byproducts of combustion are simply water vapour and carbon dioxide they can do no harm and may actually be beneficial, since carbon dioxide in the air is the source of all the carbon which plants use in manufacturing complex organic molecules. There are, however, other byproducts of combustion, largely determined by the heat of the flame: at low temperatures hydrocarbons such as ethylene are produced; at high temperatures, nitrogen oxides. All of these can be harmful to plants; but heat-exchanging flues may reduce their concentration. However, some ventilation is essential when burning any fuel inside a greenhouse. Apart from this, natural gas is a highly convenient method of heating. Small portable stoves can be placed inside the greenhouse and be controlled by built-in thermostats. Cost of stoves and installation is moderate and, where North Sea gas is available, this can be the most economical method of warming a small greenhouse.

Electricity scores for cleanliness and convenience and light, portable, fan-assisted heaters are available which can be moved about as freely as paraffin stoves. But electricity is not an economical means of producing heat. Costs can be reduced by using thermostatic control, so ensuring that stoves are only switched on when necessary, but even so electricity is unlikely to compare favourably with other fuels on running costs. Nevertheless, it is likely to remain a favourite means of heating small greenhouses because of its convenience. It is essential that all electrical fittings, including power sockets, are completely waterproof. Installation should always be carried out by someone with experience of this specialized work.

Solid fuel boilers are less convenient to manage than most other types of greenhouse heating and are fairly costly to install but may be economical to run especially if more or less continuous heating is required for fairly long periods. They are less satisfactory for intermittent heating and are most likely to be worth consideration for greenhouses that are to be run at intermediate or warm temperatures.

Do not overlook the fact that heat can be conserved by concentrating it where it is most needed. It may be possible to divide the greenhouse internally so that one section is kept warmer than another. The more tender plants and the early seedlings can be kept in the warmer section until it is safe to move them on to the other. Alternatively, a small frame with its own heating system can be placed inside the greenhouse. Various propagators are made expressly for this purpose, some with air or soil warming usually by means of electrical cable or tungsten filament bulbs. Water, warmed by small immersion heaters similar to those used for tropical aquariums, is also used. The small volume of air inside such frames can be warmed very economically, especially when it has the additional protection of a greenhouse, and temperatures of around 18 °C can be maintained in which most seeds will germinate rapidly. However, it is wise to bear in mind the fact that the seedlings will grow fast and soon require much more room and if the temperature of the greenhouse is very much lower than that of the frame it may be difficult to make the transition from one to the other safely.

There are those who contend that soil temperature is more important than air temperature in determining the time and speed at which plants grow and that it is more economical to warm the soil than the air. They usually advocate warming the soil inside the greenhouse to a temperature of about 18 °C with special electrical cables buried 10–15 cm below the surface and only using enough air heating to exclude frost. Undoubtedly this works well for some plants though not necessarily for all.

When thermostats are built into a heating apparatus, as they usually are with small gas and electrical appliances, one must accept them as they are but realize that they may not register the true temperature of the house. They are likely to be too close to the source of heat for this and they may even be in the direct flow of an expeller fan which will falsify the reading. A little experiment using a maximum/minimum registering thermometer as a check, should reveal the nature and extent of the error and make it possible to decide on a setting that will give reasonably satisfactory results. However, the ideal is a separate thermostat placed fairly centrally in the house but screened from direct sunshine by a bright metal reflector.

Schlumbergera buckleyi (see p. 120)

Ventilation and Shading

It is easy to confuse the needs of human beings with those of plants. We require ventilation to rid the air of the carbon dioxide which we exhale and which, if allowed to accumulate too much, would kill us. Plants must have carbon dioxide which they use as food and in the process restore oxygen to the air. They also respire, i.e. give off to the air both water vapour and carbon dioxide, so that they are quite capable of maintaining a stable atmosphere and living indefinitely in an almost completely closed place, such as a bottle garden or plant cabinet.

So the primary purposes of greenhouse ventilation are not to provide fresh air to prevent suffocation but to control temperature and humidity – two factors of vital importance to plant health.

The problems are greater in small greenhouses than in large ones since small volumes of air can change their temperature and their moisture content more rapidly than large ones. Moreover there is a tendency for small houses to be underequipped with ventilators usually because manufacturers try to cut costs to undersell their competitors. Some offer additional ventilators as an optional extra and it may be well worthwhile to invest in these. To keep the temperature of a small greenhouse down to acceptable levels for most plants on sunny summer days it may well be necessary to be able to change the air inside the house every two minutes and one small ventilator in the roof of a 10×8 ft greenhouse is not sufficient for this unless the door is also left wide open. Many of the troubles that occur in small greenhouses are due to rapidly rising temperatures in the early morning when the sun is shining brightly but before anyone is about to open the ventilators. Unless a maximum/minimum registering thermometer is installed in the house and is reset every morning and evening these sudden changes in temperature may not be suspected and symptoms such as singed leaves, bud dropping and other ills are likely to be wrongly ascribed to disease or other causes.

Didiscus caeruleus (see p. 56)

One way of controlling temperatures in bright weather is to fit ventilators with automatic openers controlled by the temperature of the air inside the house. Most of these operate on a simple piston and lever mechanism, the cylinder in which the piston fits being filled with a compound which expands considerably when warmed. These excellent devices are completely independent of electricity and, once correctly adjusted to open directly a required temperature is reached, they require virtually no attention. An alternative is to equip a greenhouse with one or more electrically operated extraction fans but the small fans used for domestic ventilation may not be adequate for the task and it is wise to obtain equipment designed for greenhouses. The fan should be controlled by a thermostat placed inside the house in a place where it will give a reasonably true reading of the temperature.

Failing any form of automatic control it is usually wise in summer to err on the side of over-ventilation, maybe opening the ventilators wide early in the morning before leaving for work and not closing them until about an hour before sunset. At this season too much heat is usually more likely to cause damage than too little. It is when the temperature rises to 30 °C and more that serious harm can be done. By contrast in winter it is wise to err on the side of under-ventilation since at this season cold is more likely to do the damage.

Humidity and temperature are closely interlinked since the air will tend to become dry as it warms up and to remain damp when it is cold. This may suit some plants but by no means all. Many tropical plants like to grow in warm, steamy air and to maintain this in a greenhouse may not be all that easy. Plants can be syringed with water several times a day, walls and stagings can be soaked with water or shallow troughs filled with water can be placed in the house, possibly accommodated under the staging. But if the temperature rises too much and the ventilators are opened to cool it the moist air will escape and may be replaced with drier air from outside. Shading may then provide the best solution since this, too, is at least in part a device to control temperature though it is also necessary for some plants which actually prefer to grow in the shade.

There are numerous ways of shading greenhouses, from the very simple method of spraying or painting the glass with limewash or a proprietary shading compound to highly sophisticated systems employing coloured fluid running over the glass. Shading compounds suffer the drawback of being semi-permanent. They are usually applied in May or early June and washed off in September or early October. More serviceable are blinds that can be raised and lowered at will and many greenhouse manufacturers supply blinds to fit their houses. It is an advantage if they can be inside where they are protected from the weather. For some plants which like dappled light, such as would occur naturally beneath fairly widely spaced trees, more permanent lath shading may be ideal. Many greenhouses designed for orchids are equipped with such shading, the laths spaced a few centimetres apart and fitted 10–15 cm above the glass on the sunny side of the house.

In the autumn and winter damp air can be more of a problem than dry air and can encourage fungi of many kinds to attack plants that are not used to it. It may then be necessary to use a combination of internal heating and ventilation to dry the air inside the house without making it too hot. This is a skill which can only be learned by experience though experts can help by giving advice about the means which should be used and indicating which plants like relatively dry air and which prefer moist.

A slight complication is that though most people are familiar with thermometers, know how to read them, and understand precisely what is meant by instructions such as 'average temperature 15–18 °C', few know much about hygrometers and even expert gardeners seldom express humidity requirements in terms that can be read on such instruments. They talk about a 'humid atmosphere' or a 'buoyant atmosphere' without explaining (or perhaps even knowing) precisely what they mean. For convenience such terms are used in this book and I shall now define them as follows: humid = relative humidity 70–80 per cent; buoyant = 50–60 per cent; dry = 30–40 per cent. Small hygrometers are readily available at a modest price in most garden shops and one placed inside each greenhouse will provide a useful guide to the humidity of the air.

Gesneria cardinalis compacta (see p. 63)

2 Cultivation

Soil Mixtures for Greenhouse Plants

When outdoors, plants are usually grown in the natural soil of the site, well cultivated and suitably enriched with manure and fertilizers. In greenhouses this is only advisable when the plants are growing more or less unrestrictedly in beds on the ground. Directly they are confined to pots or containers it becomes necessary to prepare special mixtures for them. The reason for this is that soil isolated in this way behaves in a different way from soil that is in contact with all the surrounding soil, including the subsoil, down below. It easily loses its texture and its plant foods; it can quickly become sour or impoverished or it may become so consolidated that neither air nor water can penetrate it.

To overcome these difficulties gardeners have always taken care to choose suitable kinds of soil for pot plants and have added other materials to improve its porosity. Years ago they used leaf mould, particularly that made from rotted beech or oak leaves, and this is still an excellent material if it can be acquired in sufficient quantity. Because this was often not possible, peat was substituted for leaf mould and has the advantage that it decays more slowly and so maintains a good spongy texture for a longer period. But peats come from many environments and differ greatly in character. Some are very fine and dusty when dry, others are much coarser and more fluffy. It is these latter kinds, usually sphagnum peats, that are the most suitable for pot plants.

Another traditional ingredient of soil mixes was sand, the coarser and grittier the better as then there was no danger of its binding as some very fine sands can. Such sands are still widely used, though because suitable grades are sometimes difficult to find, they are challenged by new materials such as perlite, polystyrene fragments or vermiculite. None of these has any nutrient value. They are used solely to give the soil mixture a suitable porous texture.

However, soil itself is now challenged as a base, partly because it is a heavy and rather dirty material to handle, partly because it varies so greatly in character. Peat can be standardized much more readily than loam, the particular kind of soil most favoured for seed and potting mixtures. Loam is a natural mixture of clay, sand, and humus (decaying organic matter) but the proportion of each can vary greatly and so can the loam's chemical content and its acidity or alkalinity, all of which affect the way plants grow.

As a result mixtures without loam have become very popular, usually based on peat with or without sand, perlite, or something of the kind, and always with added plant food since peat is very deficient in this. Peat mixtures work well, especially for some plants and for relatively short periods, but they do not retain plant food as long as do loam mixtures, and they break down more rapidly. As a result plants grown in peat mixtures usually require feeding earlier and more frequently than similar plants grown in loam mixtures and they are likely to require repotting more frequently. It is also even more necessary to ensure that they do not dry out as some peats are very difficult to moisten again.

So there are pros and cons for both soil and soilless mixtures and it becomes a personal choice which suits one best. Many gardeners will probably find, as I do, that peat mixtures are fine for seed sowing and for growing young plants but that soil mixtures are easier to manage when plants are to be grown in pots for a long time.

Many attempts have been made to standardize seed and potting mixtures, some of which are kept secret for commercial reasons. The most famous of those formulae that are free for anyone to copy are the John Innes Seed and Potting Composts and the University of California (UC) peat mixes. The former are based on loam, the latter on peat.

There are three basic John Innes formulae, one for seeds, one for potting, and one for cuttings, and also a number of variations on the potting compost.

Ingredients for the John Innes Seed Compost (JIS) are:

> 2 parts by bulk medium loam
> 2 parts by bulk granulated peat
> 1 part by bulk coarse sand

To each 10 l of this mixture is added 12 g of superphosphate of lime and 6 g of ground limestone or chalk. If intended for lime-hating plants the limestone or chalk should be replaced with 6 g of flowers of sulphur.

The ingredients for the basic John Innes Potting Compost (JIP No. 1) are:

> 7 parts by bulk medium loam
> 3 parts by bulk granulated peat
> 2 parts by bulk coarse sand

To each 10 l of this mixture is added 6 g of ground limestone or chalk and 30 g of John Innes Base Fertiliser which is itself prepared by mixing the following chemicals:

> 2 parts by weight superphosphate of lime
> 2 parts by weight hoof and horn meal
> 1 part by weight sulphate of potash

For lime-hating plants the ground limestone or chalk is replaced by 6 g of flowers of sulphur.

Richer variations of this mixture are recommended for certain hungry plants, and for plants as they grow bigger and need more food. The proportions of loam, peat and sand remain the same; it is only the quantities of base fertilizer and limestone, chalk or flowers of sulphur that vary as follows:

JIP No. 2 60 g of base fertilizer and 12 g of ground limestone, chalk, or flowers of sulphur per 10 l.
JIP No. 3 90 g of base fertilizer and 18 g of ground limestone, chalk, or flowers of sulphur per 10 l.
JIP No. 4 120 g of base fertilizer and 24 g of ground limestone, chalk, or flowers of sulphur per 10 l.

It is recommended that all loam used in John Innes composts should first be sterilized, preferably by steaming until it attains a temperature of 93 °C which should be maintained for about twenty minutes. This is sufficient to kill spores of fungi, pests, weed seeds, and many harmful bacteria, but not to destroy the texture of the soil.

There are also a number of University of California mixtures devised for particular purposes but the one that is most generally useful for greenhouse pot plants is made with equal parts by bulk of medium grade sphagnum peat and fine (but not binding) sand. To each litre of this mixture is added 1.5 g of hoof and horn meal, 0.15 g of nitrate of potash, 0.15 g of sulphate of potash, 1.5 g of superphosphate of lime, 4.5 g of finely powdered magnesium limestone and 1.5 g of finely powdered chalk or limestone. For a richer mix suitable for hungry plants or those that are in fairly large pots simply double up on the quantity of hoof and horn meal. Peat mixes containing hoof and horn meal do not store well and should be mixed as required and certainly used within a week. If to be mixed in bulk and stored omit the hoof and horn meal and add it later when the compost is to be used. Alternatively the mixture without any hoof and horn meal can be used and is excellent for young plants but will quickly run out of nitrogen and require supplementary food.

John Innes composts can be purchased ready for use but some that are sold under this name do not entirely follow the John Innes formulae. Many proprietary peat or other soilless mixes are also available but the formulae of these are hardly ever disclosed. There are also other proprietary mixtures on the market for some of which the formulae are stated.

A difficulty underlying all these attempts to standardize seed and potting mixtures is the impossibility of completely standardizing loam or even peat. Inevitably samples differ from place to place and even from time to time, particularly according to the weather prevailing when they are dug or cut. So the end products differ despite all efforts to the contrary.

Fortunately plants are very adaptable things and they can usually survive quite wide variations without suffering too badly. As the cost of proprietary mixes rises many gardeners may prefer to economize by making simple mixes at home and this is entirely possible. Ordinary garden soil, if reasonably good, can be used as a base with peat or leaf mould, sand and a mixed fertilizer. Such a homemade mix, which I use a lot myself, is prepared with 2 parts by bulk soil, 1 part by bulk sphagnum peat and slightly less than 1 part coarse sand. I do not follow these quantities slavishly but vary them a little according to the character of the ingredients. When well blended I squeeze and rub the mixture with my hands and like it to feel smooth and velvety yet with a touch of grittiness. After a little experiment, and watching the way plants and the soil behave, one gets the idea of what is required. The essential thing is that after several months of watering, the mixture must still be porous so that water drains through it quite quickly, yet this must be achieved without adding so much sand that the mixture dries out very fast and retains little plant food. I do not attempt to sterilize the soil because I find this so difficult to do properly but to avoid the danger of importing disease I do try to get my soil from some part of the garden where there has been no observed trouble. Weed seedlings are rather a nuisance but if they are pulled out while still very small they do no harm and homemade composts can save a great deal of money if one is growing a lot of plants or seedlings. To provide adequate plant food in this homemade mixture I add about 25 g of a good compound fertilizer such as Phostrogen or Vitax Q4 to each 10 litres of potting mixture.

For seeds and cuttings I use a mixture of equal parts of sphagnum peat and coarse sand without fertilizer but it is necessary to transplant from this early, as soon as cuttings or seedlings are well rooted, as it contains little plant food and plants

Veltheimia (see *p. 87*)

starve in it quickly. To overcome this some gardeners may prefer to add a light peppering of finely ground bone meal. All seed and potting mixes should be stored under cover. Outdoors rain will wash the soluble chemicals out of them and may spoil their texture. To preserve this they should be moist but not wet and this is the best condition in which to use them. If too dry the mixes will run about too freely and it will be impossible to make them suitably firm around roots. If too wet they will be sticky and difficult to handle and are very likely to become caked in the pots after a few weeks.

Most mixes (except where otherwise indicated) can be kept for quite a long time but do not improve with age and it is really better to make sufficient for a few weeks and then mix again.

It is possible to grow plants without any soil, with their roots suspended in, or constantly irrigated by, water containing all the necessary nutrients. Such systems of hydroponics require constant chemical monitoring and are not very practicable for untrained persons but a simple adaptation of the principle, known as hydroculture, is available for everyday use. The plants are grown in leca, heat-expanded nodules of clay much used for insulation in the building industry, placed in pots or other containers without drainage holes. A nutrient solution is prepared with tap water plus a special slow release, resin-based fertilizer and a 4 cm depth of this is poured into each container. Thereafter the fluid is topped up as necessary with plain tap water. It is possible to have a simple float device which indicates the level of the water and shows when more should be added. Under average conditions topping up is required every 7–10 days. The fertilizer usually lasts about six months, when a further charge should be added. Because the nutrients are released by ion exchange with other chemicals in the tap water there is little or no danger of giving an overdose and this is as nearly foolproof a system of soilless cultivation as has yet been devised. It does not suit all plants equally well and seems specially suitable for those with rather fleshy roots or which normally grow in damp conditions.

Sowing, Pricking Out and Potting

For seed sowing, especially if the seeds are very small, the soil or peat mix needs to be more finely broken than for potting. It can be rubbed through a fairly coarse sieve, say one with a 1 cm mesh, so that the fibre in the loam or peat is broken up and not left behind. It is valuable in preserving the spongy texture that is so necessary for good germination and growth.

Seed can be sown in pots, pans or seed trays, whichever is most convenient. (Corms can also be

Begonia corms are planted in peat to sprout.

Propagators provide an economical way of maintaining higher humidity and temperatures for seeds and cuttings. The cover ensures that no moisture is lost.

planted in pots or pans to sprout, as in the illustration opposite.) All should be filled level with the rim, then given a few sharp raps on a wooden bench or other firm surface to settle them down without making them hard. Finally the surface is pressed gently with a small wooden block to make a level bed to receive the seeds.

These may be scattered evenly over the surface, or they can be sown in tiny drills drawn with a pointed stick (a pencil will do), or they can be spaced evenly a few millimetres apart. Most seeds are then covered by sieving or scattering just a little more of the soil or peat mix over them, but the tiniest seeds, such as those of begonias, need no covering at all other than a sheet of glass and maybe on top of that a piece of newspaper placed over the container but out of contact with the soil. Even quite large seeds need only be covered to about their own depth when sown under glass since they need no protection from the weather and are more likely to germinate quickly if quite near the surface.

Whether they will germinate faster in light or darkness depends on the species but most seeds prefer the dark, and all like the soil to remain moist. The covering of glass is to retain the moisture in the soil and the sheet of newspaper to shield the seeds from sunshine but both need to be removed when the seeds germinate: the paper immediately the emerging seed leaves are seen, the glass a day or so later.

Most seeds germinate readily in a temperature around 18 °C and this is economically maintained in a propagator or small frame placed inside the greenhouse. Higher temperatures, up to 30 °C, are usually only necessary for the seeds of tropical plants and can actually retard the germination of some seeds. Low temperatures are also to be avoided, except for a few seeds, and scarcely any, even of quite hardy plants, germinate at temperatures of 10 °C or less.

As soon as the seeds have been sown, they should be well watered from a watering can fitted with a fine rose (spray) if they are medium to large size seeds, but by holding the container almost to its rim in

Pricking out with a dibber: seedlings are separated and dropped into holes, and the soil is pressed around their roots.

water if they are very tiny seeds. This is to prevent washing them out, as is possible when watering from above, but it is still necessary to take care that the rising water in the semi-immersed pot or pan does not float the surface right off, which can be just as damaging.

Some seeds germinate best if sown directly they are ripe; some are better kept until spring, when temperatures are rising and days are lengthening; and a few will not germinate until they have passed through a prolonged process of chilling. This is a natural defence against premature germination before winter and the seed seems capable of timing so many weeks of cold before the spring and favourable conditions have arrived. It is possible to provide the cold artificially by keeping the seeds for three or four months in an ordinary domestic refrigerator at 3–4 °C before sowing them. It is mostly tree and shrub seeds from species native to cold regions that have this safety mechanism, but some alpines and perennials also possess it. Delphinium seed germinates freely when first ripe in late summer and autumn but loses its vitality rapidly during winter if stored at normal room temperatures. Kept over winter in a refrigerator it will germinate in spring almost as freely as it would have done the preceding autumn.

By sowing thinly one can delay the time at which the seedlings have to be given more room but even so they should not be left more than a few weeks, since the soil mixes used for seeds contain little reserve food. Most seedlings are transplanted (pricked out) a few centimetres apart into shallow seed trays, but very fast growing kinds, such as tomatoes, can go immediately into small pots, one seedling in each. With a few kinds – notably large seeded vegetables such as marrows, cucumbers, sweet corn and beans – it is even worth sowing direct into small pots, one or two seeds in each, to avoid the trouble and check to growth caused by pricking out.

Most seedlings need good light and one of the hazards of sowing in autumn rather than in spring is that they run into shortening days instead of lengthening ones. It is possible to overcome this with artificial lighting but this introduces a new expense and more complicated techniques which are probably best left to experienced gardeners.

Many half hardy annuals need to be sown in February or March in order to get them flowering outdoors early in the summer. Tomatoes, melons, and cucumbers need to be sown at about the same time if they are to start cropping reasonably early and just a few species are really best sown in January. For all these a considerable saving in heat can be effected by germinating them in a small

Pricking out with fingers: the same system applies.

propagator in which the required temperature can be maintained but it must be borne in mind that once they have germinated the seedlings will soon require a great deal more room and it may be impossible, without some artificial heat in the greenhouse, to maintain the necessary temperatures before mid-spring. It is very easy to get a good start in a propagator and then find that everything has been lost for lack of adequately warmed growing space for the young plants.

The technique of pricking out is simple yet very important. The seedlings must be lifted from, or tipped out of, their container with as little damage to their roots as possible and then be carefully separated (this will be much easier if the seeds were sown thinly) and re-planted in the trays or other containers in which they are to be grown on. They can be held by their leaves, so that their roots hang down ready to be dropped into little holes made with the forefinger or with a pointed stick (dibber), or with a sharpened wooden plant label. A special tool, known as a Widger, is also excellent for this work. The soil is then gently pressed around the roots. When all the seedlings are in, they should be watered from a can fitted with a fine rose (spray). This will settle the soil around them still more and will freshen them up and ensure that they do not flag unduly from lack of moisture. If the weather is bright it may be necessary to shade the pricked-out seedlings for a few days with newspaper or butter muslin until they stiffen up and are obviously growing again.

Potting is done when seedlings have filled the space in the trays or boxes in which they were pricked out or when plants have filled with roots the pots they already occupy. Occasionally it pays to let a plant get pot bound, i.e. really jam its pot with tight packed roots. This can have the effect of forcing some plants to flower but it should not be done unless it is known to be a suitable treatment.

In general plants are moved on to larger pots as soon as the soil in the smaller ones is comfortably filled with roots. Usually the move is into a pot one or two sizes larger than that it already occupies or, if it is a seedling coming from a pricking-out tray or a cutting newly rooted and in need of more room and a richer soil mixture, into the smallest size pot that will contain its roots with just a little space all round. It is rarely wise to put small plants straight away into large pots because, even with good porous soil or peat mixtures, the compost confined in a pot tends to become sour unless there are active roots in it. Again there are occasional exceptions. Some very strong growing plants, such as tomatoes and cucumbers, may go straight from 7·5 cm diameter pots to 20 cm diameter pots, but it is the exception which should only be practised when it is known to be safe and useful.

(a)

The potting process. (a) The plant is in need of repotting, having rooted through the drainage holes in its present pot. (b) It is gently tapped out of the pot. (c) Its roots are tightly coiled together. (d) The plant is placed in a larger pot and more soil is run in around its roots. (e) The new soil is firmed with the thumbs. (f) The repotted plant: the soil level is a little below the rim of the pot. (g) A repotted plant should be watered immediately to settle the soil around the roots.

Nowadays, pot sizes are always referred to by diameter across the rim. The most useful sizes are from 6 to 20 cm in diameter but large pots, tubs or other containers may be necessary for some purposes, particularly for shrubs and other large plants. All pots and containers must be provided with drainage holes in the bottom to allow surplus water to escape. Pots and bowls without drainage holes are sometimes used indoors to avoid the danger of water trickling onto furniture, carpets, etc, but then ordinary soil or peat mixtures should be replaced by a special mix, known as bulb fibre, consisting of peat, crushed shell and crushed charcoal. Even so, great care should be taken when watering to moisten this bulb fibre without giving so much that water collects in the container. Roots need air and if they are immersed in water they literally die of drowning from lack of air.

When potting, place a little of the soil or peat mixture in the bottom of the pot or other containers and stand the plant on this. There should be just enough to bring the top of the root ball 2 cm (a little more for larger pots, slightly less for very small ones) below the rim. Then run in more compost all round, pressing it in with the fingers or giving it an occasional sharp rap on a firm surface, such as a wooden bench, to settle the mixture in. Continue until the uppermost roots are just covered but never fill a pot right to the rim. There must be a space to hold water when the plant is watered otherwise most of it will run uselessly over the sides.

Soil mixtures should be made fairly firm though I have never seen the need for the hard ramming with a short length of old broom handle which used to be recommended for chrysanthemums and a few other plants. Soil soon finds its own firmness according to its texture and if it is heavily rammed all that happens is that its texture is destroyed. So, as a rule, firming with the fingers and by rapping is quite sufficient. Even this can be too much for peat mixtures which should only be firmed by rapping and light pressure with the fingers. They are open textured by nature and even those plants which are supposed to require firm soil do not seem to mind this.

Plants that are growing rapidly – seedlings for example and vigorous cuttings – may require repotting every few weeks, but many permanent plants, such as shrubs and herbaceous perennials, only require an annual repotting and there are a few that can be left even longer than that. The best time for the work is usually just as the plants start into new growth, which for a great many plants means early spring. However, there are exceptions, the greenhouse cyclamen for example, which starts to grow in late summer or autumn. It is usually wise to avoid potting in late autumn and winter, when short days and poor light give plants little encouragement to make new roots quickly and, as I have already explained, soil in pots that is not fairly quickly occupied by some roots is liable to become sour and unhealthy.

After potting it is nearly always wise to give an immediate and thorough watering. This helps to settle the soil even more closely around the roots and prevents, or at any rate curtails, any temporary leaf flagging due to the root disturbance. As a rule roots should be kept as intact as possible during repotting and the soil already around them should be retained. If the old pots are clean as they should be, when the time comes for repotting roots and soil will slide out cleanly and easily if each pot is turned upside down and the rim is rapped on a firm bench. While doing this, place one hand under the plant to steady and hold it as it slips out. Just occasionally it may be better, having removed the plant,

Capillary watering in conjunction with a misting frame in a greenhouse at Wisley. Water rises through the soil by capillary attraction from wet sand, pea gravel, or plastic matting.

Left: hand watering. Plants are watered directly from the spout beneath the leaves so that the water does not hit the soil with too much force.

Right: one method of automatic watering: a 'spaghetti' tube is placed in a plant pot (see overleaf).

to shake off some of the soil or, if it is very firm, to tease it away with a pointed stick. This is most likely to be necessary with large plants which are to go back into the same size containers or where the existing soil is in bad condition or is believed to contain pests. But then it is more than ever important to do the work at the season most favourable for rapid recovery and new growth.

Watering

There is a good deal of mystique about the watering of pot plants, much of it unjustified. I knew one commercial tomato grower who would delegate every job in his nursery except the watering which he considered so important and so difficult to get done properly by hired hands that he invariably did it himself. Well, I would not deny that watering is of vital importance. Without it plants die, most of them quite quickly, and with an inadequate supply they slowly starve to death, since every bit of food that a plant takes from the soil must be in solution. At the other extreme, too much water will drive out most of the air from the soil and roots will die of drowning, for like leaves they must have air to survive though they do not need so much of it. The only exceptions are aquatic and bog plants which have adapted themselves to grow in water and to obtain their oxygen from it.

So it follows that plants must have enough water but not too much. The old rule-of-thumb used to be to give sufficient at each watering to soak the soil right through, until surplus commenced to dribble out of the drainage holes, and then to give no more until the soil began to get dry. If one is watering with a can or a hose it is still a good rule, though now that most potting composts are so much more open textured than they used to be I would err on the side of watering too much or too frequently rather than too little. If the soil or peat mixture is right it will only retain a reasonable amount of water and any surplus will quickly drain away.

But nowadays many gardeners do much of their watering by capillary benches and that completely contradicts the old idea that plants should be alternately rather wet and just a little dry. Capillary watering means that the soil is kept constantly moist by contact with a layer of wet sand or pea gravel or a mixture of the two or from matting made of rot-proof plastic fibres. The water rises from the wet bench through the soil by capillary attraction, exactly the same force which causes water to soak upwards through a sheet of blotting paper. It is the fineness of the channels between the particles of soil that determines how far and how fast the water rises, and so how wet the soil is, and this is yet another reason for ensuring that soil and peat mixtures are of the right texture and remain in this porous condition.

Capillary watering has the merit that it can be made completely automatic. The bench can be fed with water from a small water tank connected to a mains supply and with a float-operated valve which will keep the water at any desired level. Provided the soil in the pots comes into direct contact with the wet bench or mat, or is fed from it by means of a glass-fibre or other suitable wick, one can go away for days or even weeks at a time and forget about watering. However, capillary benches do not suit all plants equally well. They are not, as a rule, very satisfactory for plants that have been recently potted (and so have not occupied all the soil with roots) and, in my view, are less satisfactory in winter (unless greenhouses are kept fairly warm) than they are in spring and summer, when most plants are growing fast.

There are other systems of automatic watering, some involving the use of electricity to control the supply either by means of a time switch or by devices which sense the rate of evaporation. Overhead misting devices usually operate on some such system and are excellent for propagating frames in which cuttings are to be rooted, but the almost constant overhead dampness is not good for all plants.

One of the most sophisticated systems, sometimes referred to as spaghetti tube watering, supplies water individually to each plant through very fine bore plastic tubes which are plugged into a large supply pipe. Again there are various ways of controlling the supply of water – some electrical, others mechanical. The merit of the system is that the water supply can be varied from plant to plant (two or three tubes for a thirsty plant; only one for a moderate supply; none for one that needs to be dry). Its principal drawbacks are initial expense and the necessity to check the fine tubes quite frequently to ensure that they have not become blocked or airlocked.

Inserting a probe into the soil. The probe illustrated indicates not only the degree of moisture in the soil, but also the light intensity.

So for many people it will be hand watering much or all of the time. Choose a can that is easy to handle, not so small that one has to be constantly going back to the tap or tank for a refill, not so large that it is really hard labour to stretch out to water plants at the back of the staging or above one's head. A fairly long spout is useful and some makers offer a spout extension which can be slipped instantly over the shorter one. All cans should have a fairly fine 'rose' (the attachment for the end of the spout) which will give a spray instead of a spout of water. This spray is needed for watering seed pans and trays before and after sowing, for watering seedlings, and very small plants, for keeping cuttings moist, and for dampening the floor and stagings in the greenhouse to increase atmospheric humidity when this is necessary. It is hardly ever required for watering plants that are well established in pots as these are far better watered direct from the spout, which is quicker and more likely to ensure that sufficient water is applied. Sprays have a deceptive habit of making the soil look very wet when really only the surface has been moistened.

When watering direct from the spout, this should be held close to the soil in the pot so that the water does not fall with such force that it washes some of the soil away. With some plants it is also an advantage to keep the leaves and crowns dry and this is another reason for holding the spout low.

It is always a little difficult to know just how wet or dry the soil really is. When plants are growing in clay pots, these can be rapped with a knuckle bone or a cotton reel impaled on a cane. A little practice will enable one to distinguish the more hollow, ringing note emitted by a pot containing dry soil from the dull thud of one containing wet soil. But this test is useless for plastic pots, nor will it work with clay pots that are cracked. In these cases one must go by appearance, or by lifting a pot and judging its weight (wet soil weighs more than dry soil), or by scratching the surface soil with a fingernail. Special probes are also available which, when thrust into the soil, indicate on a dial whether it is too dry, too wet, or just right (*see* illustration opposite). In fact, as I have already said, if the compost is right the dangers of overwatering are not great and when in doubt it is advisable to give water. Most inexperienced gardeners err on the side of underwatering.

The temperature of the water is probably not very important though some gardeners consider it should be at the same temperature as the air in the house to avoid chilling the soil. One way to ensure this is to have a dip tank inside the greenhouse which can be refilled after each watering, but in very small houses there is unlikely to be room for such a refinement.

What can be important is the quality of the water. Many plants are not fussy and will grow with almost any water that is not heavily polluted but some plants dislike hard (alkaline) water. This is true of nearly all rhododendrons, azaleas, and heathers. There is little doubt that the success of some plants in certain localities – sometimes so great that considerable commercial production has been attracted to the area – is due to the character of the local water; but this is an area in which there is more opinion than hard fact. Certainly for some delicate plants it can be an advantage to have rain water, so avoiding the twin dangers of chlorination and alkalinity.

Rooting Cuttings

Cuttings are pieces of one part of a plant severed from the rest and then induced to grow into complete new plants. If the cutting is prepared from a stem it must be persuaded to form roots; if it is made from a leaf it needs to form both roots and stems; if it is made from a piece of root it has to produce growth buds and then stems. It is this restriction to a single part of the plant that distinguishes a cutting from a division which starts with stems, growth buds and roots. It differs from a layer in being severed from the plant before it makes roots, not after they have formed.

Cuttings not only provide an economical means of increasing plants but, because of the restricted area from which they are taken, they can sometimes be used to raise healthy plants from ones that are diseased or pest infested. Because all the plant tissue in a cutting can be young, it often happens that the plant grown from it is more vigorous than its parent, which was a mixture of old and young tissues.

Stem cuttings are usually classified as soft, half ripe, or hardwooded (ripe) according to the character of the growth taken. Soft cuttings are those made from young growth, usually in the spring though this will depend upon the time of year at which the plant commences to grow. Half ripe cuttings are taken as the first flush of growth comes to an end and the stems begin to get firm and even a little woody towards the base. Hard wooded or ripe cuttings are made from stems that have completed their growth for the year.

Leaf cuttings are usually prepared from healthy, well developed leaves that are in active growth.

Root cuttings, by contrast, are generally taken when growth is more or less at a standstill, which for many plants will be in winter.

Soft cuttings lose moisture rapidly unless kept in a very still humid atmosphere. This can be maintained by inserting the cuttings in a small frame or box with a close-fitting glass or plastic cover, or by covering each potful of cuttings with a polythene bag. Special propagators can be purchased for use inside a greenhouse and some of these are fitted with their own self-contained heating. It is desirable to induce root formation quickly with this kind of cutting since roots will give it the moisture it needs and so prevent it from collapsing. As a rule roots grow fastest when the soil is a little warmer than the air and so 'bottom heat', i.e. warmth applied directly to the soil from below, is a frequent recommendation for both soft and half ripe cuttings. It is of much less importance for hardwooded cuttings which lose water far more slowly and so need not be hurried along like soft and half ripe cuttings. These hardwooded cuttings are often inserted out of doors or in unheated frames and it is for soft and half ripe cuttings that a greenhouse is most beneficial, especially if combined with a well-designed propagator with its own soil warming.

Leaf cuttings also lose a great deal of moisture rapidly unless kept in a close atmosphere, i.e. in still, damp air. They also benefit from being in a propagator with bottom heat.

Root cuttings are kept moist by soil so they do not lose moisture rapidly, and do not as a rule need a propagator though the protection of a greenhouse can be useful against frost and heavy rain.

Cuttings have little need for food until they have formed roots and rich soil can actually inhibit or slow down the process of rooting. Gardeners have many different ideas about the ideal 'soil' to use for cuttings. That known as John Innes Cutting Compost consists of 1 part by volume medium loam, 2 parts peat and 1 part sand with no fertilizers of any kind. Some gardeners use nothing but sand or perlite but this dries out rather rapidly and is most suitable if some kind of automatic misting or watering is available. Other gardeners use peat or well sifted leaf mould but for some plants this may be a bit too loose in texture and it can become soggy if overwatered. I generally use a mixture of half and half sphagnum peat and coarse sand and find this satisfactory for most purposes. However, peat, sand and perlite contain little or no plant food, so once cuttings are rooted they must be moved quite quickly to a richer mixture or they will starve. One merit of the John Innes Cutting Compost is that the 25 per cent loam it contains will feed the cuttings for a while if there is delay in moving them out of the cutting bed or propagator.

Stem cuttings. The stem cutting has been made and is inserted into the sand and peat mixture deeply enough to hold itself erect.

Stem cuttings of all kinds, soft, half ripe, and hardwooded, are usually severed cleanly just below a joint or node, i.e. the point at which a leaf or leaf stalk joins the stem. Sometimes half ripe and hardwooded cuttings are made from short side stems pulled away from a main stem with what is termed a 'heel' of the older growth right at the bottom. If this heel is ragged or carries a strip of bark this should be trimmed cleanly before insertion. Just a few plants root better from what are termed internodal cuttings, i.e. shoots severed between joints, not immediately below a joint, but as a rule it is at the joint or around the 'heel' of a pulled-off cutting that roots form most rapidly. This seems to be because it is at joints that there is the greatest concentration of those plant hormones that trigger off root formation, but the amount of hormone occurring naturally varies from week to week and from one part of the parent plant to another, which can explain why, out of a batch of cuttings all treated in the same way, some root faster or better than others.

The effect produced by natural hormones can be duplicated by synthetic hormones and these can be purchased in powder form ready for use. When the cutting has been prepared, it is dipped in water and then the base of the cutting is pushed into the rooting powder so that it picks up a little all around

Stem cuttings. To maintain humidity, a polythene bag is slipped over a pot of cuttings.

(a)

(b)

(c

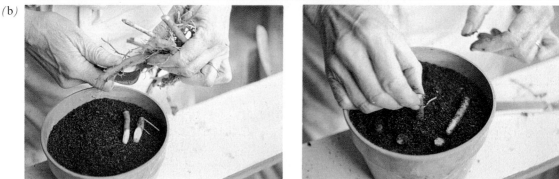

*Root cuttings. (a) A sloping cut is made at the bottom end of the root. (b) A suitable length of root is cut off –
straight across at the top to identify the correct way up. (c) The cutting is inserted into soil, in a small pot.*

the cut surface and the bottom joint. Some brands of rooting powder also contain a fungicide to
protect the cutting from soil-borne diseases. Some manufacturers also offer several different strengths
of rooting powder: a weak mixture for soft cuttings, a medium one for half ripe cuttings, and a higher
concentration for hardwooded cuttings.

As a rule the lower leaves, if present, are removed, before the cutting is inserted. It is pushed
sufficiently deep into the soil to hold itself erect. The forefinger (perhaps protected with a finger stall)
may be used to make a little hole for the cutting and then to firm it in, or a special dibber about as thick
as a pencil can be used or, if the rooting medium is loose (peat for example), and the cuttings are fairly
stiff, they can simply be pushed into it. They can go into pots, pans, or seed trays filled with the rooting
medium or directly into a bed of it made in the greenhouse or propagator. Whichever system is used,
the cuttings should be well watered from a can fitted with a fine rose which will not disturb them but
will settle the soil, sand, or whatever rooting medium is being used, closely around the cuttings.

Subsequently the cuttings must be kept moist until they are rooted, which they will signal by
commencing to grow again. If they are in a well-made propagator or are well sealed inside a polythene
bag they will lose very little water and may need no more for several weeks but they must be examined
fairly frequently to make certain that all is well. Shading will reduce loss of water but may also delay

root formation, so whether it is used or not must depend upon circumstances. As a general rule soft cuttings are likely to need some shading such as a single thickness of newspaper or butter muslin, but half ripe cuttings may need little or no shading and hardwooded cuttings are almost certain to require little to none.

Automatic misting devices are available to keep cuttings constantly damp (*see* illustration p. 22). Some are controlled mechanically, some electrically. The frequency of misting may be determined on a time basis or according to the rate of evaporation. Cuttings rooted under mist do not, as a rule, need to be kept in an especially close atmosphere or require any shading and often the misting units are installed above the open staging of the greenhouse which carries a cutting 'bed' into which the cuttings are inserted. Because of the constant moisture it is essential to use a very porous mixture, usually either fine sand or perlite or a mixture of either of these with peat. The most tricky stage in mist propagation is often the weaning of the rooted cuttings from the constant moisture of the mist bed to the normal atmosphere of the greenhouse. Professionals sometimes use special weaning beds as an intermediate stage in which the cuttings are still dampened automatically but less frequently. Gardeners usually have to manage with one piece of apparatus, either adapting it to do two jobs or acclimatizing the rooted cuttings by careful watering, shading (if necessary), and syringing.

Even when cuttings are rooted in propagators the change to the open greenhouse staging and a richer potting mixture can be tricky. Peat composts may prove easier to manage at this stage than soil mixtures and in any case the fertilizer content should be kept low to begin with. The rooted cuttings are best potted singly so that they can be given individual attention and, though they should go first into small pots, they will need to be moved on into larger ones as the pots fill up with roots.

Exactly the same treatment applies to leaf cuttings, the sole difference being in the method of preparation. Some leaves, those of saintpaulia for example, are taken with a leaf stalk which is then pushed into the soil just like a stem cutting. Just a little of the leaf can be in the soil as well as the stalk. Some big leaves, such as those of *Begonia rex*, are laid flat on the compost and slits are made with a penknife across the leaf veins. Hairpins or pebbles are then used to hold their cut veins close to the damp soil and it is from the healing wounds that roots will form and new leaves appear. A number of tiny plants can be produced in this way from a single leaf and, when they can be handled fairly easily, they are carefully excised from the parent leaf and potted individually.

Root cuttings are nearly always made from plants with fairly fleshy or thongy roots. These are cut into short lengths and are then either laid flat on the surface of a cutting soil mixture and covered with about 2 cm of the same or are dropped into dibber holes sufficiently deep to take the whole cutting and cover it to a depth of about 1 cm. If this latter method is used the root cuttings must go in the right way up so it is wise to indicate which end is which when preparing the cuttings. A simple method is to make a straight cut at the top end and a sloping cut at the bottom end.

Layering is a method of making stems form roots before they are severed from the parent plant. In many respects the techniques resemble those used for cuttings. The stems chosen for layering should be fairly young and they must be wounded where they are to form roots. A healing callus will form over the wound and roots will grow from this just as they do from the callus which seals the end of a cutting. The wound should be made just below or through a joint either by drawing a knife blade around the stem to cut through the skin or bark but not into the harder wood beneath, or by drawing the knife diagonally through the joint without severing the stem. Either way it will help to wet the wound and then dust it with hormone rooting powder before covering it with soil or a mixture of peat and sand. This can be in a pot placed in a convenient position, or in a bed of soil if the stem being layered is sufficiently flexible and low down to be brought to ground level. It can be held in place with a piece of stiff wire bent like a large hairpin or with a stone placed over it.

Alternatively, if it is inconvenient to layer either in pots or the soil, the wounded area can be covered with damp sphagnum moss over which a polythene film sleeve is then drawn and tied tightly at each end. Yet another method is to put the sleeve on first, tie it at one end, fill it with moist peat or a mixture of peat and vermiculite and finally tie the other end. It may take some months for roots to form but when they can be seen curling around inside the polythene sleeve the stem can be severed just below the rooted area, the sleeve carefully removed and the layer potted or planted in the same manner as a rooted cutting.

Hardening Off

Plants do not like sudden changes of climate. Inside a greenhouse there may be several different climates, one that is fairly warm and humid inside the propagator and then a range of diminishing temperatures in the greenhouse itself the further one gets from the heating apparatus or the nearer one approaches the covering whether it be of glass or plastic (note that the air close to the glass or plastic is always cooler because it loses heat to the air outside by conduction). A clever gardener uses all these variations for the good of the plants, moving them from one climate to another according to the need of the moment.

The biggest and most difficult change of all comes when plants have to be moved from the greenhouse to the open air. This may happen because they have been raised under glass with the express purpose of planting them out later (early vegetable seedlings, for example, or half hardy annuals and summer bedding plants) or because the greenhouse has become too full and more space must be found by taking the hardier plants elsewhere.

Losses can be prevented, or at the very least reduced, if plants are prepared gradually for this change of climate. It is the process gardeners call 'hardening off' and it is an important operation.

For many plants hardening off begins directly they come out of the propagator. They are moved every week or so to cooler parts of the greenhouse, or to a cooler greenhouse if more than one is available. Then, three or four weeks before they are due to go outdoors, they are transferred from the greenhouse to a frame. The advantage of this is that the frame 'light', the glass or plastic cover for it, can be removed altogether or be swung so widely open that, for all practical purposes, the plants inside the frame are completely exposed. Of course this is not done all at once. For the first few days the frame lights are opened a little to give a temperature not more than a few degrees below that of the greenhouse from which they have come. Then, as the plants become acclimatized, increased ventilation is given, especially on mild days, until it is safe to open the frame up completely by day, and even give a good deal of ventilation at night, though in late spring one must always be watchful for night or dawn frosts, caused by clear skies allowing great loss of heat from earth to sky by radiation. Such frosts are usually forecast on radio and television and these warnings should be heeded. Plants that are being hardened off should be protected with their frame light, and if the frost threatens to be severe, additional protection can be given with mats, sacks or even newspapers spread over the lights. Only when this process of acclimatization is complete and there is little further risk of frost should half hardy plants be risked in the open without any protection.

Frames are of many types and sizes and may be constructed with wooden, concrete or metal sides. The 'lights' with which they are protected may be glazed or made of plastic and some of the more sophisticated models are fitted with their own heating by means of electric cable – either to be buried a few centimetres below the surface of the sand, gravel or soil in the frame, or lapped around the inside wall of the frame. Lights may be hinged or made to slide. With so much variation it is really best to visit a garden centre of a greenhouse stockist where a range of models can be inspected and the one most convenient for the site and the type and number of plants likely to be grown can be selected.

Plants can be hardened off even if no frame is available though this is a little more difficult. First of all the temperature in the greenhouse must be lowered as much as is safe for other occupants that are not being hardened off. It may well be that at the door end of the greenhouse a lower temperature can

Clematis indivisa (see p. 51)

be maintained by day by leaving the door open. Shelves fitted below the ventilator may also be cooler than the stagings or the floor of the house.

When all that is possible has been done by these means, the plants can be stood outdoors in the most sheltered place available, maybe near the foot of a sunny wall. If there is a cold wind by day, polythene sheets may be spread over the plants and held down with bricks, stones, planks or soil. At night this polythene does not afford much protection, especially from radiation frost, but brown paper is quite good and can be spread over the plants where there is danger. Fortunately the worst late spring frosts usually occur when there is little or no wind, which makes it easier to hold the paper in place. Gradually the protection can be reduced and, as the weather should be getting warmer, the process of acclimatization can be completed successfully.

3 Pests and Diseases

Plants grown under glass are just as likely as those outdoors to be attacked by pests and diseases but the emphasis and the timing can be different. For example, red spider mites are much more likely to be troublesome in a greenhouse than in the garden because the atmosphere so easily gets hot and dry and these are just the conditions red spider mites enjoy.

Aphids of all kinds (and the name covers various species of greenflies, blackflies and other plant lice) are likely to appear earlier under glass than out of doors; indeed in a warm house they may be there all winter and the same is true of the whitefly, one form of which is more or less confined to greenhouse plants since it is incapable of surviving outdoors in really cold weather.

There is also a difference in the treatment of pests and diseases between outdoors and under glass. In the open spraying is the most favoured method of applying insecticides and fungicides whereas aerosols are more popular in greenhouses. The still air prevents the very fine particles carried in the aerosol vapour being blown away uselessly and there is no water spray on the leaves to cause trouble. Aerosols are very easy to handle, always ready for instant use at the first sign of trouble, and this is inportant under glass where populations of invading insects built up rapidly. Infestation is nipped in the bud and a great deal of subsequent trouble can be avoided. Aerosols differ from sprays in that the active chemical is dissolved in a highly volatile solvent which is broken up into such tiny particles by the force of ejection that it evaporates almost instantly leaving the chemical to settle evenly over the plants. These solvents can be damaging to foliage or flowers if they come into contact with them so aerosols should not be discharged very close to plants. They should be held at least 30 cm away and with some it is even better to hold them a little above the plants, but makers' instructions should be consulted about such matters.

Fumigation is a method of control very difficult to apply outdoors but easy and highly efficient in a greenhouse. Smokes or vapours quickly penetrate into every nook and cranny and circulate around every leaf, stem, flower or fruit. It is possible to get a better coverage by this means than with any spray, or even with an aerosol, and it is possible to install apparatus which will maintain a constant fumigation of the greenhouse without harm to the plants or to anyone working among them. This apparatus usually consists of a small electrically warmed container into which a volatilizing chemical is placed. Vapour is given off slowly and the vessel is recharged from time to time according to manufacturers' instructions.

Smoke generators for use in small greenhouses are usually prepared as pellets. On the container there will be instructions saying how many cubic feet or cubic metres each pellet will fumigate effectively. To calculate this, measure the length, breadth, and height of the greenhouse to a point midway between eaves and ridge and multiply the three figures together. If the measurements are in feet the result will be in cubic feet; if in metres, in cubic metres.

To use smoke generators of any kind the required number should be spaced out fairly evenly along the central path or on the floor of the house. Then they are ignited, starting at the end furthest from the door and working back rapidly so that the house can be vacated before it is filled with smoke. Doors and ventilators should be kept closed for about half an hour and can then be opened to allow any remaining fumes to escape. If possible fumigate towards evening and avoid midday or periods when the sun is shining brightly on the greenhouse.

Here are some of the pests and diseases most frequently encountered in greenhouses and the best methods of preventing, controlling or eliminating them. The pests are dealt with first, the diseases second – and both are listed in alphabetical order.

Pests

Ants

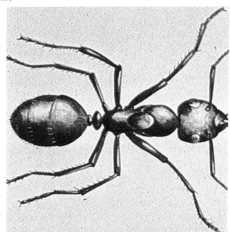

These are mainly a nuisance rather than a direct threat to plants. They make their nests in the soil, loosening it, disturbing roots, and preventing any secure root hold. Seedlings and small plants can be thrown right out of the ground or buried beneath the ant hills. Fortunately ants are readily killed with BHC dust purchased in puffer cans from which it can be blown directly into the ants' nests or wherever ants are seen moving or congregating. Treatment should begin as soon as ants are seen, and can be repeated daily until they are eliminated.

Aphids (Greenflies, Blackflies, etc.)
These are plant lice which live on the sap of plants, attacking principally the succulent young shoots and multiplying rapidly under favourable conditions. A large number of chemicals are available to kill them, including derris, diazinon, dimethoate, formothion, lindane, malathion, pirimicarb and resmethrin. Most are sold under trade names but the chemical name will appear somewhere on the pack, though probably in small type. Some are available as liquids for dilution with water and application as sprays, some as aerosols or in puffer packs ready for immediate application, and lindane is also sold in pellets which, when ignited, will produce volumes of smoke carrying the chemical to all parts of the greenhouse. The package will state the cubic capacity which one pellet will treat effectively.

Aphids on cyclamen

Capsids

These are plant lice not unlike greenflies but larger and much more active. They suck the sap and cause leaves to pucker and develop dry brown patches. They can be controlled by fumigating with lindane, by using a pirimiphos-methyl aerosol, or by spraying with diazinon, lindane or pirimiphos-methyl. (*Illustration: capsid damage to hydrangeas.*)

Earwigs

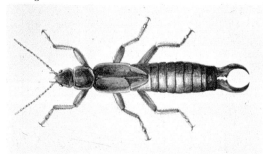

These can cause quite a lot of damage to carnations, chrysanthemums and some other plants, eating the petals and the edges of leaves and causing damage very similar to that caused by slugs. Earwigs feed at night and mostly hide by day in dark places. They can be trapped in small, inverted flower pots stuffed with hay or straw or they can be killed with lindane dust blown on the plants or on the soil wherever earwigs have been seen.

Eelworms

These are also known as nematode worms. Some of the larger species are scavengers and do not damage growing plants but some of the very small, microscopic kinds are serious pests, entering roots and stems in great numbers, causing the formation of cysts and swellings, or distorting and in other ways disrupting growth. One of the worst in greenhouses is the root knot eelworm which attacks the roots of tomatoes, checking their growth and covering them with small swellings. The chemicals used by commercial growers to control eelworms are too poisonous to be used in home greenhouses and the best way to keep these pests under control is to use fresh soil annually, taking it from some place where a similar crop has not been grown in recent years. Alternatively tomatoes, cucumbers, and other susceptible crops can be grown in plastic bags filled with sterile peat soil mixture, which is kept out of contact with the soil in the house by remaining in the bags.

Leaf Miners

Various small grubs tunnel through the leaves of some plants leaving telltale snaky white lines which show where they have been. If the leaf is drawn between the fingers it is probable that the grub will be felt inside. Chrysanthemums and cinerarias are particularly subject to attack. On a small scale, and if tackled almost immediately infestation occurs, the grubs can be killed by feeling for them and piercing them with a pin or the point of a penknife. On a larger scale leaves should be sprayed with diazinon, lindane or malathion. (*Illustration: leaf miner damage.*)

Mealy Bugs

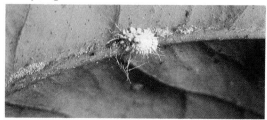

These bug-like insects suck the sap of many plants, move very slowly and protect themselves with a white secretion which looks like tufts of cotton wool. This makes it difficult to get any insecticide into contact with them and so, on a small scale, it is best to remove them individually by hand or with a brush dipped in soapy water. On a larger scale mealy bugs can be killed by spraying with diazinon or malathion or, more effectively, by brushing this into the woolly patches with a stiff paint brush.

Red Spider Mites

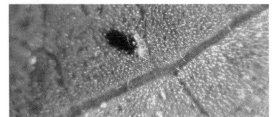

These pests are not spiders, despite their name, and they are rusty coloured or even yellowish rather than red. They are also very minute, only just visible with the naked eye though easily seen with a hand lens. They prefer the under sides of leaves, particularly the succulent veins from which they suck sap. A telltale indication that red spider mites are at work is a distinctive grey or bronzy mottling of the leaves.

Red spider mites thrive in hot, dry conditions and can be controlled by keeping the air cooler and moister but this may not be sufficient to eliminate them completely. They can be killed by spraying with derris, diazinon, dimethoate or malathion.

Thrips

These very active insects attack many greenhouse plants and sometimes severely disfigure the flowers of chrysanthemums and carnations. They suck the sap and produce silvery or brown streaks on stems, leaves and petals. They hide so efficiently that it is usually difficult to see them but if a damaged flower is shaken over a sheet of paper the thrips will fall on to it and scurry away – little yellow, brown or black insects very narrow in proportion to their length. Fumigation with lindane will destroy them or a malathion or pirimiphos-methyl aerosol can be used. Lindane, derris, malathion and pirimiphos-methyl sprays may also be used but sprays are less effective unless they are driven well into the crevices in which the thrips are concealed. Thrips thrive in the same hot, dry conditions that favour red spider mites. (*Illustration: petal bleaching due to thrips feeding.*)

Weevils

These are beetle-like insects but they differ from beetles in having long snouts and in being vegetarian rather than carnivorous. Several species attack garden plants, including the vine weevil. Weevils eat leaves, particularly the edges of leaves, giving them a scalloped appearance. Their white larvae eat into fleshy roots and tubers, and the under surface of the tubers of cyclamen are frequently attacked. As the grubs are completely out of sight, the cause of poor growth and wilting leaves may be a puzzle unless the soil is shaken from the roots and the holes in the tubers are discovered.

Adult weevils can be killed by spraying with lindane, carbaryl or trichlorphon. Weevils in the soil can be killed with bromophos. (*Illustration: weevil grub.*)

Whitefly

These very small, white insects can become so numerous that, when disturbed, they fly out in clouds. They lay eggs on the leaves of plants and these later develop into scales, like tiny grey limpets, firmly attached to the leaves. Finally the adult insects emerge. Sap is sucked from the leaves and they also become covered in a sticky secretion which encourages the growth of sooty mould, further disfiguring and weakening the leaves. Neither eggs nor scales can be readily killed with insecticides but the adult insects can be killed by fumigation with lindane, by using malathion or pirimiphos-methyl aerosols or by spraying with lindane, malathion, pirimiphos-methyl, resmethrin or bioresmethrin. It is necessary to repeat the treatment at intervals of a few days for several weeks to catch successive broods of adult whiteflies as they emerge from the scales and before they have time to lay more eggs.

Whitefly can also be controlled with a natural parasite, a small insect named *Encarsia formosa*. This lays its eggs in the whitefly scales and its larvae, on hatching out, destroy the scales. Leaves bearing parasitized whitefly scales must be obtained and suspended in the greenhouse. If there are plenty of whiteflies and the temperature is 18 °C or more the parasite will feed rapidly and will keep down the whitefly population, though it will never completely destroy it as that would eliminate the parasite also, since it has no other food for its young. It will die out quite rapidly as the temperature falls in autumn or as the whitefly population decreases. As a rule it is necessary to re-introduce the parasite every year, towards the end of spring or early in summer when greenhouses are warm and the whitefly population is increasing. *Encarsia* is available from the Royal Horticultural Society's laboratories at Wisley, Surrey,

Spraying to kill whitefly.

and from some commercial sources; but the demand usually exceeds the supply.

Woodlice

These are often found in considerable numbers in greenhouses. They do little or no damage to large plants but sometimes eat small seedlings. Numbers can be reduced by removing decaying wood and other organic refuse. Woodlice can be trapped, like earwigs, in inverted flower pots stuffed with straw or hay or in potatoes or carrots cut in half and laid on the soil. They can also be killed with bromophos, carbaryl, lindane or trichlorphon.

Diseases

Botrytis

This is one of the commonest diseases under glass and it is known by various names according to the

symptoms it produces. Thus the black decay of stems particularly common on pelargoniums in winter, is often called 'blackleg', whereas the fluffy outgrowth which occurs on the leaves and stems of many plants is called 'grey mould'. Botrytis thrives when the air is cold and damp, so raising the temperature and avoiding unnecessary splashing of water will help to prevent it spreading. It is a difficult disease to control once it gets a hold but spraying with benomyl (Benlate) will help.

Damping off

This is an omnibus name for a number of soil-borne diseases which are particularly destructive to seedlings though they do occasionally attack older plants. The fungi invade the seedlings at or near soil level causing rapid decay so that the seedlings topple over while still green and apparently healthy. Closer inspection will reveal the rotted stems at the base. Damping off diseases flourish in damp, overcrowded conditions. Thin sowing, early pricking out, careful watering, good lighting, and adequate ventilation will all help to keep them at bay. So will sterilized soil, though it can quickly become reinfected if it comes into contact with

Effects of damping off diseases.

soil or plants containing any of the fungi which cause damping off.

When an attack does occur the best way to contain it is to water soil and seedlings with Cheshunt Compound or to spray them thoroughly with quintozene.

Leaf Mould (Cladosporium)

This is a disease confined to tomatoes in greenhouses and it can be one of the most damaging. First khaki-coloured patches appear on the under surfaces of the leaves, matched by yellowish patches above. These can spread rapidly until the whole leaf is enveloped and withers. Leaf mould is encouraged by overcrowding, poor light and a damp, stuffy, ill-ventilated atmosphere. It can be checked by spraying with benomyl, copper fungicide or maneb but it is really more sensible to avoid it altogether by spacing plants well, ventilating properly, and growing tomato varieties that are resistant to the disease.

Mildews

It is the powdery mildews that are most troublesome in greenhouses and they are worst when the house is badly ventilated and the air stuffy. Dry soil, combined with a damp atmosphere, will also encourage mildews and they tend to reach a peak in late summer and early autumn. Leaves, and sometimes stems as well, are covered with a white powdery outgrowth as though they had been dusted with flour and, if the attack is severe, the leaves will wither and die. Adequate watering and good ventilation will help to reduce mildew. If it occurs plants should be sprayed with benomyl, dinocap or thiram.

Virus Diseases

Numerous viruses attack greenhouse plants causing various symptoms, including yellow or yellowish-green mottling of leaves, leaves closely bunched or divided into narrow, sometimes thread-like segments, dry brown spotting and stunted growth. Similar

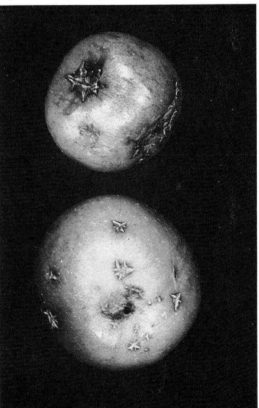

symptoms can be caused by mineral deficiencies in the soil, by excessive heat, by selective hormone weed-killers (even the small residue left in straw can affect sensitive plants such as tomatoes), poor cultivation and so on. So it is often difficult to diagnose virus infections with certainty and it is wise to consult an expert when in doubt. (*Illustration: Star Crack Virus.*)

There is no easy way of curing affected plants and,

38

since infection may be carried from them to healthy plants by sucking insects such as aphids, blades of knives or secateurs used in pruning, or even on the fingers of anyone working among the plants, it is wise to remove and burn infected plants as soon as diagnosed. Tobacco is a common source of virus infection so it is unwise to smoke in greenhouses or when handling plants. Spraying or fumigating to kill sucking pests will also limit the spread of these diseases.

Table of Pests, Diseases and other Hazards to Greenhouse Plants

Name	Symptoms	Remedies
ants	soil disturbed, greenflies 'farmed'	dust with HCH
aphids (greenflies, blackflies, etc.)	lice clustered on young stems and under side of leaves	spray with pirimiphos-methyl, resmethrin or other aphicides
botrytis (grey mould)	black decay followed by fluffy white outgrowth	raise temperature; improve ventilation; spray with benomyl
capsid bugs	leaves cockled and cracked, with brown patches	use pirimiphos-methyl aerosol or HCH smoke generators
damping off	seedlings rot at soil level and collapse	use sterilized soil; water with Cheshunt Compound
earwigs	flowers and leaves gnawed and deformed	dust with HCH
leaf miners	snaky white channels tunnelled in leaves	spray with HCH or malathion
mealy bugs	white tufts on leaves and stems, protecting cream-coloured bugs	brush with malathion
mildew (powdery)	white, mealy covering on leaves and stems	spray with benomyl or bupirimate
red spider mites	grey or bronze mottling of leaves; tiny reddish creatures on undersides	increase humidity; spray with derris or malathion
scale insects	tiny limpet-like scales adhering to leaves and stems	spray with malathion or pirimiphos-methyl
thrips	small silvery or brown streaks on stems, leaves, and petals; tiny blackish-brown insects fall out when disturbed	fumigate with HCH
virus	leaves distorted and/or with yellow mottling. Plants dwarfed. Flowers of chrysanthemums deformed. Small dry spots on leaves	destroy plants immediately; spray against aphids
weevils	leaf edges eaten by adult weevils and roots attacked by grubs	use HCH smoke generators; water with HCH
whitefly	tiny white 'flies' on plants which become sticky and covered with black mould	spray frequently with pirimiphos-methyl or resmethrin; or use *Encarsia formosa*
woodlice	small seedlings eaten	use HCH dust
excessive cold	flower buds and leaves fall; growth ceases. If severe or prolonged, plants die	raise temperature to recommended levels
excessive use of fertilizers	large, dry, brown areas on leaves similar to those caused by fumes	soak with clear cold water to wash out excess; use fertilizers according to label instructions
fumes from oil or gas stoves	dry brown areas on leaves larger than the dry spots caused by some virus infections	open ventilators a little; clean stoves and burners; fit heat exchange flues
sun scorch	leaves and young growth withering, the former usually from the edges inwards. Grapes may collapse as a result of stems being killed	shade from direct sunshine
watering too little	plants wilt and collapse	water more freely and frequently; make soil more retentive with extra peat or leaf mould
watering too much	leaves turn yellow and growth ceases; many roots dead	reduce water supply; improve drainage

4 Flowering Plants

The plants described in this chapter are those that are grown primarily for their flowers, an arbitrary but convenient division. If their foliage is good – and in some varieties, the silver-leaved cyclamen for example, it is very good – it is nevertheless regarded as a bonus rather than an alternative to flowers.

On the whole these are plants which require a fair amount of light, though by no means all appreciate strong sunshine, particularly in summer when it may scorch their leaves or flowers. Because of this light requirement they are in general less suitable for growing in rooms (where the light intensity is often low and rarely controllable) than in greenhouses, conservatories, and other structures made expressly for plant cultivation.

These are plants that exhibit a great deal of individuality since they come from many parts of the world in which climates may vary from temperate to tropical; rainfall may be anything from almost non existent to torrential; and air conditions range all the way from dry desert to humid swamp. Most puzzling of all is the way in which the flowering of some of these plants is controlled by day length so that they resolutely refuse to bloom when the ratio of day to night differs markedly from that in their native habitat.

For all these reasons these are fascinating plants to grow and one has never finished learning new things about them.

Abutilon

Abutilon

Shrubby, sun-loving plants some of which can be grown outdoors in mild places. The best for greenhouses are hybrids of *A. striatum* with bell-shaped flowers produced continuously from late spring to autumn, and even a few in winter if the temperature does not fall below 10 °C. They make big, loosely branched shrubs if left to grow unchecked but can be made shorter and bushier by annual pruning in early spring, when stems can be shortened considerably. Alternatively the long, flexible stems can be trained to wires or trellis work against the wall of a conservatory or in any other convenient place. So long as frost can be excluded, they will come to no harm but a minimum temperature of around 10 °C will produce better results. Water rather sparingly in winter especially if the greenhouse is not well warmed. One kind, *A. striatum thomsonii*, is grown primarily for its

Acacia dealbata

green and yellow mottled leaves and is often planted outdoors in summer bedding displays. Another species, *A. megapotamicum*, has dangling scarlet and yellow flowers like little lanterns and thin stems which can be tied to supports or allowed to hang over the edge of staging.

All can be grown from summer cuttings in a propagator or from seed sown in a temperature of 15–18 °C in spring.

Acacia (Wattle)

Trees and shrubs, mostly with very small yellow flowers in little ball or cylinder-shaped clusters. Some make good pot plants or can be planted in a bed of soil on the greenhouse or conservatory floor and allowed to grow into larger specimens. All can be grown in ordinary peat or soil mixtures in any well lighted structure from which frost can be excluded. But the most popular winter-flowering species, such as *A. dealbata*, often erroneously called 'mimosa', with

sweetly scented flowers; *A. armata* and *A. drummondii* will do better in a winter temperature of 10–15 °C. Water carefully in winter, especially if the temperature drops below 5 °C, when plants should be rather dry. Long stems can be shortened or removed after flowering. Increase by seed sown in a temperature of 15–18 °C in spring or by summer cuttings in a propagator.

Achimenes

Low growing or sprawling herbaceous plants with showy trumpet-shaped flowers produced continuously all summer. Colours include pink, red, violet or purple, and white. All make excellent pot or hanging basket plants. When grown in pots they may need a few branching twigs to support their thin stems or they can be made stiffer and more compact if the tips of stems are pinched off occasionally to encourage branching. All make little cylindrical tubers which can be stored dry in winter in a minimum temperature of

Achimenes 'Early Arnold' and 'Minuet'

7 °C and then be restarted during the spring months in a temperature of 15–18 °C. Pot the tubers 2 cm deep and 5 cm apart in peat potting compost or a soil mixture containing a liberal amount of peat and/or leaf mould. Water sparingly for the first few weeks after starting, then freely as the plants begin to grow fast, but gradually reduce the water supply in early autumn until soil is quite dry. Shade from strong sunshine in summer.

Achimenes can be raised from seed sown in a temperature of 21–27 °C in spring.

Acidanthera

The kind commonly grown, *A. bicolor murieliae*, looks like a gladiolus with a few sweetly scented, white, maroon-blotched flowers clustered at the top of the stem rather than spread out in a spike. It is nearly hardy but often flowers so late outdoors that its flowers are spoiled by autumn gales. Under glass it will flower late in summer. It makes corms like a gladiolus and these can be stored dry in winter in any frostproof place. They are potted in early spring 2½ cm deep, four or five corms in each 10 cm pot or they can be planted in a bed on the greenhouse floor in ordinary soil or peat potting mixture. They like sunshine, a temperature of 13–21 °C (it can rise higher on sunny days) and plenty of water while growing.

The corms increase in number naturally and plants can also be raised from seed sown in spring in a temperature of 15–18 °C but seedlings will not flower the first year.

Agapanthus (African Lily)

Some kinds are fairly hardy but *A. africanus* (also known as *A. umbellatus*) will not survive much frost

Agapanthus africanus

and is usually grown as a cool greenhouse or conservatory plant or is stood outdoors in a sunny place in summer but overwintered in a frostproof greenhouse or conservatory. It makes large clumps of strap-shaped leaves and has big heads of violet blue or white flowers in summer. It does not make bulbs but forms a mass of white, fleshy, roots which make the division of old plants rather difficult. Plants can also be raised readily from seed sown in spring in a temperature of 15–18 °C but seedlings will not flower during their first year.

All kinds of agapanthus are easily grown in any sunny, frostproof conservatory in large pots or tubs, or planted in beds of soil. They will grow in all fertile soils and need plenty of water in spring and summer, but should be watered sparingly in winter especially if temperatures drop below 10 °C.

Allemanda

This name is often erroneously spelled allamanda. The

Allemanda

kind usually grown is *A. cathartica*, a very vigorous climbing plant most suitable for large greenhouses or conservatories where it can be planted in a bed of soil and allowed to ramble at will. However, it can also be grown successfully in large pots or tubs in fairly rich soil (John Innes No. 2 or similar), watered freely in spring and summer, and moderately in autumn and winter. It likes a warm atmosphere and temperatures should not fall below 13 °C in winter. The shiny, yellow, trumpet-shaped flowers are produced from spring to early autumn. The slender stems should be tied to wires, trellis work, or some other support, and can be cut back in late winter. Tips of stems that threaten to grow too far can be nipped out any time in summer. Increase is by cuttings in summer in a warm propagator.

Anthurium (Flamingo Plant, Tail Flower)
The flowers of these very showy plants are highly distinctive, consisting of a broad, coloured, tongue-like spathe, often held downward, with a slender yellow spadix projecting like a stiff tail from it. The spathe is usually some shade of red but there are also pink and white varieties. The largest flowers are produced by *A. andreanum*. Another species, *A. scherzerianum*, with small scarlet spathes, is more tolerant of dry air and so makes a better house plant. All kinds grow well in pots in peat potting mixture or soil mixtures containing quite a lot of peat in temperatures 13–18 °C in winter, rising with sun heat in summer. Plants should be shaded from direct sunshine from late spring to early autumn. Water

freely in summer, moderately at other times and maintain a damp atmosphere, particularly in spring and summer. Repot in spring, when large plants can be divided. Anthuriums can also be raised from seed sown in a temperature of 24–26 °C in spring but seedlings may take a few years to reach flowering size.

Arum Lily. *See* Zantedeschia (*page 87*)

Azalea
It is the evergreen 'Indian' azaleas, garden varieties of *Rhododendron simsii*, that are mainly grown as pot plants under glass and for house decoration. They are short, well branched shrubs with small leaves and usually double flowers freely produced in winter and spring. The colour range is mainly various shades of pink and red, often with white, and there are also pure white varieties. Time of flowering is controlled in part by variety, in part by temperature. All varieties are nearly hardy and can be grown in any structure from which frost can be excluded, but for winter flowers a temperature of 13–15 °C is required. All are lime haters and so require a moderately acid soil mixture from which lime and chalk are excluded. They all grow well in peat mixtures provided they have adequate nutrients and no lime or chalk, or a mixture of 3 parts peat, 1 part lime-free loam and 1 part calcium-free sand. Water fairly freely in spring and summer when plants will also benefit from overhead spraying with water. Water moderately in winter but never let the soil become dry. Shade lightly in summer or, better still, stand plants outdoors in a shady but not dark

Anthurium andreanum

place. Increase is by summer cuttings or by grafting but neither is easy.

Babiana (Baboon Root)

Small South African plants which produce corms and carry their blue, purple or crimson flowers in short spikes in spring or early summer. They are nearly hardy and make attractive pot plants for a sunny, frostproof greenhouse. Pot the corms in autumn, 5 or 6 in each 10 cm pot, covering them well and using a rather porous soil mixture. Water moderately at first, freely in spring and early autumn but after midsummer reduce the water supply and keep quite dry for a few weeks before shaking out the corms and repotting in early autumn. The corms increase naturally and plants can also be grown from seed sown in a temperature of 15–18 °C in spring but seedlings will not flower the first year.

Begonia

Some begonias, and most notably all varieties of *B. rex*, are grown for their ornamental leaves and so are described in Chapter 5. Those grown primarily for their flowers are best divided, for cultural purposes, into two major groups: one with tuberous roots and the other with fibrous roots.

  B. semperflorens, which belongs to the second group, is a low growing plant with small flowers produced almost continuously in dense sprays. Because of this habit it is very popular for summer bedding, when it is usually treated as a half hardy annual to be renewed each year from seed sown in a warm greenhouse in late winter or early spring. In fact it is a perennial and, if kept in a greenhouse with minimum temperature of about 13 °C it will continue to flower much of the autumn and winter.

  The most popular tuberous rooted begonias are manmade hybrids and they produce their large, usually double flowers all summer. They can also be used for summer bedding though their big flowers are much more vulnerable to wind and rain than the small single flowers of *B. semperflorens*. The finest results are obtained by growing them as greenhouse pot plants. Though tender, they do not need much heat as they rest during the winter, when the tubers can be stored dry in any frostproof place such as a cupboard indoors. They are then re-started into growth in late winter or early spring by being bedded in moist peat in a temperature of 16–18 °C. As soon as each tuber has formed two or three leaves it is potted individually in a 9 cm pot in a fairly rich, spongy compost such as John Innes No. 1 plus a little extra peat or some leaf mould, so that it is just covered. Later it is moved into 13–15 cm pots as seems necessary.

  From midspring onwards little artificial heat will be required as these begonias thrive best in a fairly cool house with shading from direct sunshine in summer. They are watered fairly freely in summer and fed

Begonia crispa marginata

occasionally with liquid fertilizer but in early autumn watering is gradually reduced, the leaves are allowed to die down and eventually the tubers are removed from the soil and stored dry. The heavy flowers of some varieties need individual supports, either small split canes or special wire supports which can be obtained from some garden shops. There are also varieties with smaller flowers and longer, pendulous stems which are best grown in hanging baskets or in pots stood on pedestals so that the stems can hang down freely. Otherwise cultivation is the same as for the erect growing varieties.

  A third race, known as *B. multiflora*, is intermediate in habit and flower size between *B. semperflorens* and the hybrid tuberous rooted begonias. Varieties of this type can be used for summer bedding or can be grown as pot plants. They also make tuberous roots which can be stored dry in winter and re-started early the following year.

  All these begonias can be grown from seed sown in spring but it is almost dust-like and requires no soil covering. It should be sown on the surface of a peat compost in pots or pans which should then be covered with glass and newspaper to keep the peat moist and the seeds dark. As soon as seedlings appear the paper must be removed. A few days later the glass can be tilted to let in air and still later removed completely.

The tiny seedlings must be pricked out carefully and, when sufficiently large, potted singly, first in 6 cm pots, later in larger pots as necessary. If seed is sown in mid to late winter in a temperature of 16–18 °C, plants should flower the first summer.

Yet another race of begonia, usually known as 'Gloire de Lorraine' after the most popular variety, flowers in winter. Seed can be sown in spring as described for other begonias and the seedlings pricked out and later potted in a similar manner. However, these are fibrous rooted begonias with no complete resting season so they must be watered and kept growing all the year. In winter they like a temperature of 16 °C or more but will come to no harm if it occasionally falls to 13 °C. The flowers are single and produced in large sprays on plants that can be 30 cm high and as much or more in diameter. 'Gloire de Lorraine' has pale pink flowers but there are also white-flowered varieties.

These begonias can also be grown from cuttings of young shoots in a warm propagator in spring and this is the best way to grow another race of winter flowering begonias, of which pink flowered 'Optima' is a favourite variety, which have larger flowers and semi-tuberous roots. These are more difficult to manage than 'Gloire de Lorraine', requiring slightly higher temperatures and more careful watering, especially after flowering when the soil should be no more than just moist for a few weeks.

Beloperone

Beloperone (Shrimp Plant)

This is a good perennial in flower most of the year and it is safe in any house in which a minimum winter temperature of 7 °C can be maintained, though it is more likely to bloom in winter if the temperature is 13 °C or more. The popular name refers to the shape and colour of the curving flower spikes, the flowers themselves being white but almost enveloped in overlapping, shrimp-coloured bracts. There is also a very distinctive variety with lime-green bracts and a dwarf variety only about 30 cm high against the normal 50–60 cm. All will grow in ordinary soil or peat mixtures and should be watered all year, more freely in spring and summer, when they are growing, than in autumn and winter.

Cuttings root readily in a propagator in summer or plants can be raised from seed sown in a temperature of 16–18 °C in spring but the dwarf and lime-green varieties are unlikely to breed entirely true from seed.

Billbergia

Among the easiest to grow of this large family of bromeliads is *B. nutans*, a distinctive plant with narrow, rather stiff leaves and slender, arching, 30 cm high stems bearing drooping clusters of tubular green and blue flowers emerging from pink bracts. It will grow in any greenhouse with a minimum winter temperature of 7 °C or indoors, preferably near a window. In greenhouses it will appreciate shading

Billbergia nutans

from strong sunshine in summer. It will grow in ordinary soil or peat mixtures, and should be watered rather sparingly in winter but normally at other times of the year. Increase is by division when repotting in spring.

Bougainvillea

These are the vigorous climbers which, in warm countries, cover walls and buildings with sheets of rose and magenta. The true flowers are inconspicuous and it is the bracts that surround them that make the display. Bougainvillea can be grown in any greenhouse or conservatory in which the temperature does not fall below 7 °C but higher temperatures are appreciated and plants must have sunshine if they are to flower freely. If planted in beds of soil on the floor of the house they grow very vigorously and can cover the back wall of quite a large conservatory; or they can be trained beneath the rafters of a greenhouse. In fairly large pots or tubs they can be kept more under control, especially if some of the less vigorous garden varieties are grown such as orange-coloured 'Mrs McLean' or 'Orange King'. 'Mrs Butt', with deep rose-coloured flowers, is the most commonly seen. All will grow in soil or peat mixtures which should not be too rich. Plants should be watered freely from spring to early autumn but sparingly in winter. To restrict growth side growths can be cut back in early spring to within 3 or 4 cm of the main stems. Cuttings of firm young shoots will root in summer in a warm propagator.

Bouvardia

Evergreen shrubs with clusters of small, tubular, starry-mouthed and sweet-scented flowers which may be scarlet, pink or white, single or double. They are showy plants, flowering in winter when colour is at a premium, but they need a minimum night temperature of 13 °C rising by day to 16–21 °C to keep them growing and flowering happily. In summer they are no problem and can even be stood outdoors in a sunny sheltered place if there is no room in the greenhouse. They make good pot plants in a moderately rich peat- or soil-based mixture with plenty of water most of the time but very little for three or four weeks in spring, after flowering, when the plants need to rest. This is the time to cut back the stems, if the plants are becoming too big.

Cuttings of firm young shoots will form roots in a warm propagator in summer or root cuttings can be taken in winter and started in a similar propagator.

Browallia

These are annuals which must be renewed from seed every year. If two sowings are made, one in late winter or early spring, the second in late spring or early summer, the plants will flower successively from about midsummer until autumn. A temperature of about 18 °C is necessary for germination and seedlings can be grown in ordinary soil or peat potting mixtures. One

Bougainvillea

A hybrid Bouvardia

plant will fill a 10 cm pot. Grow in a light greenhouse, water normally and discard plants when the last flowers fade. *B. speciosa major* and *B. viscosa* 'Sapphire' are the best varieties. Both grow 25–30 cm high and have violet-blue flowers.

Brunfelsia

Brunfelsia calycina

The kind most usually seen is *B. calycina*, a small, evergreen shrub with sweetly scented flowers which will go on opening throughout the year if a minimum temperature of 13 °C can be maintained. Plants will survive in any frostproof greenhouse but if the winter temperature is low flowers will cease and some leaves may fall. A variety named 'Floribunda' will flower with less warmth than the common type. It can be grown in pots or in beds in ordinary peat or soil mixtures with normal watering but if the temperature does fall below 13 °C in winter the water supply should be reduced and the soil kept just moist, no more. There are other species, some with white flowers, but they are larger and less suitable for use as pot plants. All kinds can be grown from summer cuttings rooted in a warm propagator and all can be pruned a little each spring to keep them tidy.

Calceolaria

The most popular kinds for greenhouse cultivation are the large-flowered biennials, known as *C. herbacea*, which flower in spring and early summer. The flowers are pouched, closely clustered in quite large heads and are strikingly coloured yellow, orange, red or crimson often with a dark shade heavily spotted on a lighter ground colour. Normally plants are about 40–45 cm high but there are also dwarf varieties little more than half this. All are grown from seed sown in late spring or early summer in an unheated greenhouse. Seedlings are pricked out into boxes filled with a soil or peat seed mixture and, when these are filled, are potted singly into a normal soil or peat potting mixture. As they are nearly hardy, they can be grown in an unheated frame all summer but are best returned to a light, airy, frost-proof greenhouse in autumn before there is risk of frost. Throughout the year they should be watered normally but with care to keep water as far as possible off the leaves and crowns of the plants. The largest plants may need to be moved on into 15 cm pots for flowering but the smaller ones will be satisfied with 13 cm pots. After flowering the plants are discarded.

There are also perennial calceolarias, including a semi-shrubby kind named *C. integrifolia·* which is much used as a summer bedding plant. It has much smaller but similarly pouched yellow or bronzy-red flowers and can either be raised from seed sown in early spring in a temperature of 16–18 °C or from cuttings of young growth in a propagator or pot covered with a polythene bag in spring or summer. The plants are nearly hardy and will survive for years outdoors in mild places but severe frost will kill them. They will grow and flower in full sun or partial shade in all reasonably fertile soils.

Callistemon (Bottle Brush)

The flowers of these evergreen shrubs are composed mainly of long, bristle-like stamens clustered in a dense cylindrical spike like a bottle brush. They may be pink, scarlet, crimson, yellow or white according to their kind. All are rather too big to make convenient pot plants but, where there is room for them, they are very showy and distinctive. All dislike chalk and lime and should be grown in moderately acid peat- or soil-based mixtures. They like sunshine, are nearly hardy and can be grown outdoors in some sheltered places.

Calceolaria 'Victoria Prize'

Callistemon citrinus

In a greenhouse it is only necessary to exclude frost and to water rather sparingly when the weather is cold. In summer plants can stand outdoors. They do not much like being pruned but some stems can be removed in spring if the plants get too large. Cuttings of firm young shoots will root in summer in peat and sand in a propagator.

Camellia

Camellia japonica

These handsome evergreen shrubs are sufficiently hardy to be grown outdoors, except in the coldest places, but their flowers come early, some in winter, many in early spring and they can be spoiled by frost,

wind or heavy rain. The very early flowering or very large-flowered varieties are most at risk and are often grown in greenhouses or conservatories either as pot or tub plants or in beds of soil. They can be trained against the back walls of conservatories or allowed to develop into large bushes.

All kinds dislike lime and chalk and are best grown in a mixture of 2 parts by bulk lime-free loam and 1 part peat. They can be stood outdoors all summer. They need quite a lot of water, especially in summer when they can also be fed once a week with a little liquid fertilizer. If left in the greenhouse all summer they should be shaded from direct sunshine. Any pruning necessary to keep them shapely or within bounds should be done immediately the flowers fade.

Increase is by cuttings or by mature leaves inserted in peat and sand in summer in a propagator. Seeds will also germinate in similar compost in a frame or cool greenhouse in spring but it will be several years before seedlings grow large enough to flower.

Campanula

Campanula isophylla

Two very different kinds of campanula are grown in greenhouses. One of them, C. isophylla, is a trailing perennial with starry blue or white flowers produced continuously in summer and early autumn. This is an excellent plant to grow in hanging baskets or in pots placed at the edge of the greenhouse staging so that the stems can hang down. It is nearly hardy, will thrive in any frost-free house in sun or partial shade, in ordinary soil or peat potting mixtures. It needs normal watering and can be raised from seed sown in a greenhouse or frame in spring or by cuttings in late summer or early autumn in a propagator or in a pot placed inside a polythene bag.

The other kind popular for greenhouse cultivation is C. pyramidalis, a biennial sometimes called the Chimney Bellflower because of its tall, narrow spikes of blue or white flowers. It is renewed annually from seeds sown in spring in a temperature of 15 °C. Seedlings are potted singly in a soil- or peat-based potting mixture and are grown in a cool house or, during the summer months, in a frame outdoors. They will need to be moved on to larger pots and may need pots 25 cm in diameter by the autumn or following early spring. In winter they need a light, frostproof greenhouse. After flowering in early summer the plants should be discarded.

Campsis radicans

Campsis (Trumpet Vine)

Vigorous climbers sometimes known as *Bignonia* or *Tecoma*. The showy, trumpet-shaped flowers are produced in clusters in late summer and early autumn. *C. grandiflora*, with orange-red flowers and *C.* 'Madame Galen', with deep salmon-red flowers are the two best kinds to grow under glass. They can be grown in large pots or tubs but are happier in a bed of reasonably good soil. They are almost hardy and will survive in any frost-free greenhouse but they need plenty of warmth and sunshine to make them flower freely. They should be watered fairly freely in spring and summer, sparingly in autumn and winter and can be cut down to within 30 cm of ground level in late winter. They are to some extent self-clinging to walls but it is advisable to supply wires or trellis to which their long stems can be tied. Stem cuttings root readily in a propagator in summer and plants can also be grown from root cuttings in winter or from seed sown in a temperature of 16–18 °C in spring.

Canna (Indian Shot)

These very showy plants with broad, upstanding leaves and stout spikes of flamboyant flowers in summer are much used for subtropical bedding effects and can also be grown as greenhouse pot plants. Colours include yellow, orange and red, often with one colour splashed on another.

Cannas make fleshy roots which can be stored dry in

winter in any frostproof place, to be restarted in early spring by being potted, watered and placed in a temperature of 16–18 °C. Increase is by division or by cutting the roots in sections, each having a growth bud. Plant these in late spring when the soil has warmed, covering them with about 10 cm of soil. Plants can also be raised from seed but the seeds are hard coated and rather difficult to germinate. They should be soaked in warm water for 24 hours, then the coat of each seed should be punctured with the point of a penknife, after which the seeds can be sown in a temperature of 25–28 °C.

Cannas enjoy rich soil and plenty of water while they are growing. Those to be used for summer bedding should be carefully hardened off in late spring for planting out in early summer. Those to be flowers indoors should be moved into larger pots or small tubs in good soil- or peat-based potting compost and when well established in these, can be fed once a week with liquid fertilizer. Watering is reduced in autumn so that leaves can die down and roots can be stored dry in a frostproof place.

Carnation

There are numerous different types of carnation, but only two, the Perpetual Flowering Carnation and the Malmaison Carnation, are commonly grown in greenhouses. Both are nearly hardy and plants can be stood outdoors in summer if there is no room for them inside, but they need protection in winter, which is when the flowers of perpetual carnations are most valuable.

A third group, the Chabaud carnations, are grown as half hardy annuals for summer flowering outdoors. They have large, double, sweetly scented flowers in a variety of colours and make excellent cut flowers besides being very decorative in the garden. They are reared annually from seed sown in later winter or early spring in a temperature of 16–18 °C. Seedlings are pricked out and grown on under glass but are hardened off in time to be planted outdoors in a sunny

Carnation 'Grenadin'

place in late spring or early summer. They succeed in most soils but have a special liking for those containing lime.

Perpetual and Malmaison carnations can also be raised from seed treated this way but seedlings vary in colour and quality and so the named varieties are increased vegetatively, the Perpetuals by cuttings, taken in winter or early spring, Malmaisons usually by layering in summer as soon as the flowers fade. Cuttings are prepared from short side shoots midway up the flowering stems, broken away where they join the stem and inserted in sand or sandy soil in a propagator. When rooted, they are potted singly in a good soil compost containing lime or chalk, first in 8 cm pots but, when they have filled these with roots, in larger sizes until they reach the 15–20 cm pots in which they will flower. The top two joints of each young plant are broken out when it has made about eight pairs of leaves to make it branch, and this 'stopping' is repeated on the secondary stems when they have made about eight pairs of leaves. Plants should not be stopped after midsummer if winter flowers are required.

Carnations like a sunny, airy house. No extra heat is required in summer, and in winter it will be sufficient to prevent the temperature falling below 7 °C though artificial heat, combined with a little top ventilation, may be necessary in damp weather to keep the air fairly dry and circulating. When flower buds appear it is usual to retain only one at the tip of each stem and nip out side buds below the terminal buds so that a large flower is produced, but this is not done with American Spray varieties. Plants can grow quite tall and need careful staking. Throughout soil should be kept nicely moist, never waterlogged, and from about midsummer onward plants can be fed every seven to ten days with a carnation fertilizer. Perpetual carnations are seldom retained after their second flowering season as plants deteriorate in vigour and often become infected with disease.

Malmaison carnations only flower in summer and are usually renewed annually by layering. Soil and watering requirements are the same as for Perpetual carnations but, since they do not flower in winter, there is not the same necessity to keep the temperature up, and provided they do not actually freeze, they will come to no harm. The most convenient way to layer these carnations is to plant them in a bed of soil, either outdoors or in the greenhouse, directly they have finished flowering and peg the best non-flowering stems into the soil around each plant. If a slit is made through a joint where the stem is to be pegged to the soil and the wound is dusted with hormone rooting powder, good roots will be formed in about six weeks, when layers can be lifted and potted directly into the 13–15 cm pots in which they will flower the following year.

Red spider and thrips can be troublesome summer pests of carnations if the air becomes too hot and dry.

This is one good reason for standing the plants in a frame or outside in summer. Occasional late spring and summer spraying with derris, diazinon or malathion will also help to prevent these pests establishing themselves.

Cassia

The kind most commonly grown, *C. corymbosa*, is a sprawling evergreen shrub which, in greenhouses and conservatories, is best treated as a climber, its flexible stems tied to wires or trellis. The yellow flowers, borne in loose clusters in summer and early autumn, are very showy. It is almost hardy and will survive so long as it does not freeze, but for good flower production it must have sunshine. Plants are best grown in beds of good soil but they can be grown in large pots or tubs in an ordinary soil-based potting compost. Water fairly freely in spring and summer, just sufficiently to prevent the soil becoming dry in autumn and winter. If plants grow too large stems can be cut out or shortened in early spring or seed will germinate in spring in a temperature of 18–20 °C.

Celosia

Celosia 'Dwarf Geisha'

There are two totally distinct kinds of celosia: one, known as *cristata*, with tiny flowers crowded into sinuous heads which have earned it the popular name Cockscomb; the other, known as *plumosa*, with flowers in feathery plumes, for which reason it is sometimes called Prince of Wales' Feather. The colours of the flowers can be very brilliant and include yellow, orange, salmon, scarlet, carmine and crimson.

Both are half hardy annuals occasionally used for summer bedding but more often grown as pot plants. Seed is sown in late winter or early spring in a temperature of 16–18 °C. Seedlings pricked out and later potted singly in soil or peat potting compost will require no artificial heat from late spring onwards. They should be watered fairly freely and fed with weak liquid fertilizer once well established in the pots in which they will flower.

Celsia

Celsia arcturus

The kind commonly grown, *C. arcturus*, makes a rosette of leaves from which come narrow spikes of yellow flowers like those of a short verbascum. It is a perennial but is often treated as an annual or biennial since it grows readily from seed and can flower in six months from sowing. If seed is sown in early spring plants will flower in autumn, if sown about midsummer they will start to flower the following spring. Seed germinates in a temperature of around 15–16 °C and in winter only sufficient heat is required to exclude frost. The house should be sunny, the soil porous but reasonably good. Plants will flower well in 13–15 cm pots.

Cestrum

These are climbers or whippy stemmed plants easily tied to wires or trellis. The flowers are small and tubular, produced in clusters in summer. One of the best is *C. aurantiacum* with orange-yellow flowers. *C. purpureum* is reddish purple. All are nearly hardy and can be grown in any sunny greenhouse or conservatory from which frost can be excluded. Plant directly in a bed of good soil or grow in large pots or tubs in an ordinary soil-based potting mixture. Water normally and in early spring thin out or shorten stems as necessary to keep plants within bounds. Cuttings root readily in summer in a propagator.

Chrysanthemum

One can have a lot of fun growing greenhouse chrysanthemums from seed but, except for a few special types – like the bushy, single-flowered Charm varieties and the semi-weeping Cascade chrysanthemums – the habits, flower forms, and colours of chrysanthemums raised from seed vary so much that it becomes rather like a lucky dip. One may get what one is looking for or one may not. The only way to be quite certain is to obtain 'named' varieties and increase them by cuttings.

Cuttings can be rooted at any time of the year but, for the home greenhouse, late winter and early spring is the most convenient period. The best shoots to choose are the young ones then coming up freely through the soil direct from the roots. If they are severed when 5–7 cm long, and the base of each is dipped in hormone rooting powder and then inserted in sandy soil in a propagator, they will root in a few weeks. Cuttings should then be potted singly in a good soil-based potting compost, such as John Innes No. 1, in 7–8 cm pots. They will need to be moved on periodically to larger sizes and richer soil until, by late spring or early summer, they reach the 18–22 cm pots in which they will flower. Late struck cuttings can be flowered in smaller pots. All plants can be fed weekly with liquid fertilizer once they are established in their final pots but feeding should cease when the flowers begin to open.

Chrysanthemums are nearly hardy and require little artificial heat. All summer they can stand outdoors in a sunny place but they should go into a greenhouse in autumn before there is danger of frost, which can damage the flower buds, and even more easily, the opening flowers, of early varieties. In winter a minimum temperature of 7 °C is enough but a little more will be helpful while plants are coming into bloom to keep the air fairly dry and prevent attacks by botrytis (grey mould) which can rot the flowers.

As a rule the tips of the growing plants are nipped out when they are 20–23 cm high to make them branch and, if very bushy plants are required, the resultant stems may themselves be pinched when about 10–12 cm long. Some chrysanthemums, particularly those with large flowers, are restricted to one flower per stem, all side buds and growing shoots which form around or below this flower bud being removed at an early stage. Other varieties are grown for spray flowers, i.e. clusters of smaller blooms. These may be allowed to develop quite naturally or the central flower bud in each cluster may be removed leaving the rest to develop, since, if left, it will open earlier than the others and may already be fading by the time they are opening, so spoiling the effect of the spray. Nearly all varieties require careful staking and tying from the time they reach their final pots. Big plants may need several canes with encircling ties.

After flowering most of the plants are discarded, only sufficient of each variety being retained to give cuttings for the following year. The old flowering stems are cut off a few centimetres above soil level and the pots can then be packed close together to economize on space. The soil should be kept just moist and the temperature maintained at 15 °C. Cuttings can be taken as they become available and, when sufficient have been secured, the old plants should be thrown away.

If chrysanthemums are to be grown from seed, this should be sown in late winter or early spring in a temperature of 15–18 °C. Seedlings are treated in a similar way to rooted cuttings except that those of Charm and Cascade varieties may be pinched more frequently to increase the number of branches they make. No disbudding is carried out with these varieties and the stems of Cascade chrysanthemums can be tied downwards to wires or canes to exaggerate their natural cascading habit.

Outdoor or Border chrysanthemums are simply varieties that bloom sufficiently early to be planted outdoors with reasonable expectation of a good display before autumn frosts spoil the flowers. They may be grown from cuttings or from seed just like the greenhouse chrysanthemums but in late spring they are planted outdoors instead of being moved on into larger pots. After flowering a few plants of each variety are cut down, almost to soil level, lifted, and either potted or packed into boxes, with soil around the roots, as stock plants from which cuttings will be taken later. It is best to give them greenhouse protection in winter just like the indoor varieties.

Korean chrysanthemums flower in autumn but are less sensitive to frost than most other kinds and so can be flowered outdoors. They grow well from seed and also from cuttings.

Cineraria

The greenhouse cinerarias are among the showiest of all flowers that can be grown with just sufficient heat to exclude frost. Though perennial, they are invariably grown as annuals from seed sown in late spring or early summer to give plants that will start to flower in the autumn from the earlier sowings or in late winter from the last sowings. They make big, branching sprays of single, daisy type flowers in various shades of blue, pink, carmine, scarlet, crimson and purple often with a white zone around the centre of the flower. There are several types, the Grandiflora varieties

Cineraria dwarf

having large flowers, the Multiflora varieties having medium size flowers and the Stellata varieties, small flowers. Heights, also vary from 30 to 60 cm.

No artificial heat is required to germinate the seed and all summer the seedlings can be grown in a frame if there is no room for them in the greenhouse. Only in autumn and winter do they need protection from frost and even then should be grown in quite cool conditions, temperature 13–18 °C. Some heat may be needed to keep the air dry and circulating as decay at the crowns can occur in damp, cold conditions. Water should be applied direct to the soil, not splashed over the leaves, and plants should be given plenty of room and all the light possible.

Seedlings are pricked off in the ordinary way and then potted singly in 7 cm pots and moved on as necessary into the 12–15 cm pots in which they will flower. They grow well in both soil and peat mixtures.

Clematis (see illustration p. 31)

Only a few kinds are sufficiently tender to require greenhouse protection but one that will not survive much frost and is both beautiful and early flowering is C. indivisa. Its white flowers are not very large but are freely produced in loose clusters in spring. It only needs protection from frost, will grow in any reasonably good soil and can be allowed to climb on wires or trellis up the back wall of a conservatory or in any other reasonably light place. It should be watered normally and can be pruned after flowering as necessary to keep it in bounds. It can be raised from seed sown in spring or from cuttings taken in summer and rooted in a propagator. Cuttings should be severed mid-way between joints, not immediately below a joint as is usual with most plants.

Clerodendrum

Two species are commonly grown in greenhouses and conservatories, one a climber the other a shrub. The climber is *C. thomsoniae*, a twining plant with clusters of red and white flowers in summer. The shrub is *C. speciosissimum*, often known as *C. fallax*, with scarlet flowers in erect, spike-like clusters, also in summer. Both can be grown in a minimum temperature of 10 °C but will appreciate more. *C. thomsoniae* can be grown in a large pot, a tub or in a bed of soil and will need something to twine around. It can be used to clothe the back wall of a conservatory or can be trained on wires beneath the rafters, but quite often it is allowed to grow over a crinoline-like frame of wire so that the plant forms a large dome. It can be pruned as necessary to keep it shapely in spring and is usually increased by cuttings in summer in a warm propagator.

C. fallax can also be raised from summer cuttings but is more often grown from seed sown in late winter or early spring in a temperature of 18–21 °C. If grown in a fairly warm temperature the seedlings will flower the first year.

Both species will grow in peat potting mixtures but, because of their permanence, are really better in a good soil potting mixture such as John Innes No. 2. They are watered fairly freely in spring and summer, moderately autumn and winter.

Clianthus (Lobster Claw, Parrots' Bill)

The popular names refer to the unusual shape of the flowers which are scarlet in the ordinary form of *C. puniceus*, white in variety 'Alba'. The two look well planted together. The evergreen leaves are composed of numerous small leaflets and are decidedly decorative. The stems are rather weak and sprawling and so *C. puniceus* is usually grown as a climber, tied to wires, trellis or any other convenient support. It is nearly hardy and can be planted outdoors in mild, fairly frost-free places but it makes an excellent plant for a sunny greenhouse or conservatory with just sufficient heat available to exclude frost. It likes reasonably good but porous soil and can be grown in large pots or tubs but is really happier planted in a bed on the greenhouse floor. Plants should be watered fairly freely in spring and summer, rather sparingly in autumn and winter. If they grow too large some stems can be cut right out in spring.

Increase is by seeds sown in a temperature of 18–21 °C in spring or by cuttings of short side shoots in summer in a warm propagator. Slugs and snails are fond of clianthus and, if troublesome, should be killed with a methiocarb or metaldehyde slug bait.

Clivia

The kind commonly grown is *C. miniata*, a plant with fleshy roots and broadly strap-shaped leaves. The orange or yellow, funnel-shaped flowers are produced in spring in close clusters on 30–45 cm stems. Clivias make excellent pot plants for a greenhouse or conservatory with a minimum temperature around 10 °C though they will survive lower temperatures provided they do not actually freeze. They are best grown in an ordinary soil-based potting mixture in pots just sufficiently large to contain their roots comfortably. They should be watered fairly freely from spring to autumn, sparingly in winter though the soil should never be allowed to become quite dry. In summer they should be shaded from direct sunshine.

Seeds will germinate in spring in a temperature of 16–18 °C but seedlings may take a few years to reach flowering size. Large plants can be divided when repotting immediately after flowering in spring.

Cobaea (Cathedral Bells)

This is one of the fastest growing climbers, its slender stems being capable of extending 4–5 m in a year. Because of this speed and the ease with which it can be raised from seed, it is often grown as a half-hardy annual, seed being sown in early spring in a temperature of 16–18 °C, seedlings potted singly in an ordinary peat or soil potting mixture and hardened off for planting outdoors in late spring or early summer. It will quickly cover an arch or grow along a fence or wall. If the position is warm and sunny it will produce its bell-shaped, violet-purple, or white and green flowers freely in summer. However, it is not an annual but a perennial and in a frost-proof greenhouse or conservatory will live for years. In such a place it is best planted in a bed of good soil and pruned each spring as necessary to keep it in bounds.

Columnea

There are numerous species, most of them handsome, trailing or semi-shrubby plants. The kind most commonly grown is *C. gloriosa*. This is ideal for a hanging basket in a fairly warm greenhouse as the slender stems hang straight down and the orange-red, hooded flowers stand out from them. It needs a minimum temperature of 13 °C and is even happier with a few degrees more. It also likes a fairly humid atmosphere, plenty of water in spring and summer and a moderate amount in autumn and winter. A rather spongy mixture of equal parts by volume soil, peat and chopped sphagnum moss suits it and most other species well. Cuttings taken in summer will root in sand and peat in a warm propagator.

Coronilla

An evergreen shrubby species, *C. glauca* makes a good pot plant and there is also an attractive variety with cream variegated leaves. Both can be grown with little or no heat, though if they can be given a minimum of 7 °C they will continue to produce their small, yellow, sweetly scented flowers most of the winter as well as in summer. Both will grow in any reasonably good soil-based potting mixture, should be given as much sun-

Below: Cobaea scandens

Top right: Columnea gloriosa

Middle right: Clerodendrum thomsoniae

Bottom right: Clivia miniata

shine as possible and watered normally. Alternatively they can be planted in a bed against the back wall of a conservatory and trained to wires or trellis which they will clothe very attractively. Stems can be shortened or cut out in spring. Cuttings will root in summer in a propagator.

Crassula

All the crassulas are succulents and they are much confused with other closely allied plants such as Rochea and Kalanchoe. One of the most attractive kinds is *Crassula falcata* which has greyish leaves and showy clusters of orange-scarlet flowers on stems 30–60 cm high in summer. It should be grown in a

Crassula argentea

rather gritty compost in the smallest pots that will contain its roots comfortably. Water fairly freely in spring and summer but sparingly in autumn and winter. Grow in the sunniest position possible and maintain a minimum temperature of 7 °C, more if possible. Increase by cuttings rooted in sand, or a mixture of sand and soil, in late spring or summer.

Crocus

All kinds of crocus, both the delicately formed wild species and the more amply built garden hybrids, look charming grown in half pots or pans and flower early in an unheated, or very slightly heated, greenhouse. A 13 cm pan or half pot will take from 7 to 9 corms planted in any porous peat or soil-based potting mixture. A mixture of 2 parts peat, 1 of soil and 1 of coarse sand will do well. The corms should be potted in early autumn, just covered with soil and then placed in any cool place for 8–10 weeks to form roots. They will need to be protected from mice during this period for

these regard the corms as a delicacy. Then, as shoots appear, the crocuses must be given all the light possible. The compost should be kept nicely moist throughout. In early summer the leaves will die down and little or no water need be given for a few weeks until the corms are shaken out and repotted or are planted out of doors.

Crossandra

These small evergreen shrubs make excellent pot plants for a well warmed greenhouse. They require a minimum temperature of 18 °C and a moderately rich potting mixture, such as John Innes No. 2, with the addition of a little extra peat or leaf mould. Water is required freely in spring and summer, rather sparingly in autumn and winter though the soil must never get dry. The atmosphere should be rather humid and the plants shaded from direct sunshine in summer. Cuttings will root in a warm propagator in spring or summer or seeds can be germinated in a temperature of 21–23 °C.

One of the best kinds is *C. infundibuliformis* with short, crowded spikes of orange-red flowers on 30 cm stems in spring.

Cuphea (Cigar Plant)

The popular name refers to *C. ignea* because of its curious little tubular scarlet flowers which are ringed with black and white, like ash, at the mouth. It makes a good pot plant which will be continuously in flower from spring to autumn in a sunny greenhouse or conservatory. It is hardy enough to be planted outdoors in summer but frost will kill it, so it should be kept in a greenhouse from early autumn until late spring with a minimum temperature of 7 °C. It will grow in any good soil or peat potting mixture, with normal watering. Seed germinates readily in spring in a temperature of 16–18 °C or cuttings can be rooted in summer in a propagator. Good plants can be grown in 9 cm pots.

Cyclamen

The greenhouse cyclamens will live for years, their

Cyclamen 'Decora'

bun-shaped tubers gradually increasing in size until it becomes awkward to contain them in pots. Better results are obtained by renewing the plants from seed annually, or at most every second year. Seed can be sown at the end of the summer, in late winter or early spring in a temperature of 16 °C. Germination is often slow and erratic and some seedlings from a late summer sowing may be little ahead of those from a late winter sowing. Others will be more forward and by that date can have been pricked out into trays for 2 to 3 months and be nearly ready for the next move into 7.5 mm pots. The little tubers should be kept sitting on top of the soil.

Whichever sowing date is preferred, the aim should be to keep the seedlings growing steadily in a temperature of 13–16 °C in a good soil potting mixture, such as John Innes No. 2 with the addition of a little extra peat or some well-rotted beech or oak leaf mould. The soil must be kept moist throughout this first year. Plants will be moved on to larger pots as necessary until they reach the 10–13 cm pots in which they will flower. During the summer they will be better in a frame, or even stood outside in a semi-shady place, as greenhouses can get too hot and dry for them, but they should be back under cover before there is any danger of frost. Plants can be fed with liquid fertilizer every 10 days or so from the time they are well established in their flowering pots. A winter temperature of 13–15 °C will be sufficient for the flowering plants and it will not matter if it drops occasionally to 7 °C.

If plants are kept for a second year they should be removed to a frame or semi-shady place outdoors in early summer and remain there until the end of the summer when most of the old soil can be shaken off the tubers so that they can be repotted in fresh soil. During this second summer the plants will be resting, most of the leaves will die down, and only just sufficient water should be given to prevent the soil becoming quite dry, until they restart into growth in late summer or early autumn when normal watering should be resumed.

There are numerous strains, some with handsomely silvered leaves, some with scented flowers, some relatively dwarf, some with very large flowers. The colour range is in many shades from pale pink to crimson plus white.

Cytisus canariensis

Datura suaveolens

Cytisus (Genista)

The pot plant with small scented yellow flowers which most people call 'Genista' is, in fact a cytisus. It is a popular spring flowering evergreen shrub which is almost hardy, can be grown in any sunny greenhouse from which frost can be excluded, and is not in the least difficult to manage. It will grow in any good soil or peat potting mixture, should be watered fairly freely in spring and summer, moderately in autumn and winter and can be pruned after flowering as necessary to keep it in shape. Cuttings of young side shoots taken in summer, preferably with a heel of older growth, will root in sandy soil in a propagator. The correct botanical name of this plant is *Cytisus* × *Spachianus* and it is a hybrid.

Datura

There are numerous kinds of datura but by far the best for greenhouse cultivation are the three that share the popular name Angel's Trumpet. They are *D. arborea*, *D. cornigera* (often known as *D. knightii*) and *D. suaveolens*. All are big bushy plants, semi-shrubby, with large leaves and big, pendant, trumpet-shaped flowers which are double in some varieties and are always very sweetly scented. They are hardy enough to be grown outdoors in summer but frost will kill them, so they must have the protection of a frost-proof greenhouse or conservatory in winter. Young plants can be grown in pots but they increase in size quickly and will eventually require tubs or other big containers.

Cuttings of firm stems root readily in summer and can be grown on in any good soil-based potting mixture. Plants need plenty of water in spring and summer, enough to keep the soil just moist in autumn and winter. They can be pruned to shape and size in spring. They enjoy all the light that is going and can be fed weekly in summer with liquid fertilizer. Tub- or container-grown plants make fine summer decorations for a patio or terrace.

Didiscus (Blue Lace Flower)

The kind cultivated, *D. caeruleus*, is an attractive annual with flat clusters of pale lavender-blue flowers carried on 45-cm stems in summer. It is easily raised from seed sown in spring in a temperature of 16–18 °C and will grow in a peat or soil potting mixture. Seedlings are pricked out when large enough to handle and later are either potted singly, first into 7.5 cm pots, later into 10–12.5 cm pots in which they will flower, or they are hardened off for planting outdoors when there is no longer any danger of frost. Pot plants are very attractive and easily managed. They should be watered normally, kept in a sunny place and be discarded when the flowers fade. (*See* illustration p. 11.)

Dipladenia

These are slender evergreen twining plants with trumpet-shaped flowers in summer. Two kinds are cultivated, *D. boliviensis*, with white flowers and

Eccremocarpus scaber

Dipladenia splendens

D. splendens, normally with pink and white flowers though there are also deep rose, carmine and crimson forms of this species. All like a fairly warm greenhouse, one with at least a minimum winter temperature of 13 °C but preferably rather more. Otherwise they are not at all difficult to grow, either in beds of good soil or in pots or tubs filled with a soil or peat potting mixture. Plants should be watered fairly freely in spring and summer, when a fairly moist atmosphere is desirable, and shaded from direct sunshine; watered moderately in autumn and winter, when the air can be a good deal drier, especially if it is difficult to maintain the ideal temperature. Plants will take all the sunshine that is going. In late winter all previous year's growth should be cut back to within a few inches of soil level. Plants should have wires, trellis or canes up which to climb. Cuttings will root in summer in a warm propagator.

Eccremocarpus (Chilean Glory Flower)
There is only one kind, *E. scaber*, a most attractive climber with finely divided leaves and clusters of tubular, orange or orange-red flowers produced all summer. It is a slightly tender perennial with fleshy roots. If the temperature falls close to freezing point the top growth dies but, provided the roots do not freeze, new shoots will appear in spring and quickly attain a height of 3 m or more. In a warmer

temperature eccremocarpus will retain its old growth and go on flowering well into the autumn. Plants are readily raised from seed which is produced freely. It should be sown in early spring in a temperature of 16–18 °C, seedlings being potted singly in 9 cm pots in any good soil or peat potting mixture. Later they can be moved on into larger pots or tubs but best results are obtained by planting in a bed of good soil on the greenhouse or conservatory floor. Water fairly freely in spring and summer, sparingly in autumn and winter. Provide wires, trellis or other suitable support for the tendrils to cling to. Thin out or cut back growth in early spring as necessary to keep plants within bounds.

Epacris (Australian Heath)
Small evergreen shrubs which look like erect heathers in leaf and habit but have tubular flowers. They make attractive pot plants but need very careful watering, never being allowed to become either sodden or dry. Grow in an acid mixture, either peat-based or containing a lot of peat and some lime-free loam, in a sunny greenhouse with minimum temperature of 7 °C. Prune to shape in spring after flowering. Seeds, if available, will germinate in peat and sand in a temperature of 16–18 °C in spring or cuttings can be rooted in a similar mixture in early summer in a propagator. *E. longifolia* has crimson and white flowers, *E. purpurascens* purple and white flowers, both in winter.

Epacris longiflora

Erica hyemalis *(see overleaf)*

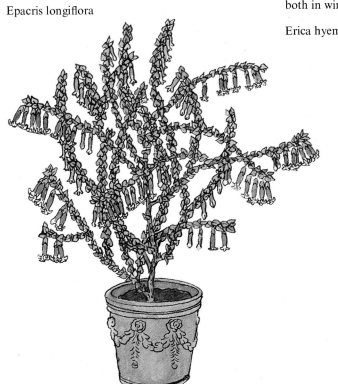

Eucharis grandiflora

Euphorbia splendens

Erica (Heath, Heather)

The kinds grown in greenhouses are all winter flowering and come from South Africa. They are evergreen shrubs, too tender to be grown outdoors except in a few exceptionally mild places but under glass they like cool conditions and only require enough extra warmth to keep out frost. They are sensitive to watering, especially in winter when the soil must be moist right through but never really wet or dry. In summer they will be happier in a frame or with their pots plunged to the rims outdoors rather than in a greenhouse which may get too hot on sunny days. All kinds dislike lime in any form and should be grown in peat with a little coarse sand or grit. Cuttings of young shoots will root in summer in peat and sand in a propagator. The three favourite kinds are *E. canaliculata*, often called *E. melanthera*, white or pink with dark anthers; *E. gracilis*, rosy purple and *E. hyemalis*, pink and white.

Erythrina (Coral Tree)

Many of these are trees, too large to be grown in ordinary greenhouses, but *E. crista-galli* can be cut hard back each spring and will then make strong growths from the base with handsome leaves and spikes of large, crimson flowers shaped rather like the claws of a lobster. It is a very handsome plant but it makes a big, fleshy root which is difficult to

accommodate in a pot. It can be grown in a tub but is really happiest planted in a bed of good soil or the floor of the greenhouse or conservatory. In winter it only needs sufficient heat to exclude all frost and should be kept almost dry but in spring and summer it can be watered freely, should have all the sunshine available and, at least in early spring, a little extra warmth to give it an early start. It will appreciate weekly feeding with liquid fertilizer from late spring until late summer. Seeds, if available, will germinate in a temperature of 18–21 °C. Cuttings of young shoots, taken in spring with a heel of older growth, will root in a warm propagator.

Eucharis (Amazon Lily)

These are tender, bulbous-rooted plants producing very richly scented white flowers which individually resemble those of a narcissus but are carried in nodding clusters. They are mainly white but in the kind most commonly grown, *E. grandiflora*, they are delicately tinged with green.

These are easy plants to grow in a warm greenhouse but they do need a winter minimum of 15 °C rising to a fairly steady 26 °C in summer. Pot the bulbs in spring in a good soil or peat potting mixture, one bulb in each 15 cm pot or several bulbs in larger pots. Water moderately at first, freely as growth appears and until the autumn, when watering should be reduced for a

Exacum affine *(see overleaf)*

Francoa ramosa *(see overleaf)*

few weeks to allow bulbs to ripen. Subsequently the amount of water required will depend on the warmth available. If there is plenty the plants will go on growing and flowering and may produce three flower crops in a year. Shade from direct sunshine in summer. Increase is by separating the bulb clusters when repotting, but it is not desirable to repot annually, though older plants may require fairly frequent feeding while in growth. Seeds, if available, will germinate in a temperature of 28–30 °C but seedlings will take several years to attain flowering age.

Euphorbia (Poinsettia, Crown of Thorns)

Three very different kinds are grown in greenhouses but the most popular of them all, *E. pulcherrima*, is hardly ever known by that name and is familiar to everyone as the Poinsettia, with rosettes of large coloured bracts in midwinter. The other two kinds are *E. fulgens*, with slender arching stems bearing, in winter, small orange-scarlet flowers and *E. splendens*, the Crown of Thorns, a very spiny, angularly branched, succulent plant with scarlet flowers produced most of the year if the temperature does not fall too low.

Poinsettias can be grown in a minimum temperature of 13 °C, in any fairly rich soil- or peat-based potting mixture. Plants are grown from cuttings of young growth rooted in a warm propagator in late spring or early summer. When rooted they are potted singly in 10 cm pots and are moved on to larger sizes as necessary. They are watered freely and given light shading from direct sunshine in summer and the air is kept fairly moist. Feeding with liquid fertilizer will be

necessary once a week from the time plants are established in their final pots until the bracts begin to colour in autumn. After flowering the tops are cut off and the soil is kept just moist for a few weeks while plants rest. Then the stems are cut back to 10–12 cm, the temperature is raised a little and normal watering resumed so that growth re-starts. When cuttings have been taken the old plants are often discarded but they can be kept from year to year if large plants are required. If to be retained plants should be repotted as soon as they have been cut back, the old soil being shaken off their roots and replaced with a fresh mixture.

If poinsettias are grown in rooms it is important not to expose them to artificial light in the evenings or at any time during the night in autumn. Flowering, and consequently the formation of the colour bracts, is controlled by night length, which must be at least 12 hours, and if this is curtailed by artificial lighting it is probable that there will be no bracts, only green leaves. Poinsettias are naturally rather tall plants and the relatively dwarf plants produced commercially are treated with chemicals to limit their growth. These chemicals are poisonous and are not available for use in private gardens.

E. fulgens is grown in the same way, except that it prefers a slightly higher temperature, especially in winter, and is usually kept for many years as it does not grow so large as the poinsettias.

E. splendens will survive a minimum temperature of 7 °C but is unlikely to produce winter flowers if the temperature falls below 13 °C. It likes a much drier atmosphere than the poinsettia, needs less water, especially in winter, and appreciates a grittier compost. Cuttings will root in sand in a propagator in spring or summer. Plants can be pruned in spring if they get too large.

Exacum

The kind grown, *E. affine*, is a bushy annual with scented lilac-blue and yellow flowers. If seed is sown in a temperature of 16–18 °C in early spring the plants will start to flower in late summer and continue well into the autumn and early winter. Exacum will grow in any good soil- or peat-based mixture, should be watered fairly freely throughout and kept in a light place. No artificial heat is required in summer. Seedlings can be potted individually in 7.5 cm pots and moved on to 12 cm pots for flowering. They are discarded after flowering.

Francoa (Maiden's Wreath, Bridal Wreath)

These are herbaceous perennials, hardy enough to survive some frost and so capable of being grown out of doors in many places, but one kind, *F. ramosa*, makes such a good pot plant that it is frequently grown in this way. It will thrive in almost any place from which severe frost can be excluded, such as an unheated greenhouse, a conservatory or a window. It makes a clump of deeply lobed leaves from which come, in summer, slender 60 cm sprays of white flowers. It is best grown in a soil-based mixture, should be watered fairly freely in spring and summer, moderately in autumn and winter and can be increased by division when repotting in spring, but annual repotting is not usually necessary.

Freesia

Freesia

No flowers have a sweeter or more penetrating perfume than freesias and this, combined with the lovely colours now available and their slender stems and elegant form, makes them favourite cut flowers. They are easily grown from seed sown any time in spring in a temperature of 16–18 °C. For the later sowings no artificial heat will be necessary and throughout the summer the plants will be happier in a frame or outdoors than in a greenhouse which may become too hot. Before there is danger of frost in the autumn, freesias should be brought into any light, frost-proof place where they will flower during the winter or spring and then ripen their seeds and die down.

It is quite satisfactory to sow directly in the 13 cm pots in which they will flower, six to ten seeds per pot with no subsequent thinning. Water should be supplied fairly freely all summer, moderately in autumn, winter and early spring but sparingly after flowering. For a few weeks in late summer the soil can be allowed to get quite dry. Then the corms are shaken out and repotted, six to ten per 13 cm pot. Those grown on corms usually flower later than those raised from seed sown in early spring. If some corms are stored dry until later in the autumn and are then repotted they will extend the flowering season still further. Freesias will grow in any good soil- or peat-based mixture. Colours range from pale yellow, pink, and mauve, to deep yellow, blue, and carmine. There are also double-flowered varieties with stouter stems but these do not produce seed and must be increased by the natural multiplication of the corms.

Fremontia

There are two species, *F. californica* and *F. mexicana*, but they are so much alike that for garden purposes it is unnecessary to distinguish between them. Both are large evergreen shrubs with pleasantly aromatic leaves and salver-shaped yellow flowers in summer. They are sufficiently hardy to be grown in any sunny place that is nearly frost free and they make a good covering for the back wall of a conservatory if trained to wires or trellis work. They are best planted in a bed of good soil on the floor, should be watered fairly freely in spring and summer, moderately in autumn, rather sparingly in winter, and can be pruned in spring to fill the space available. Seeds germinate in spring in a temperature of 16–18 °C and cuttings of firm young growth will root in summer in a propagator.

Fuchsia

These deciduous shrubs make splendid greenhouse

Fuchsia 'Hidcote Beauty'

pot plants and those kinds with pendulous branches can be grown in hanging baskets. Hardiness varies with the type but even the most tender fuchsia can be grown satisfactorily in a greenhouse with a minimum temperature of 7 °C and many can be grown without any artificial heat at all. In a low temperature, leaves will fall in autumn and growth will become more or less dormant for several months. Under these conditions little water is required. In a higher temperature, say 10 °C or more, plants will keep on growing slowly even in winter and the soil must be kept nicely moist.

Fuchsia are readily raised from cuttings of firm young growth in spring or summer, in a propagator or in pots placed inside polythene bags. They can be grown on in any good soil- or peat-based compost but, because of their long life, soil composts are to be preferred. They need to be watered freely in spring and summer, when they are growing freely, and from late spring to late summer can be fed weekly with liquid fertilizer. In summer even the more tender kinds can be placed outdoors but for best results all should be back

under cover before there is any frost in the autumn. They will grow in sun or shade but dislike intense heat and do not flower well in heavy shade. By pinching out the tips of young shoots and by tying stems to canes or wires, plants can be trained in various ways, as standards (i.e. with a head of branches on a bare stem), cones or fans against walls or trellis work.

There are hundreds of varieties differing in habit (erect, spreading or pendulous), in size and form of flower (single, or double, widely flared or tubular), and in colour (white, pink, rose, scarlet, carmine, crimson, violet, purple and various combinations of these). Plants can be in flower from spring to autumn but summer is their high season.

Gardenia (Cape Jasmine)
Both the popular name and the full botanical name, *G. jasminoides*, draw attention to the delicious, jasmine-like perfume of this small evergreen shrub. It makes an excellent pot plant and, if the temperature does not fall below about 16 °C, flowers will be produced at intervals throughout the year. Gardenias will survive

Gardenia jasminoides

much lower temperatures, as little as 7 °C for short periods, but then flowering is likely to be confined to late spring and summer. They will grow in any good soil- or peat-based mixture but, because of their permanence, soil composts are to be preferred. Water should be supplied freely in spring and summer, moderately in autumn and winter in a warm greenhouse or conservatory, but sparingly in a cool house. In summer, plants can be stood outdoors but if kept in the greenhouse they should be shaded lightly. Plants can be pruned to required shape and size in spring. Cuttings of firm young shoots will root in summer in a warm propagator.

Gerbera (Barberton Daisy)

These elegant South African daisies have been greatly improved in cultivation, the best strains having stronger stems, larger flowers, often with several rows of petals, and a much wider colour range, which includes primrose, apricot, coral, pink, and rose, as well as the more usual scarlet. They require very good drainage and extra sand or grit should be added to the growing mixture. Good plants can be grown in 15–18 cm pots but they are usually easier to manage if planted in a bed of porous soil on the floor of a sunny, well ventilated, frostproof greenhouse. Provided drainage is good, they can be watered fairly freely in

Gerbera jamesonii

Gloriosa simplex

spring and summer but need very careful watering in autumn and winter since plants are then inclined to rot off at the collar. Plants are easily raised from seed sown in gritty soil in spring in a temperature of 16–18 °C. This is also the temperature range that suits mature plants best though it can fall a few degrees in winter.

Gesneria (*see* illustration p. 12)

The kind most commonly cultivated in greenhouses, *G. cardinalis*, may be listed in some books and nursery catalogues as *Rechsteineria cardinalis*, a more up-to-date name. It is a tender perennial with velvety leaves and tubular orange-scarlet flowers in summer. It forms small tubers and can be grown from these or from seed. Tubers should be planted in spring, one in each 13 cm pot, in a mixture of equal parts peat and sand with a half part of loam. Just cover the tubers, keep in a temperature of 16–21 °C, water sparingly until growth appears, then freely until flowering ceases, when the water supply should be slowly reduced so that the soil can be quite dry by winter, when a minimum temperature of 10 °C will be adequate. In spring the tubers are repotted. Seed is also sown in spring, in peat and sand, the earlier the better if a temperature of 18 °C or higher can be maintained. Seedlings are pricked off early and later potted singly, using the same potting mixture as advised for tubers. Flowering can be expected to commence 6 to 7 months after sowing.

Gloxinia

Gloriosa (Glory Lily, Flame Lily)

These highly distinctive plants are often called climbing lilies because they climb by tendrils and their scarlet and yellow flowers, with swept-back petals, resemble those of some lilies. In fact they are not grown from bulbs, as lilies are, but from tubers which should be planted in late winter or spring in a soil- or peat-based potting mixture, one tuber in each 15 cm pot or three in each 20 cm pot. Water rather sparingly until growth appears, then with increasing freedom but, after flowering is over, gradually reduce the water supply and keep quite dry in winter in a temperature of 15 °C. While in growth gloriosas like a temperature range from 15 to 21 °C and a light, but not scorching, place. They may need shade from direct sunshine in summer. Canes or other supports should be provided for the tendrils at the tips of the leaves to cling to. Increase is by the natural multiplication of the bulbs or by seed but seedlings may take several years to reach flowering size.

Gloxinia

Tuberous-rooted perennials which make rosettes of velvety leaves and produce large and very showy funnel-shaped flowers on short stems in summer. They require conditions similar to those which suit tuberous-rooted begonias. Seed, which is very small, can be sown in late winter or early spring on the surface of fine soil, or in a peat-based seed mixture with only the lightest of coverings but a sheet of glass and another of paper over each seed pan. Seedlings must be pricked out while quite small and then potted on as necessary in any good soil- or peat-based potting compost until they reach the 13–15 cm pots in which they will flower. From spring until early autumn they are watered fairly freely and in summer can be fed weekly with liquid fertilizer but in late autumn they are gradually dried off and are kept quite dry, preferably in their pots, in a frostproof place throughout the winter. In late winter or early spring the tubers are repotted, watering is resumed and they are restarted into growth in a temperature of 16–18 °C. This is the growing temperature they enjoy; they should not be allowed to get very hot in summer and should be shaded from direct sunshine. The colour range includes pink, violet, purple, scarlet, crimson, and white, often with the colours spotted or netted on a white base.

Haemanthus (Blood Lily)

South African bulbous-rooted plants with flowers composed almost entirely of white or red stamens, giving them the appearance of broad paint brushes. One kind, *H. magnificus*, is sometimes known as the Royal Paint Brush. All can be grown in pots in any sunny frostproof place. Pot the bulbs in early spring, one in each 8–18 cm pot, according to the size of the bulb, using any good soil- or peat-based potting mixture. Water sparingly at first, freely when leaves appear. Feed occasionally in summer with liquid fertilizer. Reduce the water supply in autumn and keep almost, but not quite dry if all leaves die down but increase again when new leaves appear, which may be in midwinter.

Hedychium
Handsome plants with broad leaves, rather like those of canna, and white, yellow, or orange-red flowers in loose terminal spikes in summer. The flowers of *H. gardnerianum*, the most popular kind, are pale yellow and scented. The roots are fleshy and they are grown in much the same way as cannas. Roots can be potted in early spring in 15–20 cm pots in any good soil- or peat-based potting mixture. They should be watered freely while in growth and fed weekly in summer with liquid fertilizer but should be allowed to die down in autumn and kept dry, in their pots, in a frostproof greenhouse in winter. While growing, they need all the light possible and a temperature between 13 and 21 °C. Roots can be divided when repotting.

Heliotropium (Heliotrope, Cherry Pie)
This favourite summer bedding plant with flat heads of small, sweetly scented, purple flowers, also makes an excellent pot plant for a cool greenhouse or conservatory. It is a half hardy perennial which, in a frostproof place, can live for many years and grow into quite a large plant but it is usually grown as a half hardy annual, raised each year from seed sown in late winter or early spring in a temperature of 16–18 °C. Seedlings are pricked out and later potted individually in any good soil- or peat-based potting compost, first in 10 cm pots, from which they can be planted outdoors as soon as there is no further danger of frost if they are to be used for summer bedding. However, if plants are to be grown throughout under glass they should be moved on to larger pots as necessary, 13–15 cm being adequate for the first year though larger pots may be needed in subsequent years. Alternatively heliotrope can be planted in a bed of good soil and trained to wires or trellis against a sunny wall or up a pillar. Water is required fairly freely in spring and summer, moderately in autumn, sparingly in winter when temperature should be maintained at 10 °C or higher. Plants can also be raised from cuttings made from young growths in spring or summer and rooted in a propagator. Old plants can be pruned in spring as necessary to keep them within available space.

Hibiscus
Two different types of hibiscus are grown in greenhouses, one an evergreen shrub the other a herbaceous perennial. The shrub is *H. rosa sinensis* and it has large, trumpet-shaped flowers, scarlet, rose, pink, yellow or buff, single or double, produced in summer. If planted in a bed of soil it will make a large bush but it can be kept much smaller in 15–20 cm pots in any good soil- or peat-based potting mixture. Plants

Haemanthus albiflos

Hibiscus rosa sinensis

require a minimum temperature of 10 °C, more if possible, plenty of water in spring and summer but only just enough to keep the soil moist in autumn and winter. Plants can be pruned to shape in spring. Cuttings will root in a warm propagator in summer.

The herbaceous kinds are *H. manihot*, with large, wide, funnel-shaped, yellow and maroon flowers in summer, and 'Southern Belle', a fine race of hybrids with very large flowers in various shades of pink and rose, plus white. If seed is sown in late winter in a temperature of 16–18 °C and seedlings are potted singly in a good soil- or peat-based potting mixture and grown on in a similar temperature they will flower

Hippeastrum

the same year in 18–20 cm pots and can be discarded after flowering. This is probably the best way to grow them as in subsequent years they get rather large for pots but they can be grown in a bed of soil if preferred.

Hippeastrum

These are bulbs, often sold under an old name, Amaryllis. The flowers are large and trumpet shaped, crimson, scarlet, pink, white or with these colours on a white base, borne in clusters on stout stems. Bulbs should be potted in autumn, late winter or early spring, singly in 13–18 cm pots in any good soil- or peat-based potting mixture. If bulbs specially prepared for Christmas flowering are obtained and potted in early autumn they can be brought straightway into a temperature of 18–21 °C and should be watered with increasing freedom as the flower stems lengthen. If ordinary bulbs are obtained they should be watered very sparingly in winter, when a minimum temperature of 10 °C should be maintained, but with increasing freedom when leaves appear some time in late winter or early spring. These bulbs will flower some time in spring or summer and quite often will produce two lots of flowers in the same year. They

should have a sunny place, be fed once every week in summer with liquid fertilizer and should not be completely dried off at any time. As the bulbs multiply they can either be separated and potted individually or the whole clump can be moved on to larger pots as necessary to contain them. The secret of successful flowering is sun, warmth and good, sustained growth.

Hoya (Wax Flower)

Two kinds of hoya are grown, one a vigorous twining plant the other a much less vigorous trailer. Both produce, in late summer or autumn, similar small hanging clusters of white and pink scented flowers which look as if made of wax. *H. carnosa* is the climbing species, *H. bella* the trailing kind and it is a little more tender. It is very suitable for growing in hanging baskets whereas *H. carnosa* should be in a large pot, a tub, or a bed of good soil. Both plants can be grown in any good soil- or peat-based compost and need to be watered fairly freely from spring until autumn but sparingly in winter. A minimum temperature of 10 °C will suit them best but for *H. carnosa* it can fall a few degrees lower without harm. This species requires some support for its stems to twine around. Bed should be shaded from strong sunshine in summer. Cuttings of young growth will root in a warm propagator in summer.

Hoya carnosa

Hydrangea macrophylla

Humea (Incense Plant)

The kind cultivated, *H. elegans*, is a tall biennial with loose sprays of small, cedar-brown flowers, but it is the leaves that are aromatic and have suggested the popular name. Seed can be sown in late spring without artificial heat. Seedlings are potted singly, in 7.5 cm pots, in any good soil- or peat-based mixture and are moved on to larger pots as necessary. By the following spring they may well require 18–20 cm pots. Plants will flower that summer and should then be discarded. A minimum temperature of 10 °C is satisfactory though a few degrees more will give better plants. Only shade lightly from really strong sunshine in summer. Maintain a buoyant atmosphere. Canes are required to support the slender stems which can be as much as 2 m high.

Hyacinthus (Hyacinth)

These popular, spring flowering bulbs make good pot plants for an unheated or slightly heated greenhouse. Bulbs should be potted in mid-autumn, one in each 10 cm pot or several bulbs, almost shoulder to shoulder, in larger pots. They can be grown in any soil- or peat-based potting mixture; if planted in undrained bowls they must be grown in special bulb fibre which contains crushed shell and charcoal to keep it sweet. It can be purchased ready for use. The bulbs need to be only just covered. They should be kept at a temperature of 10 °C or less for at least ten weeks before being brought into a greenhouse or room and during this initial cool period the bulbs can be in the dark. Water should be given sparingly at first, just sufficient to keep the compost moist throughout, but more freely as leaves and flower buds appear. When the leaves commence to die down six or eight weeks after flowering, watering can be reduced, and when all leaves have withered, the bulbs can be removed from their pots and stored dry until the autumn, when they can be planted outdoors. It is unwise to grow the same bulbs two years running in pots.

Hydrangea

It is the large-flowered varieties of *H. macrophylla* that make the best pot plants. They can be grown very easily from cuttings of young growth rooted in spring or summer in a propagator or in a pot placed inside a polythene bag. When rooted, the cuttings are potted singly in a fairly rich soil-based potting mixture such as John Innes No. 2. Pots 9 cm in diameter will do at first but the plants will soon need to be moved on and by the autumn may be in the 15–18 cm pots in which they will flower the following year. Plants can be grown on for many years but will need ever larger pots or tubs and for greenhouse use it is usually best to rely mainly on young plants. Hydrangeas require little heat and can be outdoors all summer but should have complete protection from frost in winter. They need to be watered freely from spring to autumn but very sparingly once their leaves fall until they start into growth in the spring. If blue or blue-purple flowers are

Impatiens 'Elfin Red'

required the soil used must be acid. Lime-free loam, peat and lime-free sand should be used and a 'blueing' compound, usually based on alum, can be added to the water in spring and summer. In neutral or alkaline soils the flowers are pink, carmine or reddish purple. White varieties are always white whatever the nature of the soil.

Hymenocallis (Spider Lily)

Bulbous-rooted plants, known as Spider Lilies because of the long narrow segments which surround the central cup-shaped portion of the flower which is always white and scented. All kinds flower in summer. Bulbs should be potted in early spring, one in each 13–15 cm pot, in any good soil- or peat-based potting mixture. Keep from the outset in a sunny, frostproof greenhouse but water sparingly at first and freely from the time leaves appear; feed weekly in summer with liquid fertilizer. When leaves commence to die down in the autumn, reduce the water supply and allow the compost to become quite dry in the winter, when the temperature should not fall below 7 °C. Bulb clusters can be separated when repotting in spring.

Hypocyrta (Clog Plant, Goldfish Plant)

The kind grown in greenhouses, *H. glabra*, is a small evergreen perennial with closely set, fleshy leaves and little orange flowers shaped rather like tiny clogs or goldfish, hence the popular names. Hypocyrta is easily grown in 8–10 cm pots in any good soil- or peat-based mixture in a greenhouse with a minimum temperature of 7 °C or in a window. It is watered normally and can be increased by cuttings in summer in a propagator or a pot placed inside a polythene bag.

Impatiens (Balsam, Busy Lizzie)

Two very different kinds are grown in greenhouses, the Balsam being *I. balsamina*, a half hardy annual which, in its cultivated forms, has spikes of double flowers, and the Busy Lizzie being *I. wallerana* (also known as *I. holstii* and *I. sultanii*) a much-branched, half hardy perennial with single flowers. Both can be grown either as pot plants or as summer bedding plants. The Balsam must be renewed annually from seed sown in early spring in a temperature of 18 °C and the Busy Lizzie, though it can be kept for years and grown from cuttings rooted in a warm propagator in spring or summer, is often treated as an annual and renewed every spring from seed. The seeds germinate best in a temperature of 21 °C.

Both kinds of impatiens will grow in any good soil- or peat-based potting mixture but the best spikes of Balsam flowers are produced in a moderately rich compost or with a fair amount of supplementary feeding. All need plenty of water while growing. Seedlings should be pricked out and later either planted outdoors when there is no further danger of frost, or potted singly in the 13 cm pots in which they will flower. Balsams are discarded after flowering. If

Hypocyrta glabra

Busy Lizzies are retained for a further year they should be overwintered in a greenhouse with minimum temperature of 10 °C and be watered rather sparingly until growth restarts in the spring.

Ipomoea (Morning Glory)

Both annual and perennial kinds are grown under glass. The best perennial is *I. learii*, a vigorous twining plant with blue, widely funnel-shaped flowers which become purple as they age. It will grow in any sunny, frostproof place but is too big for small greenhouses. In a large conservatory it can be used to clothe the back wall or be allowed to ramble over wires beneath the rafters. Because of its size, it is best planted in a bed of good soil but, if this is impossible, it should be grown in a very large pot or a tub. Water freely in spring and summer, sparingly in autumn and winter and prune as necessary in spring.

Most of the annuals are also twiners with funnel-shaped flowers, blue, purple, pink, or white according to variety; but one kind, *I. lobata* (also known as *Mina lobata*) has tubular scarlet flowers. All are suitable for cultivation in pots 13–18 cm in diameter. Seeds should be sown individually in small pots in early spring in a temperature of 18 °C. They will germinate more reliably if soaked in water for 24 hours before sowing or if the hard seed coats are chipped with the point of a penknife so that water can penetrate. Plants are moved to their flowering pots when the small ones are full of roots or are planted outdoors in a warm, sunny place when there is no further danger of frost. They are discarded after flowering.

Ismene

Bulbous-rooted plants similar to hymenocallis and by many authorities included in that genus. For greenhouse purposes the most important is *I. festalis*, a hybrid, of which a particularly fine form has been named 'Zwanenburg'. The flowers are white and sweetly scented. Cultivation is the same as for hymenocallis.

Ixia

South African plants with narrow, grass-like leaves and starry crimson, carmine, orange, yellow or white flowers carried in close sprays on slender stems in spring and early summer. They form small corms, five to seven of which can be planted in each 10–13 cm pot in autumn in any rather porous soil- or peat-based mixture. All they require is plenty of light and complete protection from frost. Any sunny, frost-proof structure will do and they should be watered sparingly at first, fairly freely as leaves appear. A few weeks after flowering the leaves will commence to turn yellow and then the water supply should be reduced and the soil allowed to become quite dry for a few weeks before repotting in early autumn. The corms multiply quite rapidly and provide the easiest means of increase.

Ixora

Evergreen shrubs with clusters of small, tubular, highly coloured flowers in summer. Colours range from yellow to crimson. Ixoras make good pot plants but need quite a lot of warmth, a minimum of 18 °C even in winter. Given this they are not difficult to grow in a soil-based mixture containing quite a lot of peat. Water freely in spring and summer, moderately in autumn and winter; shade from direct sunshine in summer and maintain a moist atmosphere. Feed once a week in summer with liquid fertilizer. Prune to required shape and size in early spring. Cuttings of firm young growth will root in summer in a well warmed propagator.

A hybrid Ixia

Jacobinia

Two very different types of jacobinia are cultivated in greenhouses and they used to be distinguished by different names which helped to avoid confusion. *J. carnea* was (and still sometimes is) called *Justicia carnea* and has short, closely packed spikes of hooded pink flowers on stout stems in summer and early autumn. *Jacobinia pauciflora* (which is alternatively known as *Libonia floribunda*) scatters its little red and yellow tubular flowers all over a bushy plant and continues to bloom all winter. Both make good pot plants for sunny greenhouses with a minimum temperature of 13 °C. They will grow in any good soil- or peat-based mixture. Both should be watered

Jacobinia pauciflora

normally except that *J. carnea* should be kept rather dry for a few weeks after flowering until it starts to grow again, when it can be cut back quite hard. Cuttings of both kinds will root in summer in a propagator.

Jasminum (Jasmine)

Two of the best jasmines to grow under glass are *J. polyanthum*, a rampant twiner with sprays of intensely fragrant white flowers in late winter or spring and *J. mesnyi*, often known as *J. primulinum*, a more shrubby plant with semi-double, yellow flowers in spring. Both can be grown in any well-lighted structure from which frost can be excluded. They can be grown in any good soil in pots, tubs or beds and require normal watering. As soon as it has finished flowering *J. polyanthum* can be thinned or cut back as necessary to keep it in bounds. It needs trellis work, wires or other support. *J. mesnyi* can also be thinned after flowering but is less likely to get out of hand. Cuttings root readily in summer in a propagator, or stems can be layered at any time of the year.

There are other more tender kinds such as *J. grandiflorum*, *J. rex* and *J. sambac*, all white-flowered climbers, but all prefer much warmer conditions with temperatures of 13–18 °C even in winter.

Kalanchoe

These are small succulent plants with clusters of brightly coloured flowers in winter. One of the most popular is *K. blossfeldiana*, with orange-red or yellow flowers, but there are also hybrids with flowers of various colours including orange, yellow, red, scarlet and rose. All can be raised from seed sown in a sandy soil, only just covered and germinated in a temperature of 18 °C. If this can be done in late winter or early spring the seedlings will flower the following winter. Plants can also be grown from cuttings rooted in sandy soil in summer. Seedlings or rooted cuttings should be potted singly in 7.5 cm pots in a rather gritty soil compost and should be moved on to larger pots as necessary, but quite good plants can usually be grown in 9 cm pots. They need all the sunshine available, should be watered carefully until well established, then fairly freely while growing in summer, but sparingly again in autumn and winter when the temperature should not fall below 7 °C. Kalanchoe can be damaged by HCH (lindane) so should be removed temporarily from the greenhouse if this insecticide is to be used for fumigation.

Lachenalia (Cape Cowslip)

The little hanging tubular flowers of some lachenalias, arranged in loose spikes, do bear a slight resemblance to those of cowslips but the plants are totally unrelated and the lachenalias are all bulbous-rooted plants from South Africa. The most popular for greenhouse cultivation are *L. aloides* (also known as *L. tricolor*), with yellow flowers tipped with red and green (there

Jasminum polyanthum

are also all-yellow forms) and *L. bulbifera* (also known as *L. pendula*), with coral-red flowers tipped with green and purple. Both make excellent pot plants for a cold greenhouse or conservatory with minimum temperatures of 7 °C and will flower in late winter and early spring. Pot in autumn in any good porous soil- or peat-based potting mixture, placing five or six of the little bulbs in each 13 cm pot or pan. Water sparingly at first, moderately as leaves appear, more freely in spring, but reduce the amount of water when the leaves commence to die down in late spring or early summer and keep almost dry for a few weeks before repotting in late summer or early autumn. The bulb clusters can be separated when repotting and this is the easiest method of increasing stock.

Lagerstroemia (Cape Myrtle)

In warm countries *L. indica* makes a very large shrub or small tree with smooth grey bark and crimped pink flowers borne along the stems in summer. But it can also be grown in large pots or tubs in sunny greenhouses or conservatories, stood outside, if desired in summer but given complete protection from

70

Top left: Lantana camerana

Bottom left: Lilium speciosum 'Melpomene'

Below: Lapageria rosea

frost in winter. There are also dwarf and prostrate varieties which may be easier to accommodate, and other colours, including red, lavender/purple and white. All will grow in any good soil-based potting mixture, watered freely from spring to early autumn, sparingly in winter. Plants can be pruned early each spring to prevent them growing too large. Autumn is the best time for repotting. Seed will germinate in a temperature of 18–21 °C in spring or cuttings will root in a warm propagator in summer.

Lantana

These are bushy evergreen plants with clusters of small flowers all summer, yellow and orange, red, pink, mauve or white. Because they flower for so long, lantanas make good summer bedding plants. They also make excellent pot plants for sunny greenhouses and can be used, in summer to decorate balconies, patios and sunny terraces. Plants can be raised from seed sown in spring in a temperature of 16–18 °C or from cuttings rooted in a propagator in summer. They can be grown on in any good soil- or peat-based potting mixture and good plants can be produced in 13–15 cm pots. They should be watered fairly freely from spring to autumn but sparingly in winter, when the temperature should not fall below 7 °C. Plants can be pruned to shape in early spring.

Lapageria (Chilean Bellflower)

There is only one species, *L. rosea*, an evergreen twining plant with large, hanging, bell-shaped flowers in late summer and autumn, but there are several varieties differing in colour. The commonest colour is rose but there are also pink varieties and one that combines both pink and white. In all the flowers have a waxen texture which adds to their beauty.

Lapagerias grow best in a cool, temperate climate not very hot in summer; but not cold in winter. A temperature range from 7 to 21 °C will suit them well with plenty of water in spring and summer, enough to keep the soil just moist in autumn and winter and shade from direct sunshine in summer. Stems can be layered in summer to produce new plants. Lapagerias can be grown in large pots or tubs but are better in a bed of soil, which must be lime-free and moderately acid. They need wires, trellis work or some other support for their slender stems. Little or no pruning is required.

Leptospermum (South Sea Myrtle)

These New Zealand shrubs with small evergreen leaves and sprays of white, pink or crimson flowers in spring or early summer, are sufficiently hardy to be grown outdoors in many places but they also make good pot plants for sunny greenhouses and require little or no artificial heat. They can be planted in large pots, tubs or beds but the soil must be peaty, lime-free and moderately acid. They need moderate watering in spring and summer but the soil should be no more than just moist in autumn and winter. No shading is required at any time. Cuttings will root in a propagator in summer and seeds will germinate in a temperature of 18 °C in spring. One of the most spectacular varieties is 'Red Damask', with double, garnet-red flowers. There is also a dwarf variety named 'Nanum' which can be grown in 13–15 cm pots.

Lilium (Lily)

Any lilies can be grown in pots or tubs in a greenhouse or conservatory but most would do at least equally well outdoors. Those that actually benefit from pot cultivation are the more tender kinds or those that flower very early or late when weather might easily spoil them. The most important of these are the Easter Lily, *L. longiflorum*, with long white trumpets any time from early spring until early summer according to the warmth available, and *L. speciosum* and its varieties which produce hanging flowers, with swept-back petals, in late summer and autumn. Typically these are white flushed with pink but some are much redder and others entirely white. Other good lilies to grow in pots are *L. formosanum*, with narrowly trumpet-shaped white flowers in late summer; and *L. auratum*, with very large bowl-shaped flowers in late summer. These may be white, variously speckled with gold and red, or may be heavily striped with red.

All lily bulbs should be potted as soon as available, which may be any time from early autumn until late winter according to the place from which they come. All should be grown in moderately acid, lime-free soil, either a mixture of soil, peat and sand or a compost based on peat as the major ingredient. Bulbs should be well covered and be grown in cool, but not frosty, conditions until well rooted, after which they can come into a temperature of 16–21 °C. Lilies should be watered sparingly at first, freely while in growth; but in autumn the soil should be allowed to become nearly but not quite dry. All kinds should be repotted in autumn, after flowering, and can be increased by separating the bulb clusters. Many can also be grown from seed sown in spring in peat and sand in a temperature of 16–18 °C but *L. formosanum* is the only one likely to flower the first year from seed.

Limonium (Sea Lavender)

For many years these plants were called Statice and the name is still frequently used in gardens. Most kinds are fully hardy but *L. suworowii* and *L. profusum* are rather tender and so are frequently grown as pot plants. They are very different in appearance and requirements.

L. suworowii is a half hardy annual with small pink flowers arranged in slender branched spikes. It is renewed annually from seed sown in spring in a temperature of 16–18 °C, the seedlings pricked off and later potted singly in 10–13 cm pots in any good soil- or peat-based potting mixture. They are watered moderately and grown throughout in a sunny greenhouse or they can be planted outdoors when there is no further risk of frost.

L. profusum is a perennial with large, leathery leaves and dense sprays of small violet-blue and white flowers in late summer and autumn. It can be grown from seed but is usually increased by root cuttings in winter. It is best grown in a fairly porous soil-based potting mixture, in the smallest pots that will contain its roots, in a sunny greenhouse with minimum temperature of 7 °C. Water fairly freely from spring to autumn, sparingly in winter. Do not shade at any time.

Luculia

The kind most commonly grown, *L. gratissima*, is a semi-evergreen shrub with heads of very sweetly scented, rose-pink flowers in autumn. It can be grown in pots in any good soil-based potting mixture and its roots should not be given too much space as this encourages growth at the expense of flowers. It needs a minimum temperature of 7 °C, as much light as possible at all times and it should be watered fairly freely from spring until the flowers fade, sparingly from then until growth re-starts the following spring. Stems can be cut back quite severely after flowering. Cuttings will root in a propagator in summer.

Mandevilla (Chilean Jasmine)

The kind cultivated is *M. suaveolens*, a slender deciduous twining plant with white, trumpet-shaped, sweetly scented flowers in summer. It is nearly hardy and can be grown in any well-lighted structure from which frost can be excluded. Plant in autumn, either in a bed of good soil or a large pot or tub in any good peat- or soil-based potting mixture. Water sparingly in autumn and winter, freely in spring and summer. Old

Limonium suworowii

Medinilla magnifica

Mandevilla suaveolens

growth can be cut back almost to soil level each year in late winter. Increase is usually by summer cuttings in a propagator but seeds, if available, will germinate in a temperature of 16–18 °C.

Manettia

These are climbing plants with slender twining stems and little tubular flowers produced successively for much of the year if the temperature remains at about 15 °C or higher. The two kinds most often grown are *M. bicolor*, with flowers half red, half orange, and *M. inflata* in which the flowers are red with just a little orange. Both can be raised from seed germinated in a temperature of 18 °C or from summer cuttings in a warm propagator. They will grow in any good soil- or peat-based mixture in large pots or beds and should be watered fairly freely in spring and summer, moderately in autumn and winter. Canes, wires or trellis are needed for support. Stems can be cut back in late winter as necessary to fill available space.

Maurandya

These are herbaceous climbers running up quickly to a metre or more in summer but dying down in winter. The flowers are trumpet-shaped, rather like those of a penstemon, violet-purple in *M. barclaiana*, carmine in *M. erubescens*. They are nearly hardy, can be grown in any sunny, frostproof structure in any reasonably good soil, either in pots or beds, and are easily raised from seed sown in spring in a temperature of 18 °C. Plants should be watered freely in spring and summer while growing, but in winter only just sufficiently to prevent soil becoming quite dry.

Medinilla

The kind grown is *M. magnifica*, a very handsome plant with large evergreen leaves and, in late spring and early summer, hanging trusses of pink flowers on pink stems and with large pink bracts. The total effect is striking and unique. The plant needs warmth, with minimum winter temperature of 15 °C rising to 21 °C or more in spring and summer, when it should be watered freely and kept in a fairly humid atmosphere. In autumn the water supply should be reduced and in winter the soil should be just moist, no more. Medinilla likes a spongy compost with plenty of peat and with regular feeding in summer. Cuttings will root in summer in peat in a really warm, moist propagator.

Mesembryanthemum

To botanists this name is now almost meaningless but for gardeners it remains a useful omnibus name for a number of allied but distinct genera including *Carpobrotus*, *Dorotheanthus* and *Lampranthus*. All have succulent leaves and flowers which have a superficial resemblance to daisies though they are structurally quite different. All are sun lovers and native to dry, semi-desert places. Some are on the borderline of hardiness and all can be grown in sunny greenhouses in which the temperature never falls below 7 °C. All can be raised from seed sown in sandy soil in a temperature of around 18 °C and also from cuttings rooted in sandy soil in summer without extra heat. They will grow in a rather gritty, soil-based potting mixture, watered normally in spring and summer but very sparingly in autumn and winter. Most flower in spring and early summer but some flowers may be produced later.

Mesembryanthemum 'Dorotheanthus'

A hybrid Mimulus *(see overleaf)*

Mimulus (Monkey Flower, Musk)

Two very different kinds of mimulus are grown in greenhouses. One is *M. tigrinus*, a race of hybrids with large, showy, trumpet-shaped flowers in various shades of yellow, orange, pink and coppery red, often with one colour splashed and spotted on another. Though perennial, they are almost invariably grown as annuals since they are readily raised from seed sown in spring in a temperature of 16–18 °C. They like a spongy soil with plenty of peat, enjoy abundant moisture while growing and, once danger of frost is over, are often planted outdoors beside streams or pools.

The other kind is *M. aurantiacus*, often known by its old name *Diplacus glutinosus*. This is semi-shrubby, has sticky leaves and either yellow or coppery red flowers all summer. It loves warmth and in summer should be given the sunniest place possible. It can be planted outdoors when danger of frost is over. In winter it needs a minimum temperature of 7 °C and only sufficient water to prevent the soil becoming quite dry. It is usually increased by summer cuttings inserted in a propagator or a pot of sandy soil slipped inside a polythene bag.

Narcissus (Daffodil)

All kinds of narcissus can be grown in greenhouses and none requires any artificial heat, though the very early flowering Polyanthus varieties, such as 'Scilly White' and 'Soleil d'Or', are better without any frost. These two, if potted in early autumn and grown on in a light greenhouse with average temperature range of 10–16 °C, can be in bloom by Christmas or soon after. They are

A hybrid Narcissus

the only kinds that do not require an initial period of cold before being brought into leaf and flower. All other kinds should be potted as early as available, and then, for the next ten to twelve weeks, kept as cool as possible in a frame or outdoors. Only when they have more or less filled their pots with roots should they be brought into a greenhouse or room with temperatures of 13 °C or higher.

All can be grown in any good soil- or peat-based potting compost. Bulbs should be obtained in September and can be potted singly in 10 cm pots but it is usually more effective to use larger pots and pack in several bulbs almost shoulder to shoulder, with their tips just showing through the surface. Water moderately at first, fairly freely once the bulbs are growing and are inside the greenhouse or room. About six to eight weeks after flowering leaves will commence to yellow and then watering can be reduced but it is not necessary to dry off narcissus bulbs completely. In late summer they can be tipped out of their pots and planted outdoors. It is unwise to use the same bulbs for pot cultivation two years running.

Nerine (Diamond Lily)

The popular name refers to the sparkling colour of the

Nerine bowdenii

flowers which are carried in clusters on bare stems in autumn. The hardiest kind is *N. bowdenii* and it also produces some of the largest flowers but the colour range is limited to pink and white. Most of the cultivated greenhouse varieties are hybrids with flowers of various colours including white, pink, rose, scarlet, carmine and mauve. They should be grown in a rather gritty soil mixture, the bulbs no more than half buried and the pots just large enough to contain them comfortably. Late summer is the best time for potting.

Nerines should be watered sparingly during the autumn and winter, freely while growing in spring and summer but should be allowed to become nearly dry for a few weeks in late summer before they start to flower. Most of the time the temperature range should be from 13 to 18 °C but it will do no harm if it falls to 7 °C for a few weeks in early spring and this may help the plants to flower the following autumn.

Bulb clusters can be separated when being repotted and this is the usual method of increase. Nerines can also be grown from seed sown in spring or as soon as ripe in a temperature of 16 °C but seedlings take several years to reach flowering size.

Nerium (Oleander)
This is an evergreen shrub with clusters of showy flowers all summer. Rose-pink is the commonest colour but apricot, red, purple, cream and white varieties are also available and flowers may be single or double. All parts of the plant are poisonous.

The oleander can be grown in any sunny, frost-proof place. It is rather large to be grown in pots but does well in a tub or can be planted in a bed of good soil. It should be watered freely in spring and summer, sparingly in autumn and winter and pruned in early spring as necessary to keep plants shapely and in bounds. Cuttings root readily in a propagator in spring or summer.

Oxalis
There are a great many different kinds of oxalis, some perfectly hardy, some obnoxious weeds. Only a few make good pot plants for sunny, frostproof green-houses, the two best kinds probably being *O. deppei*, with sprays of rose-red flowers on slender stems in summer, and *O. purpurata*, a shorter, more spreading plant with rose-pink flowers. Like other species, they will grow in any good soil- or peat-based mixture. They form little tubers and it is from these that they are grown. Several can be strewn in early autumn in 10 cm pots and covered with about 1 cm of soil. Water sparingly at first, more freely when leaves appear and throughout the spring and early summer, but after flowering let the soil become nearly dry for a few weeks before repotting. No shade is required at any time.

Pachystachys
The kind most often grown is *P. lutea*, a branching plant with soft leaves and short, crowded spikes of

Passiflora caeruea

creamy white flowers almost enveloped in deep yellow bracts. It will grow in any good soil- or peat-based mixture in a greenhouse with minimum temperature of 13 °C, though a little more suits it even better. Water moderately in spring and summer, rather sparingly in autumn and winter. Give it all the light possible. Cuttings will root in a propagator in summer or seeds can be germinated in spring in a temperature of 18 °C.

Passiflora (Passion Flower, Granadilla)
Vigorous climbers mostly too large for greenhouses of ordinary size but splendid for big conservatories where they can ramble up the back walls or cling to wires beneath the rafters. The flowers are large and broadly star-shaped with a circle of coloured filaments, some-times of considerable length, as in *P. quadrangularis*, the giant granadilla. *P. antioquiensis*, has rosy red flowers, *P. allardii,* white, pink and deep blue flowers and there are many more. Several species, including *P. edulis*, the purple granadilla, have edible fruits.

Most will grow in a minimum temperature of 7 °C but a few degrees more suits the more tender kinds better. All are best grown in beds of good soil rather than in pots though they can be managed in tubs. They need supports for their tendrils to cling to. All should be watered fairly freely from spring to early autumn, sparingly in winter and all can be pruned hard, if necessary, in early spring. Seeds will germinate in a temperature of 18–21 °C in spring or cuttings will root in a propagator in summer.

Pelargonium
These are the plants that most people persist in calling geraniums though that name really belongs to an allied race of mainly hardy herbaceous perennials. Most of

Regal Pelargonium

Plumbago capensis

the pelargoniums are half hardy sub-shrubs, bushy or trailing in habit. Some are remarkable for their long flowering season, some for their variously scented leaves, some for other qualities. Many make fine pot plants for sunny greenhouses and conservatories.

Four groups are of particular importance: the Zonal-leaved pelargoniums, which are bushy plants much favoured for summer bedding but with an even longer flowering season under glass; the Regal pelargoniums, also bushy, with larger flowers than the Zonal-leaved varieties, produced mainly in late spring and early summer; the Ivy-leaved pelargoniums, trailing plants flowering mainly in summer and highly popular for hanging baskets, window boxes and ornamental containers; and the Scented-leaved pelargoniums, most of which have small flowers and leaves of various shapes and with many different scents, including lemon, rose and peppermint.

All can be grown in pots (or the Ivy-leaved kinds in hanging baskets, if preferred) in sunny, frostproof greenhouses, in any good soil- or peat-based mixture. Use the smallest pots that will contain the roots comfortably. Though all will survive in a minimum temperature of 7 °C, winter management is easier and winter flower production from the Zonal-leaved varieties is better if the temperature range is between 13 and 18 °C. All should be watered fairly freely in spring and summer, and sparingly in winter unless fairly high temperatures keep them growing. All can be stood outdoors in summer and the Zonal-leaved and Ivy-leaved varieties are often planted out for summer bedding.

Regal pelargoniums can be pruned in summer after flowering to keep them bushy and Scented-leaved

Polianthes tuberosa

kinds can be pruned at almost any time while in growth to improve their habit. Zonal-leaved pelargoniums are best pruned when they stop flowering or are only producing a few flowers.

All kinds can be raised from cuttings of firm young growth in spring or summer and often these will root even without the aid of a propagator. Zonal-leaved pelargoniums can also be increased from seed sown in early spring in a temperature of 16–18 °C but it is important to obtain seed of varieties that flower readily the first year.

Primula obconica

Plumbago (Cape Leadwort)
The kind cultivated in greenhouses and conservatories is *P. capensis*, a climbing or sprawling plant with clusters of pale blue phlox-like flowers in summer. It is nearly hardy and will grow in any sunny frostproof structure, preferably in a bed of good soil as it makes a big plant, but if this is not possible, in a large pot or tub filled with a good soil-based potting mixture. Pot or plant in autumn, water fairly freely in spring and summer, rather sparingly in autumn and winter. Tie the stems to wires, trellis or other suitable supports and prune plants in spring as necessary to fill the space available. Cuttings will root in a propagator in summer or seeds can be germinated in spring in a temperature of 18–21 °C.

Polianthes (Tuberose)
The waxy white flowers of the Tuberose, produced in dense spikes, are among the most richly scented of all flowers and are easily produced by planting bulbs in pots and growing them in a temperature of 15 °C or more. Bulbs can be planted at any time when they are available, either one bulb in each 13 cm pot or three bulbs in a 15 cm pot, in a soil- or peat-based potting mixture. They are watered sparingly at first, freely when growth appears. The difficulty is to grow them on after they have flowered. They need to be well ripened in a warm, sunny place, with a gradual reduction of water, but even the experts cannot rely on persuading them to flower again the following year and most prefer to discard the bulbs after flowering and purchase imported bulbs, which often come from South Africa. The best varieties have semi-double flowers.

Primula
Three kinds of primula are commonly grown in greenhouses, principally for winter flowering, though one of them *P. obconica*, is almost perpetual flowering. The other two are *P. malacoides* and *P. sinensis*. All are perennial in some conditions, though usually grown for a year and then discarded since young plants raised from seed give the best results. *P. malacoides* has the smallest flowers produced in the largest sprays and is often called 'fairy primula' because of its elegance. The colour range is limited to shades of pink, carmine, rose, mauve, and white and there are double as well as single flowered varieties. The primrose-like flowers of *P. obconica* and *P. sinensis* are borne in clusters and make a fine display, the colour range being shades of pink, salmon, carmine, crimson, lavender and violet-blue with the addition, for *P. sinensis*, of orange-scarlet.

Seed can be sown in spring or summer. It can pay to make an early start with *P. obconica* but late spring or early summer are usually the best times for the other two. A temperature of 16 °C is sufficient for germination and much of the year these are plants that can be grown 'cool', without artificial heat. For winter flowering the temperature should be around 10–13 °C but it does not matter if it falls occasionally to 7 °C or even less so long as it does not freeze. In summer plants will be happy in a frame, or standing outdoors in a not too hot and sunny place, as in a greenhouse.

Grow throughout in any good soil- or peat-based potting mixture; prick out seedlings early and pot singly, when large enough, in 7.5 cm pots. Move on later to 13 cm pots for flowering (or *P. malacoides* to 11 cm pots since it makes smaller plants). Water fairly freely in spring and summer, moderately in autumn and winter. Discard the plants of *P. malacoides* and *P. sinensis* after flowering but retain *P. obconica* as long as it remains decorative.

The leaves of all these plants, but particularly those of *P. obconica*, can cause a skin rash in some people, so those known to be sensitive should wear gloves when handling them and avoid brushing against them.

Prostanthera (Mint Bush)
These are shrubs with small, evergreen, aromatic leaves, slender but wiry stems and clusters of small violet-purple flowers in spring. They make attractive plants to train against the wall of a sunny, frostproof greenhouse. They are rather large for pots and should preferably be planted in a bed of lime-free loam, peat and sand. Water fairly freely in spring and summer, rather sparingly in autumn and winter. Cuttings can be rooted in a propagator in summer or plants raised from seed in a temperature of 16 °C in spring. *P. rotundifolia* and *P. violacea* are two good kinds to grow. (*See* overleaf for illustration.)

Punica (Pomegranate)
Pomegranates are the orange-like fruits of *P. granatum*, a deciduous shrub or small tree which has scarlet or orange-red flowers in late summer and

Prostanthera rotundifolia

autumn. There are also double-flowered varieties which do not fruit but are grown solely for ornament, and a dwarf variety named 'Nana' which will not exceed a height of 45 cm and makes an excellent pot plant for a sunny, frost-free greenhouse or conservatory. It can be grown from seed sown in spring in a temperature of 18 °C. The seedlings are potted singly in any good soil- or peat-based potting mixture, first in 7.5 cm pots, later in 13 cm pots in which they will flower. Water fairly freely from spring to autumn, sparingly in winter when the temperature should not fall below 7 °C. The larger varieties can be grown in a similar way but will need large pots or tubs; or they can be planted in a bed of soil on the greenhouse floor. All kinds, including those with double flowers, can be raised from summer cuttings in a propagator.

Rehmannia
The kind most commonly grown is *R. angulata*, a tender, herbaceous perennial with metre-high spikes of purple, trumpet-shaped flowers in summer. It is not far short of hardy and can be grown as a pot plant in any well-lighted, frostproof structure. It will grow in any good soil- or peat-based mixture, watered fairly freely in spring and summer, moderately in autumn and winter. Plants can be divided when being repotted in spring but are so readily raised from seed sown in early summer in a greenhouse or frame that *R. angulata* is often grown as a biennial, raised annually from seed and discarded after flowering.

Reinwardtia (Winter Flax)
The kind cultivated, *R. trigyna*, is a small evergreen shrub with clusters of bright yellow flowers from autumn until early spring. Since it will produce this winter display in a temperature range of 10–18 °C, it deserves to be better known. It can be grown in any good soil-based potting mixture in a large pot, tub, or bed and should be watered fairly freely in spring and summer, moderately in autumn and winter. It can be pruned to size and shape in spring. The more light it gets the better. Cuttings will root in a propagator in spring or summer, or, when available, seed can be germinated in a temperature of 16–18 °C.

Rhodochiton (Purple Bells, Purple Bellerine)
There is only one species, *R. atrosanquineum* (it is sometimes called *R. volubile*), a fast-growing twiner with little mauve-pink and maroon bells hanging all along its slender stems in summer. It can be grown on from year to year provided the temperature does not fall below 7 °C but it is so fast growing and readily

raised from seed that it is often grown as an annual and discarded after flowering. If retained it should be watered moderately in autumn and winter and be pruned a little in early spring to keep it in bounds and get rid of weak or damaged growth. In spring and summer it should be watered fairly freely. It will grow in large pots or beds in any good soil- or peat-based potting mixture and light, preferably sunny place.

Rhododendron

From the botanist's standpoint azaleas are rhododendrons but gardeners consider them to be so different that they have been treated separately in this book. In general it is the azaleas that make the best greenhouse plants since many are compact, evergreen and showy and cannot be grown outdoors in cold places. By contrast many rhododendrons are large, hardy and best grown outdoors but there are exceptions, including all the Malaysian kinds (often called Javanese rhododendrons), some of which require quite high temperatures though many of the hybrids can be grown successfully in a minimum of 13 °C. More useful for ordinary greenhouse owners are some slightly tender species and hybrids such as *R. bullatum*, *R. edgeworthii*, *R. fragrantissimum* and 'R. Lady Alice Fitzwilliam'. All these are richly scented and very beautiful and only require protection from frost. They need a peaty, lime-free mixture, shade from strong sunshine and plenty of water while growing in spring and summer, with sufficient to keep the soil moist in autumn and winter. They are a little large for pots but can be grown well in tubs or beds. Increase is by

layering stems at any time of the year. Pruning is undesirable except to remove damaged or overgrown branches, and is done after flowering.

Saintpaulia (African Violet)

The cultivated varieties, some with single, some with double flowers, in many shades of blue, purple and pink, plus white, are all derived from one species native to tropical Africa, *S. ionantha*. All are small plants making neat rosettes of velvet, dark green leaves and flowering almost throughout the year if a temperature range from 16 to 21 °C can be maintained. They will survive in much lower temperatures but then stop flowering and are more liable to be attacked by fungi which rot the plants at soil level. They will grow in soil- or peat-based mixtures but if soil is used it should be mixed with more peat than in the John Innes formulae as saintpaulias like a rather spongy compost. Water fairly freely in spring and summer, moderately in autumn, very carefully in winter especially if the temperature drops below 15 °C. Apply water direct to the soil and avoid splashing it on the leaves. In spring and summer the air can be much moister than at other times. Plants should be shaded from direct sunshine. They succeed well in plant cabinets and Wardian cases in which a very even temperature and humidity can be maintained.

Seed will germinate in spring in a temperature of 18–21 °C but plants are usually increased by cuttings of well-developed leaves in summer, the stalks and

Reinwardtia trigyna

Rhodochiton atrosanquineum

Saintpaulia

Above: Salpiglossis

Below: Schizanthus

about one-third of the leaf pushed into moist peat in a warm propagator.

Salpiglossis

These half hardy annuals with trumpet-shaped flowers, often delicately veined with various colours including rose, scarlet, crimson, purple, and gold, are used mainly as summer bedding plants but they also make excellent pot plants for a sunny greenhouse. Sow in early spring in a temperature of 16–18 °C; prick out seedlings in the ordinary way but later pot them singly in 13 cm pots in any good soil- or peat-based potting mixture. Water fairly freely and keep in a sunny place in a temperature of 13–21 °C. Discard after flowering.

Schizanthus (Butterfly Flower)

These easily grown annuals have sometimes been called the 'poor man's orchid', so delicately marked are some of the butterly-like flowers carried in large sprays. They make excellent pot plants, can be grown in any good soil- or peat-based potting mixture and require little or no artificial heat. If seed is sown sometime between January and May in a temperature of 16 °C plants will flower in summer and autumn. Alternatively a sowing made in August or early autumn will give seedlings that will stand the winter in a light, frostproof greenhouse and flower the following spring. Either way seedlings should be pricked out into boxes, potted singly when large enough, first in 7.5 cm pots, and later, when these are filled with roots, into the 13–15 cm pots in which they will flower. Water fairly freely in spring and summer, moderately in autumn, rather sparingly in winter. Discard after flowering.

Smithiantha (Temple Bell)

These are tender perennials closely related to gesneria and grown in the same way either from small tubers or

A hybrid Smithiantha

Sparmannia africana

from seed. The leaves are soft and velvety, the nodding, tubular flowers carried in loose spikes in summer. Most of those cultivated are hybrids and the colour range includes cream, yellow, orange, pink, rose, and red.

Solanum (Winter Cherry)

Several very different kinds of solanum can be grown in greenhouses. One of the most popular is *S. capsicastrum*, the Winter Cherry, a bushy plant with small white flowers in summer followed by globular, orange-red fruits in autumn. It makes a good pot plant and is much used for winter decoration. It is easily grown from seed sown in spring, the earlier the better, in a temperature of 16–18 °C. Seedlings are pricked out and later potted singly, first in 7.5 cm pots; later in the 13–15 cm pots in which they will flower and fruit. They can be grown throughout in any good soil- or peat-based potting mixture. Plants are nearly hardy and can stand outdoors in a sunny place all summer. Water freely from spring to autumn, moderately in winter. Syringe with clear water daily while in flower to assist the setting of the fruits. Bring into a light greenhouse in autumn before there is danger of frost. If plants are kept for a second year they can be pruned to shape in spring when the fruits have fallen.

Very different from this are *S. jasminoides* and *S. crispum*, both climbing plants, the former a slender twiner with clusters of small, greyish-blue and yellow, or white and yellow flowers; the latter with violet-blue and yellow flowers carried on long flexible stems which need to be tied to wires, trellis or other supports. Both are vigorous, nearly hardy and are suitable for clothing the back wall of a large sunny conservatory. They are best planted in beds of good soil though they can be grown in tubs. They should be watered freely in spring and summer, moderately in autumn and winter and can be pruned as necessary in spring to fill available space. Increase is usually by summer cuttings in a propagator or by layering at any time.

Sparaxis (Harlequin Flower)

These South African plants have sprays of starry flowers in late spring or early summer. The colours of some are strongly contrasted, pink, orange, crimson, or purple with yellow or white, hence the popular name Harlequin Flower, but there are also other kinds with cream, or cream and white flowers.

All form small corms from which they can be grown. These are potted in late winter or early spring, five to seven in each 10–13 cm pot in any good soil- or peat-based potting mixture. They need sunshine and protection from frost but little artificial heat. They should be watered moderately at first, freely when growth appears but watering should be gradually discontinued in late summer and the soil kept quite dry in autumn and winter until it is time to shake out the corms and repot them.

Sparaxis can also be grown from seed sown in spring in a temperature of 18 °C but seedlings will not flower the first year.

Sparmannia (African Hemp)

The kind grown, *S. africana*, is a shrub with large, softly downy, heart-shaped leaves and sprays of white and yellow flowers produced most freely in summer though there can be some at almost any time of the year if there is enough warmth to keep the plants growing. It can be used outdoors in summer to decorate patios, terraces, etc., but does need complete protection from frost in winter. It will grow in any good soil- or peat-based potting mixture in pots or other containers large enough to hold its roots. Old plants may require tubs; young ones will grow happily in 13–15 cm pots. Water fairly freely in spring and summer, moderately in autumn, sparingly in winter especially if the temperature falls below 10 °C. Cuttings root readily in a propagator in spring or summer or seed will germinate in spring in a temperature of 16–18 °C.

Spathiphyllum (White Sails)

Perennials related to the arum lily and with flowers similar in character but much smaller, white spathes

Spathiphyllum wallisii

Strelitzia reginae

A hybrid Streptocarpus

are held erect around a narrow yellow column or spadix. *S. wallisii*, the kind commonly grown, makes an excellent house plant and can also be grown in a greenhouse with minimum winter temperature of 10 °C, with shade in summer and a fairly moist atmosphere. It will thrive in any good soil- or peat-based mixture and should be watered freely in spring and summer, sparingly in autumn and winter. The easiest way to increase it is by division when repotting in spring, when it is starting into growth. It flowers mainly in late spring and early summer but some flowers may be produced later.

Sprekelia (Jacobean Lily)
Bulbs of this handsome Mexican plant have become freely available and can be grown successfully in any sunny, frostproof greenhouse. The only species is *S. formosissima* and it has spidery, crimson flowers carried singly on short stems in midsummer. Bulbs should be obtained in spring and potted singly in 13 cm pots in any good soil- or peat-based mixture. Provided the temperature does not drop below 7 °C no artificial heat will be required. Keep throughout in a sunny greenhouse, water moderately at first, fairly freely when leaves appear, but about six weeks after flowering begin to reduce the water supply gradually and keep quite dry from mid-autumn until early spring, when the plants should be repotted.

Stocks, Winter Flowering
These are varieties of *Matthiola incana* which is also the parent of the summer-flowering stocks so popular for summer bedding. Two strains are commonly grown under glass, one known as Beauty of Nice, the other as East Lothian. Both have fine spikes of sweetly scented flowers similar to those of the summer stocks and with much the same colour range, which includes pink, red, purple, lavender and white. Good selections will produce a high percentage of double flowers. Seed should be sown from June to August in a frame or unheated greenhouse, the seedlings being pricked out into boxes as soon as they can be handled and later potted singly in any good soil- or peat-based compost in the 10–13 cm pots in which they will flower. Water fairly freely in summer and early autumn, moderately thereafter and discard after flowering. In summer plants can be in a frame or can be stood outdoors in a sunny place but from October onwards they should be in a light, frostproof greenhouse.

Strelitzia (Bird of Paradise Flower)
These very exotic-looking plants are nearly hardy and can be grown successfully with far less heat than might be supposed. They are big plants with broad, canna-like leaves except in the variety *S. parvifolia juncea*

Streptosolen jamesonii

which has rush-like leaves. The large flowers are curiously shaped, rather like a long-beaked bird, brightly coloured orange and blue, and carried on stout stems about a metre high in May and June. Plants can be divided in spring when they are repotted in a rather rich soil- or peat-based potting mixture, and can also be raised from seed sown in spring in a temperature of 18 °C but seedlings will take several years to attain flowering size. Grow in a sunny place. Water normally.

Streptocarpus
Excellent pot plants with rosettes of fairly large leaves from which come in constant succession from May to September slender stems bearing clusters of funnel-shaped flowers. One of the most popular varieties, 'Constant Nymph', is so named because it is seldom completely out of bloom. Its flowers are lavender but there are also pink, carmine and white varieties of streptocarpus.

All can be grown either from seed sown in late winter or early spring in a temperature of 16–18 °C or from leaf cuttings in a propagator in summer. Young plants should be potted singly in any good soil- or peat-based potting mixture and should be grown throughout in a frostproof greenhouse with shade from direct sunshine in summer. If autumn flowers are desired the temperature should not fall below 13 °C but plants will survive temperatures as low as 7 °C. Water fairly freely from spring to autumn, moderately in winter, or sparingly if there is not much warmth. Good plants of the larger varieties can be grown in 13 cm pots and of the smaller kinds, such as 'Constant Nymph', in 10 cm pots.

Streptosolen
There is only one kind, S. jamesonii, a sprawling South American evergreen shrub with clusters of vivid orange flowers in summer. It is best grown as a climber, its slender stems tied to canes, trellis or a wire framework. It is nearly hardy and can be grown in any light, frostproof structure, preferably in a bed of good soil but otherwise in a large pot or tub filled with any good soil- or peat-based potting mixture. Water fairly freely in spring and summer, moderately in autumn or winter, or sparingly if the temperature falls below 10 °C. Stems can be trimmed or shortened in spring. Cuttings root readily in summer in a propagator.

Thunbergia (Black Eyed Susan)
The kind cultivated is T. alata, a fast-growing perennial climber, though it is usually grown as an annual. It has slender twining stems and white, buff or orange flowers usually with a black centre. It makes an excellent pot plant if provided with two or three canes up which it can climb or it can be grown in a hanging basket and allowed to trail over the edges. Seed should be germinated in early spring in a temperature of 16–18 °C and the seedlings potted individually in small pots and later moved into 13 cm pots in which they will flower. Thunbergia will grow in any good soil- or peat-based potting mixture. It should be watered normally and, if desired, can be placed outdoors in summer when there is no further danger of frost. Plants are usually discarded in the autumn when they cease to flower, but they can be grown on in a frostproof greenhouse if preferred.

Thunbergia alata

Tibouchina semidecandra

Tibouchina (Brazilian Spider Flower, Brazilian Glory Bush)
The kind cultivated, *T. semidecandra*, is an evergreen shrub with long, lax stems, dark green, velvety leaves and violet-purple flowers produced non-stop from early summer well into the autumn according to the temperature that can be maintained. It is nearly hardy, and will survive in any completely frostproof place but needs a temperature of 13 °C or more to keep it flowering. It is best trained as a climber with its stems tied to wires or trellis and can be grown in a bed or a large pot or tub in any good soil- or peat-based mixture. Water freely in spring and summer, moderately in autumn, rather sparingly in winter especially if the temperature falls below 10 °C. If necessary stems can be thinned or shortened in February and tips of shoots can be pinched out at any time in summer to restrict growth and encourage branching. Cuttings root readily in summer in a propagator.

Tigridia (Tiger Flower, Peacock Flower)
The kind grown, *T. pavonia*, is a nearly hardy perennial bulb with flowers that look a little like widely opened tulips except that each has only three large petals. These may be red, pink, orange, or yellow, often with one colour spotted on another. Individual flowers only last a day but one plant is capable of producing a succession of flowers for several weeks.

Tigridias make good pot plants when five to seven bulbs are grown in each 13 cm pot in any good soil- or

peat-based mixture. Pot in early spring, keep in a sunny place with minimum temperature of 10 °C, and water moderately at first but freely as soon as leaves appear. A few weeks after the last flower fades, leaves will commence to die down and this is the signal to reduce watering quite rapidly so that the bulbs can be stored dry in autumn and winter. Seed germinates readily in spring in a temperature of 16–18 °C but seedlings are unlikely to flower the first year.

Torenia (Wishbone Flower)
The kind grown is *T. fournieri*, a bushy but short annual with curiously shaped violet-purple flowers marked with black and yellow. It makes an attractive pot plant and is easily grown with little artificial heat after the first few weeks. Sow in spring in a temperature of 16–18 °C; pot the seedlings singly in small pots in any good soil- or peat-based potting mixture and move on into 13–15 cm pots when the smaller ones are filled with roots. Water fairly freely throughout and grow in a sunny greenhouse until there is no further danger of frost when plants can be placed outdoors if desired. Discard after flowering.

Trachelium (Blue Throatwort)
The kind cultivated as a greenhouse pot plant is *T. coeruleum*, a herbaceous plant with clusters of small lavender-blue flowers in summer. It is nearly hardy and easily grown from seed sown in spring in a temperature of about 16 °C to give plants which will flower in 10–13 cm pots that summer; or sown in June/July to give plants that will overwinter in a frost-proof greenhouse and flower the following year in pots 15–18 cm in diameter. Either way the plants can be grown in any good soil- or peat-based potting mixture. They will need normal watering from spring to autumn, when spring-sown plants are usually discarded, and rather sparing watering in winter for the summer-raised plants. Tracheliums are seldom retained for a second flowering season as young plants make the most attractive pot specimens.

Trachelospermum (Chinese Jasmine)
Evergreen twiners with small, white, deliciously scented flowers in summer. Two kinds are commonly cultivated, *T. asiaticum* and *T. jasminoides*. They do not differ much in appearance but *T. asiaticum* is slightly hardier (it will survive some frost) and *T. jasminoides* has an attractive variety, named 'Variegatum' with leaves edged with cream, and also a little pink when the temperature falls. All can be grown in large pots in any good soil- or peat-based potting mixture, or in a bed of good soil on the floor of a frost-proof greenhouse or conservatory. Plants should be watered freely in spring and summer, and moderately in autumn and winter. A minimum temperature of 7 °C is sufficient. Cuttings will root in summer in a warm propagator. If plants grow too large they can be

Tritonia crocata

cut back in spring but generally trachelospermums are
rather slow growing and require little pruning.

Tritonia
These are perennials related to the montbretia but
more tender and fragile. Hybrids are usually cultivated
and these have loose sprays of pretty orange, cream,
pink, or rose flowers on slender 30 cm stems in
summer. They are grown from corms similar to those
of montbretia and these are potted in spring, four or
five corms in each 13 cm pot, in any good soil- or peat-
based potting mixture. Keep in a sunny, frostproof
greenhouse and water moderately at first, but fairly
freely when growth appears. In early autumn when
leaves commence to yellow, gradually reduce the water
supply and keep quite dry in winter in a frostproof
place. Repot in the spring, when the clusters of corms
can be separated.

Tropaeolum (Nasturtium)
Several kinds are grown in greenhouses and they differ
considerably in appearance and requirements. The
earliest to flower is *T. tricolorum*, a slender twining
plant with small, divided leaves and small but
abundant scarlet and black flowers in spring. It forms
little tubers from which it can be grown. They should

Tropaeolum tricolor

be potted in autumn, one in each 13–15 cm pot, in any good soil- or peat-based potting mixture, and kept in a sunny greenhouse with minimum temperature of 7 °C. They are watered moderately at first, and fairly freely when growth appears, but soon after flowering the slender stems usually die down and the soil can then be kept almost dry until it is time to repot in the autumn. Canes or other supports should be provided for the stems to twine around. *T. peltophorum*, also known as *T. lobbianum*, flowers in summer and looks much like an ordinary annual nasturtium but there are good double flower forms, both orange and scarlet. These are grown on in any good soil- or peat-based mixture in a light, frostproof greenhouse. They require little water in winter but normal quantities at other times. They also need canes for support.

T. tuberosum flowers in late summer and autumn. Its red and yellow flowers are shaped like tiny trumpets and it forms tubers which should be potted singly in 13–15 cm pots in late winter or early spring in any good soil- or peat-based potting mixture. Keep in a frostproof place, but pots can stand outdoors in summer and look pretty on balconies or hanging out of ornamental containers. Stems die down and tubers rest for a few weeks in winter, when soil can be kept nearly dry. Clusters of tubers can be separated when repotting; and all tropaeolums, except the double-flowered varieties which are grown from summer cuttings, can also be grown from seed sown in spring in a temperature of 16–18 °C.

Tulipa (Tulip)

The shorter varieties of tulip make excellent pot plants, especially the early flowering types which are often damaged by wind and rain outdoors but can be enjoyed in perfection in an unheated or very slightly warmed greenhouse or conservatory. Pot the bulbs, in October, in any good soil- or peat-based potting mixture, placing them almost shoulder to shoulder in 13–15 cm pots. For the first ten weeks keep the tulips in the coolest place available (they can stand outdoors in a shady place) and water moderately. When the pots are well filled with roots, and leaves and/or flower spikes are appearing, bring the pots into a light greenhouse or conservatory in which the temperature is around 13–18 °C by day though it does not matter if it falls to 7 °C at night. Water more freely until leaves commence to die down in late spring, when the soil can be allowed to become almost completely dry for a few weeks. In early autumn the bulbs can be planted outdoors. It is unwise to attempt to grow tulips two years running in pots.

Tweedia

The best kind, *T. caerulea*, is a twining plant with grey-green leaves and sprays of small starry flowers which start by being blue, but change to purple and finally fade to lilac. It is sometimes known as *Oxypetalum*

Vallota speciosa

caeruleum. It can be grown from seed germinated in spring in a temperature of 18 °C. Seedlings are potted singly, first in 7.5 cm pots, later in 13 cm pots in any good soil- or peat-based potting compost. From autumn to spring they should be grown in a sunny, frostproof greenhouse or conservatory but are hardy enough to be stood outdoors in summer. They will need canes or other supports. This plant can be treated as a half hardy annual, to be renewed each year from seed, or it can be kept from year to year, in which case it will need a minimum temperature of 7 °C in winter.

Vallota (Scarborough Lily)

There is only one kind. *V. speciosa*, a bulbous-rooted perennial with clusters of scarlet, trumpet-shaped flowers in late summer and early autumn. It is very easily grown in any sunny, frostproof structure. Bulbs should be potted singly in autumn, in 10–13 cm pots, in any good soil- or peat-based potting mixture. It should be watered moderately in winter, fairly freely in spring, and rather sparingly for a few weeks in early summer, when bulbs are resting, though at no time should the soil become quite dry. The bulbs increase rapidly and small ones can be detached and potted separately in autumn to increase stock. At the same time plants can be repotted but restrict them to the smallest pots that will contain their roots comfortably, with just a little extra compost around. Vallotas flower best when their roots are fairly constricted. Plants can also be raised from seed sown in a temperature of 16 °C in spring but seedlings may take several years to reach flowering size.

Veltheimia *(see* illustration p. 15)

These are attractive South African bulbs with tubular flowers in dense spikes like those of Red Hot Pokers (Kniphofias) except that the stems are no more than 45 cm high and colours are invariably soft, either pale pink with green or slightly dulled salmon-red. They make good pot plants for a sunny, frostproof greenhouse or conservatory. Pot in late summer or early autumn, one bulb in each 10–13 cm pot or three in a 15 cm pot, in any good soil- or peat-based potting mixture. Water sparingly at first, fairly freely when the leaves and flower buds appear and throughout the spring but gradually reduce the water supply in summer and keep dry for a few weeks before repotting. In winter a temperature of 13–18 °C is ideal with a minimum of 7 °C.

Bulb clusters can be separated when repotting and plants can also be raised from seed sown in spring in a temperature of 16–18 °C but seedlings will take a year or so to reach flowering size.

Verbena

The ordinary hybrid verbenas, so popular for summer bedding, also make good pot plants for a greenhouse or conservatory or for standing on balconies, in courtyards, etc. They are trailing perennials but are almost invariably grown as half hardy annuals from seed sown in late winter or early spring in a temperature of 16–18 °C. Prick out the seedlings into trays and later pot them singly in 10–13 cm pots in any good soil- or peat-based compost. Water normally and give as much light as possible. Discard in the autumn when flowering ceases. Many colours are available, including pink, scarlet, carmine, crimson, lavender, blue, and purple.

Vinca (Madagascar Periwinkle)

The kind grown in greenhouse, *V. rosea*, has now been renamed, *Catharanthus roseus*, though the old name is still generally used in gardens. It is a bushy perennial which, in a warm greenhouse, will flower almost throughout the year. The flowers are rather like those of Busy Lizzie (*Impatiens*), pale or deep pink or white with a carmine eye. It is usually grown from seed sown in spring in a temperature of 18–21 °C, but summer cuttings will root readily in a warm propagator. The seedlings are pricked out into trays and later potted singly in 13 cm pots in any good soil- or peat-based potting mixture. They are watered fairly freely and grown in a temperature of 16–21 °C. Usually this plant is treated as an annual and discarded in the autumn or winter but it can be grown on from year to year, in which case plants will need to be repotted in spring, probably in larger pots, and kept throughout the winter in a minimum temperature of 13 °C, preferably a little more.

Zantedeschia aethiopica

Zantedeschia (Arum Lily)

The common Arum Lily has had several botanical names including *Richardia africana* and *Zantedeschia aethiopica*. Its large white spathes folded around a central column (spadix) of tiny yellow flowers are well known and much used in floral arrangements. It is an easy plant to grow in any frostproof structure in full sun or partial shade. The fleshy roots should be potted in late summer in a rather rich soil- or peat-based potting mixture. At first they should be watered rather sparingly, but when growth appears, freely; and this continues throughout the spring and summer with little slackening off – except for a few weeks in summer before repotting, when most leaves die down and little water is needed. If grown with just enough heat to exclude frost plants will flower in later spring, but in a temperature of 13–18 °C they will flower many weeks earlier. Some varieties have spathes splashed with green.

There are also other species, including *Z. (Richardia) elliottiana* which is similar in character but has golden yellow spathes, and *Z. rehmannii* with smaller pink or purplish spathes. Both are more tender than the common Arum Lily and will thrive best with a minimum winter temperature of 13 °C. Otherwise cultivation is the same.

All can be increased by dividing the roots when repotting. Seeds will also germinate in spring in a temperature of 18 °C but seedlings may take a couple of years to attain flowering size.

Table of Flowering Plants

ABBREVIATIONS

Type. Sb, shrub. Hb, herbaceous plant. An, annual. Bi, biennial. Cl, climber. Bl, bulb. Cm, corm. T, tuber. Br, bromeliad. Pm, palm. Suc, succulent. F, fern. Ep, epiphyte.
Temperature. C, cold, no artificial heat. Cl, cool, minimum 7 °C. Int, intermediate, minimum 13 °C. W, warm, minimum 18 °C.
Soil. Av, average, John Innes type or peat based. S, sandy, extra sand or grit. Hm, humussy, extra peat and/or leaf mould.

Atmosphere. B, buoyant r.h. 50 to 60 per cent. H, humid, r.h. 70 to 80 per cent. D, dry, r.h. 30 to 40 per cent.
Light. Sun, no shade required at any time. Sh, shade from all direct sunshine. Semi, shade from strong sunshine in late spring and summer.
Water. N, normal watering, fairly freely in spring and summer, moderately in autumn and winter. W, keep dry in winter, water normally at other times. S, keep dry in summer, water normally at other times. PW, water sparingly in winter. PS, water sparingly in summer.

Name	Type	Temperature	Soil	Atmosphere	Light	Water
Abutilon	Sb	C	Av	B	Sun	PW
Acacia	Sb	C	Av	H	Semi	N
Achimenes	T	Int	Av	H	Semi	C
Acidanthera	Cm	C	Av	B	Sun	W
Agapanthus	Hb	C	Av	B	Sun	PW
Allemanda	Cl	W	Av	H	Sun	W
Anthurium	Hb	W	Hm	H	Sh	PW
Azalea	Sb	C	Hm	B	Semi	N
Babiana	Cm	C	S	D	Sun	S
Begonia Tuberous and Multiflora	T	Cl	Av	B	Sun	W
B. semperflorens	Hb	Cl	Av	B	Semi	N
B. 'Gloire de Lorraine'	Hb	Int	Hm	B	Sh	N
Beleperone	Hb	Cl	Av	B	Sun	N
Billbergia	Br	Cl	Av	B	Sun	PW
Bougainvillea	Cl	Cl	Av	B	Sun	PW
Bouvardia	Sb	Int	Av	B	Sun	N
Browallia	An	Int	Av	B	Sun	N
Brunfelsia	Sb	Int	Av	H	Sun	W
Calceolaria integrifolia	Sb	C	Av	B	Sun	PW
C. herbacea	Bi	C	Av	B	Sun	PW
Callistemon	Sb	C	Av	B	Sun	PW
Camellia	Sb	C	Hm	B	Semi	N
Campanula isophylla	Hb	C	Av	B	Sun	N
C. pyramidalis	Bi	C	Av	B	Sun	N
Campsis	Cl	Cl	Av	B	Sun	W
Canna	Hb	Cl	Av	B	Sun	W
Carnation Chabaud	An	Cl	Av	B	Sun	N
Perpetual and Malmaison	Hb	Cl	Av	D	Sun	N
Cassia	Cl	C	Av	D	Sun	PW
Celosia	An	Cl	Av	B	Sun	N
Celsia	Hb	Cl	S	B	Sun	N
Cestrum	Cl	Cl	Av	B	Sun	PW

Name	Type	Temperature	Soil	Atmosphere	Light
Chrysanthemum	Hb	C	Av	B	Semi PW
Cineraria	An	C	Av	B	Sun N
Clematis	Cl	C	Av	B	Sun PW
Clerodendrum thomsoniae	Cl	Int	Av	B	Sun N
C. speciosissimum	Sb	W	Av	H	Sun N
Clianthus	Cl	Cl	Av	B	Sun PW
Clivia	Hb	Cl	Av	B	Semi PW
Cobaea	Cl	Cl	Av	B	Sun PW
Columnea	Ep	W	Hm	H	Sh N
Coronilla	Sb	Cl	Av	B	Sun N
Crassula	Suc	Cl	S	D	Sun PW
Crocus	Cm	C	Av	B	Sun S
Crossandra	Sb	W	Hm	H	Sh PW
Cuphea	Hb	Cl	Av	B	Sun N
Cyclamen	T	Cl	Hm	B	Semi S
Cytisus	Sb	Cl	Av	B	Sun N
Datura	Sb	Cl	Av	B	Sun W
Didiscus	An	Cl	Av	B	Sun N
Dipladenia	Cl	Int	Av	B	Sun N
Eccremocarpus	Cl	Int	Av	B	Sun W
Epacris	Sb	Cl	Hm	B	Sun N
Erica	Hb	Cl	Hm	B	Sun W
Erythrina	Sb	Cl	Av	B	Sun PW
Eucharis	Bl	W	Av	B	Semi PW
Euphorbia pulcherrima	Sb	Int	Av	B	Semi PS
E. fulgens	Sb	W	Av	B	Sun PS
E. splendens	Sb	W	Av	D	Sun PW
Exacum	An	Cl	Av	B	Sun N
Francoa	Hb	Cl	Av	B	Semi N
Freesia	Cm	Cl	Av	B	Sun S
Fremontia	Sb	C	Av	B	Sun PW
Fuchsia	Sb	Cl	Av	B	Semi N
Gardenia	Sb	Int/W	Av	H	Semi N
Gerbera	Hb	Cl	S	B	Sun PW
Gesneria	T	Int	Hm	H	Semi W

Name	Type	Temperature	Soil	Atmosphere	Light	Water
Gloriosa	T	Int	Av	B	Sun	W
Gloxinia	T	Int	Hm	B	Semi	W
Haemanthus	Bl	Cl	Av	B	Sun	W
Hedychium	Hb	Cl	Av	B	Sun	N
Heliotropium	Hb	Cl	Av	B	Sun	N
Hibiscus						
rosa-sinensis	Sb	Int	Av	H	Sun	N
H. manihot &						
'Southern Belle'	Hb	Cl	Av	B	Sun	N
Hippeastrum	Bl	Int	Av	B	Sun	PW
Hoya carnosa	Cl	Cl	Av	B	Semi	N
H. bella	Sb	Int	Av	B	Semi	N
Humea	Bi	Cl	Av	B	Semi	N
Hyacinthus	Bl	C	Av	B	Sun	S
Hydrangea	Sb	Cl	Av	B	Semi	PW
Hymenocallis	Bl	Cl	Av	B	Sun	W
Hypocyrta	Hb	Cl	Av	B	Semi	N
Impatiens						
balsamina	An	Cl	Av	B	Semi	N
I. wallerana	Hb	Int	Av	B	Semi	N
Ipomoea learii	Cl	Cl	Av	B	Sun	PW
I. annual vars.	Cl	Int	Av	H	Sun	PW
Ismene	Bl	Cl	Av	B	Sun	W
Ixora	Sb	W	Hm	H	Semi	N
Jacobinia	Sb	Int	Av	B	Sun	N
Jasminum						
polyanthum	Cl	Cl	Av	B	Sun	N
J. mesneyi	Sb	Cl	Av	B	Sun	N
Kalanchoe	Suc	Cl	S	D	Sun	N
Lachenalia	Bl	Cl	Av	B	Sun	S
Lagerstroemia	Sb	Int	Av	H	Sun	N
Lantana	Sb	Cl	Av	B	Sun	N
Lapageria	Cl	Cl	Av	B	Semi	N
Leptospermum	Sb	C	Av	B	Sun	N
Lilium	Bl	Cl	Hm	B	Semi	N
Limonium						
profusum	An	Cl	Av	B	Sun	PW
L. suworowii	An	Cl	Av	B	Sun	N
Luculia	Sb	Cl	Av	B	Sun	PW
Mandevilla	Cl	Cl	Av	B	Sun	PW
Manettia	Cl	Int	Av	B	Sun	N
Maurandia	Cl	Cl	Av	B	Sun	PW
Medinilla	Hb	W	Hm	H	Sh	PW
Mesem-bryanthemum	Suc	Cl	Av	B	Sun	PW
Mimulus tigrinus	An	Cl	Hm	B	Sun	N
M. aurantiacus	Hb	Cl	Av	B	Sun	PW
Narcissus	Bl	C	Av	B	Sun	S
Nerine	Bl	Cl	S	B	Sun	S
Nerium	Sb	C	Av	B	Sun	N
Oxalis	T	C, Cl	Av	B	Sun	S
Pachystachys	Hb	Int	Av	B	Sun	N
Passiflora	Cl	Cl/Int	Av	B	Sun	PW
Pelargonium						
regal, zonal and scented leaf	Sb	Cl	Av	B	Sun	N
P., Ivy leafed	Cl	Cl	Av	B	Sun	N
Plumbago	Cl	C	Av	H	Sun	N
Polianthes	Bl	Int/W	Av	H	Sun	W
Primula	An	Cl	Av	B	Sun	N
Prostanthera	Sb	C	Av	B	Sun	PW
Punica	Sb	Cl	Av	B	Sun	N
Rehmannia	Hb	Cl	Av	B	Sun	N
Reinwardtia	Sb	Int	Av	B	Sun	N
Rhodochiton	Cl	Cl	Av	B	Sun	N
Rhododendron	Sb	Cl/Int	Hm	B	Semi	N
Saintpaulia	Hb	Int	Hm	B	Sh	N
Salpiglossis	An	Cl/C	Av	B	Sun	N
Schizanthus	An	Cl	Av	B	Sun	N
Smithiantha	T	Int	Av	H	Sun	W
Solanum						
capsicastrum	Sb	Cl	Av	B	Sun	N
S. jasminoides & S. crispum	Cl	C	Av	B	Sun	N
Sparaxis	Cm	C	Av	B	Sun	Sm
Sparmannia	Sb	Cl	Av	B	Sun	N
Spathiphyllum	Hb	Int	Av	B	Sun	N
Sprekelia	Bl	Cl	Av	B	Sun	W
Stocks	An	Cl	Av	B	Sun	N
Strelitzia	Hb	Int	Av	B	Sun	N
Streptocarpus	Hb	Int	Av	B	Sh	W
Streptosolen	Sb	Int	Av	B	Sun	N
Thunbergia	Cl	Cl	Av	B	Sun	N
Tibouchina	Sb	Cl/Int	Av	B	Sun	N
Tigridia	Bl	C	Av	B	Sun	W
Torenia	An	Cl	Av	B	Sun	N
Trachelium	Hb	C	Av	B	Sun	N
Trachelospermum	Cl	Cl	Av	B	Sun	N
Tritonia	Cm	Cl	Av	B	Sun	W
Tropaeolum						
tricolorum	T/Cl	Cl	Av	B	Sun	S
T. peltophorum	T/Cl	Cl	Av	B	Sun	PW
T. tuberosum	T/Cl	Cl	Av	B	Sun	W
Tulipa	Bl	C/Cl	Av	B	Sun	S
Tweedia	Cl	Cl	Av	B	Sun	N
Vallota	Bl	Cl	Av	B	Sun	PS
Veltheimia	Bl	Cl	Av	B	Sun	S
Verbena	Cl	Cl	Av	B	Sun	N
Vinca	Hb	Int/W	Av	B	Semi	N
Zantedeschia	Hb	Cl	Hm	B	Sun	PS

5 Foliage Plants

It is impossible to draw a firm line between flowering and foliage plants but one can see that certain plants are grown primarily because they have good leaves which are decorative for many months or, if they are evergreen, the whole year round. Many of these kinds also make excellent house plants since they will grow at lower light levels than those required for the majority of plants grown primarily for their flowers. This is the distinction I have tried to make in this chapter but occasionally I have felt obliged to split genera between this and the preceding chapter; e.g. *Begonia rex* varieties appear here but the tuberous, 'Gloire de Lorraine' and *B. semperflorens* varieties, appear in Chapter 4. For this reason the two chapters should really be studied in tandem.

Acalypha (Copper Leaf, Red-hot Cat-tail, Chenille Plant)
The popular names describe rather well two very different species. *A. wilkesiana* is the Copper Leaf, an evergreen shrub with quite large green or coppery-red leaves marked with pink, crimson and bronze. Its

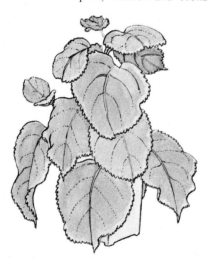

Acalypha wilkesiana oborata

flowers are inconspicuous and it is grown solely as a foliage plant. By contrast the Red-hot Cat-tail or Chenille Plant has trails of small magenta flowers that look very much as if they were made from chenille. It is a shrub with good leaves, bright green and hairy, but it is worth growing for its distinctive flowers as well as for its foliage.

Both plants thrive best in fairly warm greenhouses with minimum temperature of 15 °C and abundant moisture in the air in summer. They like a fairly rich soil- or peat-based mixture, should be watered fairly freely from spring to autumn and moderately in winter, and should be shaded in summer from direct sunshine. Seedlings will root in spring in a warm propagator.

Adiantum (Maidenhair Fern)
These are among the most beautiful of all ferns and several kinds make excellent pot plants. One, *A. pedatum*, is sufficiently hardy to be grown outdoors in many places but most require greenhouse protection in winter. *A. venustum* will grow well in a minimum temperature of 7 °C but *A. cuneatum* (also known as *A. raddianum*) and *A. tenerum* need warmer conditions and will grow most successfully when the temperature never falls below 15 °C. All like a spongy soil rich in

Adiantum venustum

humus largely composed of peat, leaf mould or a mixture of the two with just a little soil and sand and some well-broken charcoal to keep it sweet. Shade from direct sunshine throughout the year, water fairly freely in spring and summer, moderately in autumn, and rather sparingly in winter unless fairly warm conditions can be maintained. Repot when necessary in spring, growing in the smallest pots which will contain the roots completely. Increase by division when repotting.

Aechmea (Urn Plant)
These belong to a group of plants known as bromeliads, many of which are epiphytic, i.e. they do not grow on the ground but perched up on trees or rocks. Aechmeas make rosettes of stiff leaves, green or grey, often banded, striped or spotted. The flowers are small but often surrounded by pink or red bracts and sometimes followed by coloured berries. They grow best in a mixture of peat and sand with some osmunda fibre or shredded bark. The compost should be light and spongy and the plants grown in the smallest pots that will contain their roots. They like a fairly warm

Aechmea rhodocynea

temperature 16–21 °C, but it can occasionally fall to 13 °C in winter without harm. Plants should be watered fairly freely in spring and summer, moderately in autumn and winter. They like a moist atmosphere and good light, but shade from strong sunshine. Increase when plants have finished flowering by removing offsets which form around the flowering stem in spring. Pot them in 20 cm pots and discard the old plants.

Agave (Century Plant, American Aloe)
These plants are related to the aloes, but most do not make such good pot plants as their rosettes of stiff fleshy leaves are too large and often too spiny to be convenient. However, where there is room for them they can be grown in large pots, tubs or beds, in any good but porous soil-based mixture such as John Innes No. 2 plus about one-sixth its bulk of extra sand. All like air and warmth but will survive in winter with little artificial heat as long as they never actually freeze. They should be watered fairly freely in spring and summer, moderately in autumn, and very sparingly in winter, especially if the temperature falls to 7 °C or lower. Offsets can be removed and potted separately in spring.

Aglaonema
Slow-growing plants with leathery, evergreen, usually spear-shaped leaves that are often elaborately variegated with white, cream or grey. They make excellent pot plants and have become very popular as house plants since they will survive in quite poor light. They will grow in any moderately rich soil- or peat-based mixture in almost any structure with a minimum temperature of 15 °C. They enjoy a fairly moist atmosphere and, if in rooms, leaves will benefit from daily sponging and damp sphagnum moss packed around the pots to maintain a moist climate. Water fairly freely in spring and summer, moderately in autumn, sparingly in winter but do not let the soil become quite dry at any time. Plants can be divided when being repotted in spring and their tops can be removed as cuttings in spring or summer and rooted in a warm propagator.

Aloe
Plants with stiff rosettes of fleshy, usually pointed leaves, and spikes of closely packed flowers somewhat resembling those of Red Hot Pokers (Kniphofias). One of the most popular species for cultivation in pots is *A. variegata*, the Partridge-breasted Aloe, so called because the leaves are banded and speckled with white rather like the breast markings of a partridge. All are quite easy plants to grow in a rather gritty mixture, similar to that recommended for agaves to which they are related. All kinds like sun and warmth in summer but most will survive in winter in a minimum temperature of 7 °C though a few degrees more is better. Rooted suckers can be removed in spring when

Above: Araucaria excelsa

Above: Aphelandra squarrosa

Below: Ananas comosus variegatus

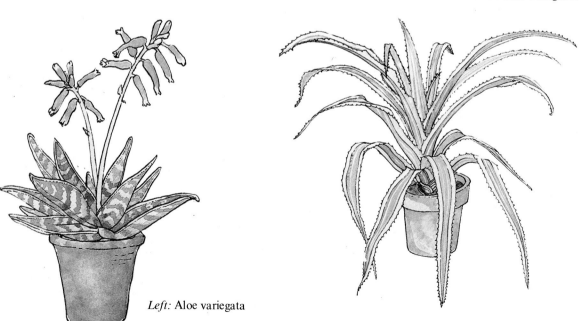

Left: Aloe variegata

repotting and grown on as new plants. Cuttings can be obtained in summer for some kinds and rooted in sandy soil. Seeds, when available, can be germinated at any time in a temperature of 18 °C.

Ananas (Pineapple)

The common pineapple, *A. comosus*, cultivated commercially in warm countries for its fruits, has a beautiful variety in which the stiff spiny leaves, arranged in elegant rosettes, are green, broadly edged with cream, often with some pink suffusion. It makes a handsome pot plant for use indoors or in a greenhouse in which the temperature does not fall below 15 °C. It will survive lower temperatures but the quality of its leaves deteriorates. It will thrive in a rather rich soil-based mixture containing plenty of peat, such as 3 parts peat, 2 parts loam, and 1 part sand with a sprinkling of bone meal or a compound fertilizer. Plants should be watered fairly freely in spring and summer and moderately in autumn and winter, care being taken to apply the water direct to the soil and not splash it over the leaves, which should be kept dry. A moist atmosphere is desirable. Tops of plants can be cut off and rooted in peat and sand in a warm propagator in summer and offsets can be detached and potted separately in spring, but this is not a particularly easy plant to propagate.

Aphelandra (Zebra Plant)

The popular name refers to the distinctive white banding of the large, dark green, shining leaves of *A. squarrosa*. The yellow flowers are also distinctive, closely packed in short spikes and enveloped in overlapping coloured bracts giving them what the Americans appropriately call a 'shingled' appearance. 'Louisae' is a compact variety of this species which makes a particularly good pot plant for warm rooms or greenhouses. Grow these plants in any fairly rich soil- or peat-based potting mixture in the smallest pots that will contain their roots comfortably (usually about 15 cm). Maintain a minimum temperature of 13 °C with average of 15–21 °C. Water fairly freely in spring and summer, moderately in autumn and winter. Plants should be shaded from strong sunshine in summer but require good light to flower and rarely do so in rooms because of the poor light. It is said that if plants are kept cool (5–10 °C) for about seven weeks in the autumn, flowering will occur earlier, in spring rather than in summer, and also that plants that are rather pot bound are most likely to flower well. Cuttings will root in summer in a warm propagator.

Aralia

See Dizygotheca.

Araucaria (Norfolk Island Pine)

Planted out of doors in a frost-free climate the Norfolk Island Pine, *A. excelsa*, will in time grow into a handsome tree twenty metres or more in height. Yet it can make an attractive pot plant and, if restricted for root room, will not exceed a metre for a good many years. Its very regular branching and small evergreen leaves give it the appearance of an exceptionally formal Christmas tree. It can be grown in any good soil- or peat-based potting mixture in any light and frostproof place and is frequently used as a house plant. It should be watered normally, only repotted when absolutely necessary and then put into the smallest pot that will contain its roots. It is usually increased by seed sown as soon as available (the fresher the better) in a temperature of 16–18 °C.

Asparagus

Three kinds of asparagus are commonly grown in greenhouses, all very different in appearance. One, *A. plumosus*, has tiny leaves closely set on flat, horizontally branched stems so that the whole looks like a fern frond. It is popularly called the 'asparagus fern' and its foliage is much used in flower arrangements. It is a climbing plant which can be grown in pots or in a bed of good soil in a greenhouse or conservatory floor, trained up a back wall or pillar.

A second popular ornamental kind is a trailing plant, *A. sprengeri*, with narrow leaves on long stems. It is an ideal plant for hanging baskets or can be allowed to hang over the edge of a staging.

A. meyerii has an upright habit with needle-like leaves arranged like long tapering bottle brushes on stiff stems up to 60 cm long. Grown in large pots or tubs it can be used as decoration for patios and terraces.

All three will grow in any good soil- or peat-based potting mixture in any completely frostproof structure, though for best winter results (the plants are evergreen) a minimum of 10 °C is required. Water fairly freely in spring and summer, moderately in autumn and winter. In summer maintain a moist atmosphere, especially for *A. plumosus* which can suffer badly from red spider if the air becomes very hot and dry. Plants can be divided when being repotted in spring and seed will also germinate in spring in a temperature of 16–18 °C.

Aspidistra

The large, broadly lance-shaped evergreen leaves of the aspidistra will survive conditions that would kill many plants. They will retain their lustrous, deep green colour even in quite ill-lighted rooms, will put up with dry air and even a great deal of neglect, so much so that this has sometimes been called the Cast Iron Plant. Yet to see it at its most handsome it should be grown in a good soil- or peat-based mixture in a not too dark place, but shaded from direct sunshine, and with normal watering throughout the year. A rather moist atmosphere is much better than a dry one and leaves will benefit from frequent sponging with water to remove grime. Plants will also appreciate feeding every ten to fourteen days in late spring and summer

Aspidistra

Asplenium nidus

with liquid fertilizer. They can be increased by division when repotting in spring.

Even better than the plain green-leaved form is the variety 'Variegata', with leaves broadly banded with white, but this has become quite a scarce plant.

Asplenium (Spleenwort)

These are ferns, some of which are hardy and suitable for planting outdoors. The two most popular as pot plants are *A. bulbiferum* and *A. nidus*, which differ greatly in appearance. *A. bulbiferum* has finely divided fronds some of which produce tiny bulbils or plantlets, for which reason it is called the Hen and Chicken Fern. If these fronds are pegged flat on the surface of a moist potting soil containing plenty of peat or leaf mould, the bulbils will form roots and can be cut out and grown on into new plants. *A. nidus* has undivided fronds, light shining green, arranged in a rosette shaped like a shuttlecock. It does not form any plantlets and is increased by spores or by division when repotting.

Both kinds like a spongy potting mixture containing plenty of humus, such as that recommended for Adiantum. They need plenty of water from spring to early autumn, and enough to keep the soil moist in winter. Both need shade from direct sunshine and make good room plants provided the air is not too dry. Both enjoy temperatures of 16–18 °C, but *A. bulbiferum* is nearly hardy and will survive temperatures of 7 °C or even less whereas *A. nidus* is a subtropical species and dislikes temperatures below the recommended range.

Begonia

Some kinds are grown exclusively for their foliage, the most useful of these being *B. masoniana* and the numerous varieties of *B. rex*. The latter have large, heart shaped leaves coloured green with silver, pink, rose, cream, etc. mixed in so many ways that it has been called the Painted Leaf Begonia. There are numerous varieties differing in leaf colour and many of these have been given distinguishing names.

There is only one type of *B. masoniana*, also with heart-shaped leaves, not so large as those of *B. rex* and green with a large black mark in the shape of a cross on each which has suggested the popular name of Iron Cross Begonia.

All can be grown in pots in any good rather spongy peat-based potting mixture, in a temperature of 16–21 °C which can drop to 13 °C in winter with little deterioration of leaf quality. They need plenty of water in spring and summer, and considerably less in autumn and winter though the soil should always be moist. They like shade from direct sunshine at all times and plenty of moisture in the air, especially in summer. They are easily increased by division when repotting in spring, or by mature leaves detached from the plant, slit with a knife through some of the main veins and then pegged to the surface of moist peat in a warm propagator.

Blechnum

These are evergreen ferns some of which are quite hardy but a few are grown as pot plants for cultivation in rooms or moderately heated greenhouses. One of the most popular is *B. gibbum* which carries simply divided fronds on a short, trunk-like stem. All like the same kind of rather spongy potting mixture recommended for adiantum and can be grown with normal watering and shading from direct sunshine in any place where the temperature does not fall below 13 °C. All like a moist atmosphere.

Because of its solitary main stem, *B. gibbum* is not a fern that can be divided and it is increased by spores

Begonia rex

Blechnum gibbum

sown on the surface of moist peat or leaf mould in a fairly warm, humid propagator.

Bryophyllum (Air Plant, Floppers)

Botanists have reclassified these plants as Kalanchoe but *B. pinnatum* is so different from the other plants gardeners think of as Kalanchoe, and the old name is so firmly established in gardens that it seems wise to retain it here. It is a rather gaunt, ungainly succulent with grey stems and leaves. Plantlets form around the edges of the leaves and when they fall off they quickly grow into new plants. It is a curiosity rather than an attractive plant, easily grown in any porous soil- or peat-based mixture in a sunny greenhouse with minimum temperature of 7 °C. Water moderately in spring and summer, sparingly in winter and autumn.

Caladium

These handsome plants belong to the arum family and have large, heart-shaped leaves similar in shape to those of the arum lily but intricately coloured green, pink, cream, rose, and white. They have tuberous roots but these should never be allowed to become completely dry. They are potted in early spring in 15 cm pots in a peat-based potting mixture or a soil mixture containing enough peat to make it rather spongy. Keep the compost just moist at first but water freely when plants start to grow strongly. In autumn gradually reduce the water supply and keep just moist in winter. Grow in spring and summer in a temperature of 18–24 °C and keep the air moist. Shade from direct sunshine but keep in good light as this helps to develop the leaf colour. A minimum of 13 °C is sufficient in winter. Increase is by division when repotting.

Calathea

The evergreen leaves of these South American plants are splashed with colour as if with an artist's brush.

Caladium

One of the most popular, *C. makoyana*, known as the Peacock Plant, has purple splashes on a background of different shades of green. In *C. rosea picta* the colours are green, pink and red with purple on the underside. There are many more colour combinations.

All can be grown in any light structure in which the temperature never falls below 13 °C. They make fairly good room plants but dislike dry air so are better in bottle gardens or plant cabinets, in which the air can be kept moist, than in the atmosphere of the room itself.

Grow in a peat-based potting mixture or a soil mixture containing a lot of peat to make it rather spongy. Water freely in summer, moderately the rest of the year. Shade from direct sunshine. Increase by division in spring, when repotting.

Chlorophytum (Spider Plant, Hen and Chickens)

The kinds cultivated are variegated varieties of a South African herbaceous perennial, *C. comosum*. It makes tussocks of rather thick-textured, grassy, light green leaves and has the following peculiarity: it puts out long runners bearing little plants which have suggested the popular names as indicated above. One variety has leaves margined with white, another has a broad band of white up the middle of each leaf. All are nearly hardy, can be grown in any frostproof and fairly light structure, and are popular and easy house plants. They will grow in any good soil- or peat-based potting mixture in pots just large enough to contain the roots. Water normally and increase by division in spring or by pegging the plantlets into small, soil-filled pots until they have filled them with roots.

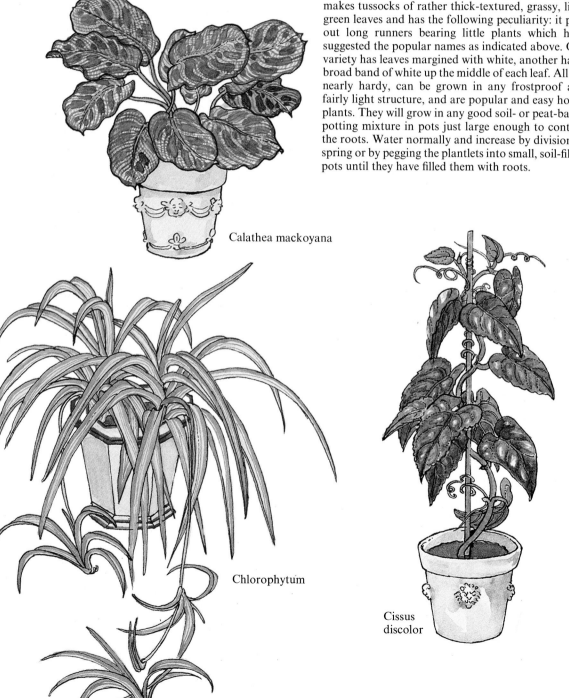

Calathea mackoyana

Chlorophytum

Cissus
discolor

Cissus

Tender vines cultivated for their foliage, which in some varieties is elaborately coloured. *C. discolor* has deep green leaves marbled with pink, purple and white and is one of the most beautiful but is considerably more tender than *C. antarctica*, the Kangaroo Vine, with plain green leaves. *C. sicyoides* has red leaf stalks and the young leaves of *C. striata* are pink.

All make good pot plants and *C. antarctica* can be grown in rooms as it does not mind relatively poor light. All can be grown in a good peat- or soil-based potting mixture. They should be watered normally and be shaded from direct sunshine. All need wires, canes, trellis or something of the kind to cling to. *C. discolor* likes a fairly warm, moist atmosphere and the temperature should not fall below 20 °C. The others are tougher and will stand temperatures as low as 7 °C. All can be increased by summer cuttings in a warm propagator.

Cocos (Coconut Palm)

The true coconut palm, *C. nucifera*, is far too large a tree to be useful in any but the biggest greenhouses and conservatories, but there is a much smaller, slower growing relative which gardeners have always called *C. weddeliana* (botanists now know it as *Syagrus weddeliana*) which can be grown in quite small pots in warm, humid greenhouses or plant cabinets. It has

Codiaeum

elegant, feather-shaped leaves, and if its roots are restricted in quite small pots it can be kept to a height of 30 cm or less for a long time. Grow it in a soil- or peat-based potting mixture kept nicely moist at all times, and shade it from direct sunshine. Increase is by seed sown in spring in a temperature of 21–26 °C.

Codiaeum (Croton)

Few evergreen shrubs can rival the crotons for brilliance and variety of foliage colour. Their leaves are large and leathery, variously shaped and shining. They can be mottled and veined with colour in all manner of ways, with greens, yellows, oranges, coppery and bronzy reds and crimson intermingling in rich and exciting combinations. They are not difficult to grow but they are tropical plants and so they do like a fair amount of warmth, around 16–21 °C most of the time, though in winter it will not matter if the temperature drops occasionally to 13 °C. Good light helps to develop the leaf colour but hot sunshine may scorch the leaves so some shading is required in summer. Water should be supplied fairly freely from spring to autumn, moderately in winter. Good plants can be grown in either soil- or peat-based potting mixtures but in the latter extra feeding will be necessary in summer. The tips of shoots can be removed occasionally to encourage branching. Increase is by cuttings in a warm propagator in summer.

Coleus

Two very different types of Coleus are grown in greenhouses. The better known is *C. blumei*, a bushy evergreen plant with nettle-shaped leaves elaborately coloured with bands or mottlings of pink, red, crimson, purple, yellow and copper or various shades of green. It is a plant that grows so quickly and readily from seed sown in spring in a temperature of about 18 °C that it is often treated as an annual and discarded in autumn when it begins to need artificial heat. Some of the colour varieties can actually be made to breed true from seed but usually seed gives mixed leaf colours, selected varieties being increased by leaf cuttings which root readily in summer in a propagator. Plants will grow well in a good soil- or peat-based mixture but may need extra feeding in summer and should be well watered from spring to autumn. In winter they can be a little difficult, inclined to rot as a result of grey mould unless very carefully watered and kept in a temperature of 13–18 °C.

Two other species, *C. frederici* and *C. thyrsoideus*, are grown mainly for their slender spikes of blue, sage-like flowers. They, too, are raised from seed and grown in the same way as *C. blumei* except that they must be kept throughout at least one winter, since that is when they flower. (*See* illustration overleaf.)

Cordyline

Many people call these plants palms but in fact they are quite unrelated to the true palms and their close

Coleus blumei

affinity is with the dracaenas (*see* page 100). They are handsome in habit, with sword-shaped leaves arranged in large rosettes, the leaves broader and more reflexing in *C. terminalis* than in *C. australis*. There are varieties with purple or variegated leaves. All are sufficiently hardy to be grown with just sufficient artificial heat to exclude frost. Otherwise cultivation is the same as for dracaena. Offsets can sometimes be detached with roots and potted separately but increase is mainly by cuttings of the roots or pieces of main stem in a warm propagator in summer.

Cotyledon

These are succulents closely allied to crassulas (*see* page 54) and much confused with them. There are a great number of species and they differ widely in character but all have fleshy leaves and some have quite attractive flowers, small, tubular, urn-shaped, carried in sprays or clusters. One of the most popular as a pot plant is *C. orbiculata*, with almost globular grey leaves and pendulous red flowers.

All kinds should be grown in a rather gritty soil-based mixture in a sunny greenhouse with minimum temperature of 7 °C. They should be watered moderately in spring and summer, sparingly in winter and can be increased by cuttings in sand in spring or summer. If seeds are available they can be germinated in spring in a gritty seed compost in a temperature of 18 °C.

Cryophytum (Ice Plant)

There is only one species, *C. crystallinum*, still known in some gardens by its old name of *Mesembryanthemum crystallinum*. It is a sprawling plant with little succulent leaves with glassy spots which have suggested the popular name Ice Plant. It is an annual to be renewed every year from seed sown in spring in a temperature of 18 °C. Seedlings are potted singly in 9 cm pots in a rather gritty, soil-based mixture and are grown in a sunny greenhouse; or they can be stood outdoors in summer in a warm sunny place. They should be watered moderately and discarded in the autumn.

Cycas (Sago Palm)

These are very primitive plants with shuttlecock rosettes of large, dark green, feather-shaped leaves. Most require a lot of room since the leaves can be several feet long. They are really best planted in a bed of good soil with plenty of peat or leaf mould but they can be grown for a while in large pots, tubs or other containers and are not difficult to manage provided a fairly warm temperature can be maintained. It should not fall below 13 °C and should be around 18–21 °C most of the time. Water freely in spring and summer, moderately in autumn and winter. Shade in summer and keep the air as moist as possible. Increase by seed sown in a warm propagator, temperature 26–30 °C in spring or by suckers detached in spring with roots and potted individually.

Cyperus (Umbrella Grass, Papyrus)

The first popular name refers to the narrow leaves held out around the flower clusters, supposedly like the ribs

Cordyline terminalis

Cycas revoluta

of an umbrella though really they more closely resemble the spokes of a wheel. The flowers themselves are unspectacular and are usually greenish or brownish but their accompanying rosettes of leaves are decidedly decorative and the tussocks of rush-like stems from the base of the plant are also attractive. The largest of the genus is *C. papyrus*, the source of the early Egyptian paper, which in favourable conditions can reach 3 m. It really likes to grow in tubs in shallow water but it can be grown by one or another of the hydroponic systems such as hydroculture (*see* page 16). Other species, such as *C. alternifolius*, about 45 cm high, and its white variegated variety, also *C. vegetus*, 90 cm, will grow in pots in any good soil- or peat-based potting mixture provided they are watered freely. *C. vegetus* is hardy and can be grown in any structure or out of doors. *C. alternifolius* needs a minimum temperature of 7 °C but for *C. papyrus* 13 °C is better, though it will survive lower temperatures. All can be increased by division in spring when repotting, and also by seed in spring, in warmth for the tender kinds.

Cyrtomium (Holly Fern)

C. falcatum is one of the easiest ferns to grow, more amenable to dry air than most and nearly hardy. The leaves are composed of several quite large segments each shaped a little like a holly leaf, though not prickly. Good specimens can be grown in 10–13 cm

Cyperus alternifolius

pots in either a peat potting compost or a soil-based one containing an extra quantity of peat and/or leaf mould. Water normally, shade from direct sunshine and keep in a minimum temperature of 7 °C.

Davallia (Hare's Foot Fern, Squirrel's Foot Fern)
Small ferns with much-divided fronds, growing from creeping, often underground stems (or rhizomes), which in some species are densely covered with hairs, suggesting some of the popular names. In the wild they grow epiphytically on tree trunks and so they make excellent plants for hanging baskets filled with peat or chopped sphagnum moss and kept constantly moist, though less so in winter than in summer. They should be shaded from all direct sunshine and kept in a fairly moist, rather warm temperature. It is inadvisable that the temperature should drop below 13 °C and 16 °C is better. All can be increased by division in spring.

Dicksonia (Australian Tree Fern, New Zealand Tree Fern)
All tree ferns are very large plants quite unsuitable for small greenhouses but magnificent where there is space for them to spread their two-metre, finely divided fronds. In time they make trunks with the fronds radiating on top. They are not difficult to grow in a spongy soil with plenty of peat and/or leaf mould, shade from direct sunshine, plenty of moisture from spring to autumn both in the soil and in the air, and complete freedom from frost. Where there is room, the easiest way to grow them is in a bed on the floor of the greenhouse or conservatory, but they can also be grown in tubs or other large containers. They are increased by spores sown as soon as they are ripe on the surface of moist soil or peat in a temperature of 16 °C.

Dieffenbachia (Dumb Cane)
One of the most popular house plants is *D. picta* which has stout, cane-like stems bearing large undivided leaves which are green, heavily variegated with white, cream, or yellow. There are numerous variations in the colour markings, all handsome, and this Brazilian evergreen is not at all difficult to grow provided a minimum temperature of 15 °C can be maintained. It will grow in any good soil- or peat-based potting mixture and does excellently in hydroculture. It should be shaded from direct sunshine and be watered fairly freely from spring to autumn, moderately in winter. Increase is usually by cuttings in spring or summer made from the thick main stem cut into short lengths and inserted in peat or leaf mould in a warm propagator.

Dizygotheca (False Aralia)
Most gardeners still call this rather strange-looking plant by its old name, *Aralia elegantissima*, but botanists now call it *Dizygotheca elegantissima*. It is a tender evergreen shrub from the Pacific, rather sparsely branched with leaves each composed of several narrow, saw-edged, reddish-bronze leaflets arranged like the ribs of a fan. It is grown both as a house plant and in greenhouses and conservatories with minimum temperature of 18 °C, but requires rather careful watering and management. It is best grown in a normal soil-based potting mixture in good light but with shade in summer from strong direct sunshine. The soil needs to be moist at all times, never dry and never waterlogged since either condition can cause the leaves to fall. It can be increased by seed sown in spring in a temperature of 18 °C or by air-layering in spring or summer.

Dracaena (Dragon Plant, Dragon Lily)
Popular as house plants, the dracaenas are quite variable in appearance. Some have leaves arranged in large rosettes like those of the cordylines, to which they are closely related and with which they are much confused; others are branched so that one kind, *D. godseffiana*, which has yellow mottled leaves, looks rather like a compact, variegated aucuba. All like fairly warm conditions with temperatures certainly no lower than 13 °C and preferably 16 °C for the most tropical species such as *D. deremensis*, *D. fragrans* and their numerous varieties. Among the most handsome are *D. deremensis* 'Warneckii', with strap-shaped, green leaves striped with cream and white; *D. fragrans* 'Massangeana' with broader leaves striped with yellow down the centre, *D. fragrans* 'Victoriae' in which the leaf is pale yellow with a central band of green, and *D. sanderiana* with greyish-green leaves margined with white.

All can be grown in any good soil- or peat-based mixture with normal watering and shade from direct sunshine. Good light will help to intensify the leaf colours and a moist atmosphere will also improve the quality of the leaves. All can be increased by cuttings in summer in a warm propagator.

Echeveria
Succulents with leaves usually in very formal rosettes so that they somewhat resemble houseleeks (*sempervivum*). One species, *E. secunda*, is popular as a summer bedding plant for edgings or groundwork. The orange-red flowers are carried in clusters on 15 cm stems and are quite attractive. *E. elegans*, sometimes called the Mexican Snowball, has small, tightly packed, slaty-blue rosettes with shining white margins and pink flowers. There are many more species.

All will thrive in pots in any good soil-based potting mixture with a little additional sand or grit, in a sunny greenhouse with minimum temperature of 7 °C, no shading at any time, normal watering from spring to autumn but only enough in winter to prevent the soil from becoming quite dry. They are easily increased by detaching offsets when repotting in spring.

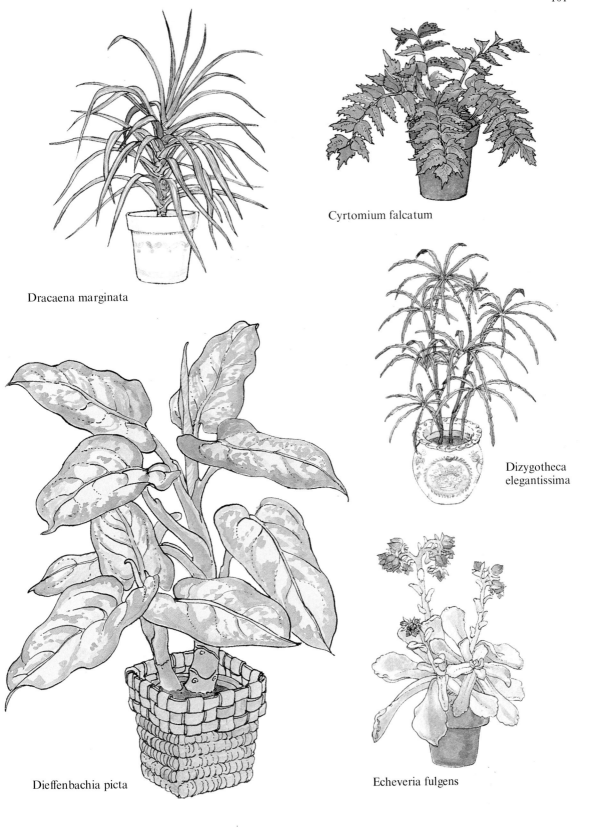

Dracaena marginata

Cyrtomium falcatum

Dizygotheca
elegantissima

Dieffenbachia picta

Echeveria fulgens

Eletaria

The kind cultivated, usually as a house plant though it can equally well be grown in a greenhouse or conservatory with shade from direct sunshine, is *E. cardamomum*. It is a soft-stemmed evergreen with lance-shaped leaves which may be shining green or nearly white splashed with green. It is an excellent house plant, easily grown in any good soil- or peat-based potting mixture and a minimum temperature of 13 °C. Water freely in spring and summer, moderately in autumn and sparingly in winter. Increase by division when repotting in spring.

Eucalyptus (Blue Gum)

All species of eucalyptus are large evergreen trees native to either Australia or Tasmania. When grown in greenhouses or conservatories, they are hard pruned in February or early March to keep them within manageable size, at any rate for a few years, and to maintain the juvenile foliage which is quite different in shape, and often more beautiful in colour, than the adult foliage. There are many different kinds, one of the most popular being *E. globulus*, with round, grey-blue leaves. Another delightful kind, more elegant in growth and similar in colour, is *E. cinerea*. All will grow in large pots or tubs in any good soil-based potting mixture. They dislike root breakage, should be raised from seed sown in a temperature of 16–18 °C in spring, the seedlings potted individually as soon as they can be handled and subsequently moved on to larger pots as necessary. Water normally from spring to autumn, sparingly in winter when the temperature should not fall below 4 °C. Keep in the sunniest place possible. Plants can stand outside in summer and make fine ornamental specimens for patios and courtyards.

Fatshedera

This is a hybrid between *Fatsia japonica* (see below) and *Hedera helix* 'Hibernica', the Irish ivy. It is intermediate in character between the two, with large, glossy, evergreen, deeply lobed leaves and long, lax stems that can be allowed to spread about or can be tied to supports; a handsome foliage plant to cover a low screen or train around a pillar. It is hardy, needs no artificial heat at any time and is easily grown in any good soil- or peat-based potting mixture in large pots, tubs or a bed on the floor of the greenhouse or conservatory. It should be watered freely in spring and summer, moderately in autumn and winter, prefers to be shaded from strong sunshine and can be pruned in spring as necessary to keep it in shape. Increase is by cuttings in summer in a frame or propagator or by layering at any time.

Fatsia (False Castor Oil Plant, Japanese Aralia, Hercules Club)

F. japonica is a hardy evergreen shrub with large, deeply lobed leaves, rather like those of a fig tree, and

Fatsia japonica

ball-shaped clusters of milky white flowers produced on stiffly branched stems in the autumn. It makes a good pot or tub plant where there is room for it and it will put up with quite a lot of shade. It will grow in any good soil- or peat-based potting mixture, should be well watered from spring to autumn and kept just nicely moist in winter. No artificial heat is required. Plants can be pruned in April to reduce their size and improve their shape. Cuttings root readily in summer in a frame or propagator.

Ficus (Fig, India Rubber Plant, Creeping Fig, Banjo Fig, Fiddle-leaved Fig)

As the popular names indicate, a number of species of Ficus are cultivated as ornamental plants. The fig itself, *F. carica*, is often trained against the back wall of a conservatory. It is a handsome evergreen shrub or small tree with large, deeply indented shining green leaves and it is very easy to grow either in a tub or planted in a border of reasonably good but not too rich soil. But it does need a lot of room and is not suitable for small greenhouses. It is virtually hardy and can be grown without heat though it is all the better (and more likely to fruit) if the temperature never

Ficus elastica

Fittonia verschaffeltii

Grevillea robusta *(see overleaf)*

drops below freezing. (For further details of fig cultivation see page 141.)

Far better as a pot plant and the most popular of the genus for the purpose is *F. elastica*, the India Rubber Plant. This, too, will grow into a large shrub or tree in time but can be kept in a pot for years and has the

merit of surviving in quite deep shade, though it will be happier and more handsome in good light. It makes an excellent house plant especially in one of its good varieties such as *decora*, which is shorter jointed and more compact; and *doescheri*, in which the leaves are variegated with white, grey and cream with the midrib and leaf stalk pink.

These plants are happiest in a minimum temperature of 15 °C. They should be watered fairly freely from spring to autumn, moderately in winter and it helps to sponge or spray their leathery leaves with water fairly frequently in summer. Increase is by cuttings in a warm propagator.

F. benjamina requires identical treatment but is a much bigger plant with smaller leaves; excellent where there is need for something 3 m high or over, but not suitable for small greenhouses. This also applies to *F. lyrata*, called the Fiddle-leaved or Banjo Fig because of the curious shape of its large leaves.

Totally different is the Creeping Fig, *F. radicans*, a small-leaved, self-clinging plant that will slowly ascend a wall like ivy. It is nearly hardy and easily grown in any frostproof house or conservatory. It should be watered normally and is best planted in a bed of good soil. It can be increased by summer cuttings or by layering at any time.

Fittonia (Snakeskin Plant, Mosaic Plant)

The popular names give some idea of the intricate and beautiful leaf markings of these creeping tropical plants. *F. argyroneura* has green leaves densely veined with silver; *F. verschaffeltii* has deeper olive-green leaves veined with pink or red. All need warmth and shade from direct sunshine but otherwise are not too difficult to grow in a rather humid greenhouse with minimum temperature of 15 °C, or in a plant cabinet indoors. Grow in any good soil- or peat-based potting mixture which should be kept evenly moist throughout the year. Increase by division when repotting in spring.

Grevillea (Silk Oak, Bark Oak)

The kind grown in greenhouses for its finely divided foliage is *G. robusta* which in the wild makes a large flowering tree. In greenhouses it is restricted in pots and discarded when it gets too big. It is an easy plant to grow from seed sown in spring in a temperature of 18 °C. Seedlings are potted singly in 8 cm pots in any good soil- or peat-based potting mixture, and are grown on in a light greenhouse which need only be warmed in winter, when a minimum temperature of 7 °C is adequate though a little more is to be preferred. Water fairly freely in spring and summer, moderately in autumn, and sparingly in winter, especially if it is cold.

Gynura

There are several species of these tender herbaceous plants, the most popular being *G. sarmentosa*. This has been called the Purple Passion Vine because its stems and deeply serrated leaves are covered with purple hairs which eventually fall from the top of the leaf though the underside remains coloured. However, it is not a vine in the sense of being able to climb, but a

sprawling or hanging plant suitable for light rooms or for greenhouses with a minimum temperature of 15 °C. It will grow in any good soil- or peat-based potting mixture, watered moderately from spring to autumn, rather sparingly in winter though the soil must never became quite dry. Cuttings will root in a warm propagator in spring or summer.

Hedera (Ivy)

All kinds of ivy can be grown in greenhouses and rooms though it is usually the more tender kinds, particularly the variegated forms of *H. canariensis*, that are most favoured. However, there are many varieties of the common ivy, *H. helix*, with small or unusually shaped leaves and some of quite compact habit, that make excellent house plants capable of putting up with a lot of shade and not too seriously affected by dry air.

All ivies will grow in any good soil- or peat-based potting mixture which should be kept just nicely moist at all times. Even the most tender varieties do not really require any warmth though they may be damaged by severe or prolonged frost. All can be shortened or cut back whenever they begin to grow too far. They are self-clinging plants which like to have something to ascend, be it a wall or a column of sphagnum moss or bark held in place with wire netting bound to any suitable support. The more bushy kinds can be grown in hanging baskets or in pots placed in raised display boxes so that they can hang over the edge. All are readily increased by cuttings or layering at almost any time.

Howeia (Sentry Palm, Curly Palm, Flat Palm, Paradise Palm)

Two species, *H. belmoreana* and *H. fosteriana*, are the most popular palms for growing in pots and using as decorations at functions but gardeners nearly always call them by a former name *Kentia*. They have broadly feather-shaped leaves and in large pots or small tubs can be kept to a height of around 2 m, though, if given free root space, they will grow far larger. Grow in any good soil-based potting mixture in a minimum temperature of 10 °C with shade from direct sunshine in summer. Water fairly freely from spring to autumn and moderately in winter but avoid all extremes of wetness or dryness, also draughts and excessively dry air which can spoil the appearance of the leaves. Increase by seed sown in spring in a temperature of 24–26 °C.

Hypoestes (Polka Dot Plant)

The popular name of *H. sanguinolenta* refers to the pink spots all over the green leaves. This is a herbaceous perennial easily raised from seed sown in spring in a temperature of 16–18 °C. The seedlings

Hedera Lelix varieties

Opposite: A superb display of Howeia belmoreana *(in foreground) among other showy plants.*

should be potted singly in 8 cm pots in any good soil- or peat-based potting mixture and can be moved on to 10 or 13 cm pots when necessary. Keep the soil nicely moist throughout and grow in a minimum temperature of 10 °C. The colouring will be best in good light but strong sunshine may scorch the leaves.

Kleinia (Candle Plant)

The plant that gardeners call *K. articulata* has been long transferred by botanists to the already overloaded genus *Senecio* but the Candle Plant is so distinctive that there seems good reason to keep it separate for horticultural purposes. It is an oddity, a succulent plant with erect, candle-shaped, grey-blue stems with a little plume of divided leaves on top, which all fall off if the plant is dry, without any harm to it. Like many succulents it will succeed in a gritty compost, something like John Innes Potting Compost plus a generous extra ration of sand and/or grit. It also likes warm sunny places and the temperature should certainly never fall below 10 °C. It should be watered moderately in spring and summer, sparingly in autumn and winter and kept in a fairly dry atmosphere at all times. Cuttings of the stems will root readily in sand.

Leucadendron (Silver Tree)

The kind cultivated is *L. argenteum*, a South African tree belonging to the Protea family with silvery leaves clustered closely around the stems. It needs a mixture of lime-free loam, sand, and peat in the proportion of 1 to 2 to 3, and must be grown in a sunny place with minimum temperature of 10 °C. It should also be watered carefully, the soil kept just nicely moist at all times but never waterlogged or completely dry. Increase by seeds sown as soon as ripe in a temperature of 16 °C.

Lippia (Lemon-scented Verbena)

The kind cultivated, *L. citriodora*, is a deciduous shrub with strongly lemon-scented leaves. The flowers are small, and pale pinkish-mauve, the leaves narrow and not particularly decorative so it is solely as an aromatic plant that it is cultivated. It is hardy enough to survive a few degrees of frost, can be grown successfully in a sunny but unheated greenhouse and is not fussy about soil. It is quite a large plant, up to 3 m high, and is best planted in a bed of soil but can be grown in a tub or large pot. It should be watered moderately from spring to autumn but very sparingly in winter when it is leafless. In March it can be thinned or cut back as necessary to keep it in shape and of manageable size. Quite often it is trained against the back wall of a conservatory. Cuttings root readily in a propagator or frame in summer or autumn.

Lygodium (Climbing Fern)

Genuine ferns that climb are a rarity, and *L. japonicum*, which does just that, is also very attractive

Maranta lenconeura

and not difficult to grow in a greenhouse or conservatory with minimum temperature of 10 °C. It likes soil with plenty of leaf mould and/or peat and is easiest to manage if planted in a bed on the floor of the house but can be grown in large pots or small tubs and needs something for its thin frond stems to twine around. It is a good plant to grow against the back wall of a conservatory with wires or trellis for support. It should be watered moderately with the soil constantly moist but never waterlogged or dry and the air in summer should be moist. Stems can be shortened in spring if desired. Increase is by careful division in spring or by spores sown as soon as ripe on the surface of moist peat or leaf mould in a temperature of 16–18 °C.

Maranta

These handsome foliage plants are much confused with calatheas to which they are related and with which they share similar cultural requirements. They are herbaceous perennials, usually with oval leaves, regularly patterned with dark blotches and silvery or pink veins on a deep velvet-green or yellowish-green ground colour, often with the whole undersurface of the leaf purplish red. Most kinds sprawl along the ground and can be grown in pots or planted in beds of either peat mixture or a soil mixture containing a lot of peat and/or leaf mould. They like to be warm and moist, minimum temperature 15 °C, with water applied moderately nearly all the year, though rather sparingly for a few weeks in winter when they are not growing. They should be shaded from all direct sunshine. Increase by division when planting or repotting in spring.

Monstera deliciosa

Musa ensete

Mimosa (Sensitive Plant, Humble Plant)

The tree with little fluffy, yellow, pompom flowers which everyone calls 'mimosa' is really an acacia, and the two true mimosas grown in greenhouses are valued solely as foliage plants, their delicately formed leaves having the curious habit of folding lengthwise if touched. There are two species which are much alike, *M. pudica* and *M. sensitiva*, the latter taller and more woody, the former not above 45 cm high and usually grown as an annual from seed sown in a temperature of 16–18 °C in spring. Pot the seedlings singly in 8 cm pots in any good soil- or peat-based potting mixture and move on to larger-sized pots if necessary. Grow in a sunny greenhouse or window, watering moderately. These are plants that love warmth. *M. sensitiva* may be kept for a year or more if desired, overwintered in a minimum temperature of 13 °C and moved on to larger pots as necessary.

Monstera

Few foliage plants can convey so exotic a background to a room as *M. deliciosa*, an evergreen climbing plant with large, heart-shaped leaves, dark and shining green, with strange perforations which gradually increase in size until the leaf splits into a number of irregular segments.

The fleshy stems ascend tree trunks by aerial roots like an ivy and, as they grow, thick white roots hang from their stems in search of moisture from the air.

Despite its tropical appearance this monstera can be grown in a minimum temperature of 13 °C in any good soil- or peat-based potting mixture, with normal watering. It needs shade from strong sunshine but does best in good light. It is an excellent house plant provided the air is not too dry and it is regularly watered. Feeding in summer with a light fertilizer will improve the size and quality of the leaves and so will frequent sponging or syringing with water. Increase by cuttings in a warm propagator in summer or by air layering at any time.

Musa (Banana)

Though all bananas have handsome leaves, most are too large to be satisfactory greenhouse plants. However, *M. cavendishii* (also called *M. nana*), is smaller than most, from 1 to 2 m high when grown in pots. It has the typical banana leaves, at first rolled up but unfolding into a broad paddle shape and a fine lustrous green. Like other bananas it likes good light, good soil and plenty of water in spring and summer while it is growing. It is hardier than some, though not as hardy as *M. basjoo*, a larger plant, and will thrive in a minimum temperature of 15 °C rising to 18–21 °C in summer. All kinds can be increased by detaching offshoots with a few roots when repotting in spring.

Neanthe (Parlour Palm)

Botanists disagree as to the exact name of this little palm, some saying that it should be called *Collinia elegans*, some favouring *Chamaerops elegans*. To gardeners it is likely to remain *Neanthe bella*, a favourite plant for bottle gardens, Wardian cases and plant cabinets. It has feather-shaped leaves and is a perfect little palm in miniature, usually no more than 30 cm high and taking years to reach even that. It should be grown in a not too rich soil- or peat-based potting mixture, kept nicely moist throughout the year, and in a temperature which should not drop below 10 °C and is better in the 16–18 °C range. It should be shaded from direct sunshine and prefers a fairly moist atmosphere. Increase is by seed sown in a warm propagator in spring.

Neoregelia

These are among the most handsome of the bromeliads, with rosettes of stiff, variously coloured leaves forming a central cup which likes to be kept full of water and in which the flowers form. The leaves of some kinds are banded with grey, or are light bronze or green striped with ivory-white, and usually they become red around the central cup. All are epiphytic in nature, living perched up in trees out of direct contact with the soil. They make good house plants so long as the position is light but not in direct sunshine. They should be grown in a peat mixture with some sand and

Neanthe bella

fibre, such as osmunda or shredded bark, and be watered moderately all the year. They enjoy a fairly warm temperature, certainly not less than 13 °C at any time, preferably between 16 and 21 °C. Increase is by offsets detached when repotting in spring, but since these plants do not take much from the soil they do not require annual repotting.

Nepenthes (Pitcher Plant)

These are among nature's oddities, tropical plants which have learned to supplement their diet by trapping and digesting small insects in pitchers developed from the elongated midribs of the leaves. These pitchers are variously shaped, some short and broad, others long and narrow, often attractively, though not spectacularly, coloured green or yellowish mottled with red or brown. Nepenthes are not the easiest of plants to grow since they require plenty of warmth and atmospheric moisture, and a specially spongy potting mixture of peat and live chopped-up sphagnum moss – about two parts by bulk of the first to one of the second – perhaps with some added fern fibre or shredded bark to make it retain its open texture longer. The temperature should not fall below 16 °C and may be considerably higher most of the time, and the more saturated with moisture the air is the better. What one is trying to do is emulate the climate of a tropical jungle. Cuttings of firm growth will root in a very warm, humid propagator, but not easily.

Nephrolepis (Ladder Fern, Sword Fern)

These are evergreen ferns with feather-shaped fronds, but the leaflets (pinnae) of the fronds are often attached to the midrib almost at right angles, giving the whole frond a ladder-like appearance. By no

Neoregelia carolinae tricolor

means all are as simply divided as this, some being cut again into smaller segments which may be so numerous and so ruffled that the whole plant has a moss-like appearance. *N. exaltata* is the species that has produced the most numerous varieties and some of these are cultivated commercially in large numbers. All are easy to grow in a peat- or leaf mould-based potting mixture in pots or hanging baskets in greenhouses, conservatories, and rooms in which a minimum temperature of 13 °C can be maintained. Plants should be watered moderately throughout the year and be shaded from strong sunshine at all times. Though they like a fairly moist atmosphere, they will put up with the dryness of living rooms better than most ferns. Increase is by division of the thin, wire-like underground rhizomes, when repotting in spring.

Nidularium

This is another of the popular genera of bromeliads closely allied to and much like neoregelias and requiring identical treatment. The central leaves around the cup are often red and the outer leaves of *N. innocenti* 'Striatum' have long, pale yellow stripes.

Pandanus (Screw Pine)

Here the popular name is misleading as these plants are neither like nor in any way related to pines nor to the pineapple to which the name really refers. They look like dracaenas with plumes of broadly strap-shaped leaves around a central stem. The leaves of the most popular kind, *P. veitchii*, have broad margins of creamy white.

This is an excellent house plant as well as being suitable for cultivation in pots in a greenhouse or conservatory with minimum temperature of 13 °C and an average of 18–21 °C. It likes good light but needs

protection from hot sunshine, can be grown in any good soil- or peat-based potting mixture, and should be watered fairly freely from spring to autumn but rather sparingly in winter, though the soil should never be allowed to become dry. Offsets from the base can be detached and potted separately when plants are repotted in spring.

Pelargonium (Scented-leaved Geranium)

The pelargoniums that are grown mainly for their foliage do not differ in their cultural requirements from those grown for their flowers (*see* pp. 75–6). They are tender, sun-loving plants and must be protected from all frost but they are easy to grow in any good soil- or peat-based potting mixture and most make excellent room plants provided they can be kept near a sunny window. They need to be watered moderately from spring to autumn, rather sparingly in winter, particularly if little warmth is available, but in a

Nephrolepsis exaltata

Nepenthes

Pandanus vandermeeschii

Pelargonium radens

Philodendron bipinnatifidum

Peperomia caperata

temperature of 13 °C or more they will keep growing even in winter and will need more water. Warmth also helps to ward off grey mould disease which can do a good deal of damage to the plants if the air is cold and damp. Even in summer pelargoniums are plants that prefer rather dry air and they can be stood or planted outdoors in a sunny place from June to September.

All kinds can be readily increased by cuttings in spring or summer in sandy soil in a frame or a pot placed inside a polythene bag. All can also be pruned to shape in March or September and some of the smaller leaved kinds, such as *P. crispum*, can be made into formal shapes, like little topiary specimens, by pinching out the tips of shoots during spring and summer. This kind is lemon scented and it has a cream variegated variety. *P. graveolens* is also lemon scented and has deeply indented leaves, rather like those of an oak tree. *P. quercifolium* is actually called the Oak Leaf Geranium and *P. denticulatum*, which is balsam scented, has even narrower leaf divisions. *P. tomentosum* has large, softly downy leaves that smell strongly of peppermint, and *P. odoratissimum* smells of apples. There are many more kinds.

Peperomia

These are soft-stemmed evergreen plants mostly small enough to be grown in 8–10 cm pots or to be planted in bottle gardens or terrariums. The species differ so much in leaf that it is not easy to recognize their relationship until they produce their curious, tail-like spikes of tiny flowers, rather like the spadix of an arum lily or an anthurium. Among the most popular are *P.*

argyreia (also known as *P. sandersii*), with heart shaped silvery leaves striped with green veins; *P. caperata*, with distinctively pleated, dark green leaves; and *P. obtusifolia*, which has a good variegated variety with pale green, cream-edged leaves a little like those of a privet but much fleshier. All make excellent house plants for warm rooms or can be grown in greenhouses in a minimum temperature of 13 °C in any good soil- or peat-based potting mixture. Water rather moderately at all times, especially in winter, shade from direct sunshine, but grow in a fairly light place. Increase by cuttings in a warm propagator or some kinds by careful division when repotting in spring.

Philodendron

This is a very big family of evergreen tropical plants, some bushy, some climbing and several popular as house plants because of the jungle-like atmosphere they can create. *P. scandens*, with laurel-green, broadly arrow shaped leaves, is one of the most popular. *P. hastatum* also has arrow-shaped leaves but of a lighter green. Both are climbers. All philodendrons like warmth and atmospheric moisture, a minimum temperature of 13 °C, preferably more, and a good peat- or soil-based potting mixture which should be kept nicely moist throughout the year. They need shade from direct sunshine and the climbing kinds like to wind around pillars or columns that are wrapped in damp moss. Increase is by summer cuttings in a warm propagator or by air layering.

Phoenix (Date Palm)

The huge, feather-shaped leaves of the date palms are exceedingly handsome and conjure up visions of sun-drenched beaches but most are too large to be attractive greenhouse plants. There is one exception, *P. roebelenii*, a relatively small species from southeastern Asia which makes an excellent pot or tub plant. Grow it in any good soil- or peat-based potting mixture in a warm room or greenhouse, shaded from strong sunshine but otherwise light, with enough water to keep the soil moist throughout the year and a minimum temperature of 13 °C, preferably a little more. Increase is by seed sown in spring in a temperature of 18–21 C.

Pilea (Artillery Plant, Aluminium Plant)

Small herbaceous plants differing greatly from one another in appearance. Several are popular and easily grown house plants and also make attractive pot plants for a greenhouse or conservatory. *P. microphylla*, also known as *P. muscosa*, has very small but rather fleshy leaves and its clusters of little yellowish-green flowers, composed mainly of stamens, emit puffs of pollen when disturbed, hence the popular name Artillery Plant. Another popular kind, *P. cadierei*, has shining, oval leaves that seem to be painted with splashes of aluminium. Both kinds prefer warm conditions but will survive in a minimum of 7 °C. They

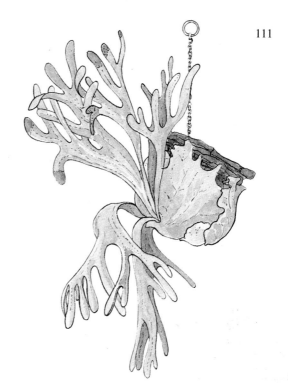

Platycerium alcicorne

can be grown in quite small pots in any good soil- or peat-based potting mixture which should be kept nicely moist throughout the year. They can be increased by cuttings in a warm propagator in summer and some kinds also by division when repotting in spring.

Platycerium (Elk's Horn Fern, Stag's Horn Fern)

These handsome ferns are unusual both in appearance and in growth. They make dome-like mounds of greyish-green, sterile fronds on which stand the antler-like fertile fronds which have suggested the popular names. They are epiphytic, living in the wild on tree trunks out of contact with soil and deriving much of their nourishment from humid air. This gives the clue to their successful cultivation in shaded greenhouses or even indoors if the air can be kept sufficiently moist. They like to grow on their sides on a pad of damp sphagnum moss and peat attached to a broad piece of bark. They must be kept moist at all times by watering, spraying or dipping in water. They need a minimum temperature of 13 °C but *P. alcicorne*, the Elk's Horn Fern, and *P. grande*, sometimes called the Regal Elk-horn, will be happier in a steady 18–21 °C. All can be increased by removing offsets in spring, also by spores sown on peat in a warm, moist propagator in spring.

Plectranthus

Herbaceous or sub-shrubby plants, mostly sprawling but some erect or bushy. They are allied to Coleus (one kind, *P. oertendahlii*, is sometimes called the 'Creeping

Pteris cretica 'Albolineata'

Rhoeo discolor 'Vittatum'

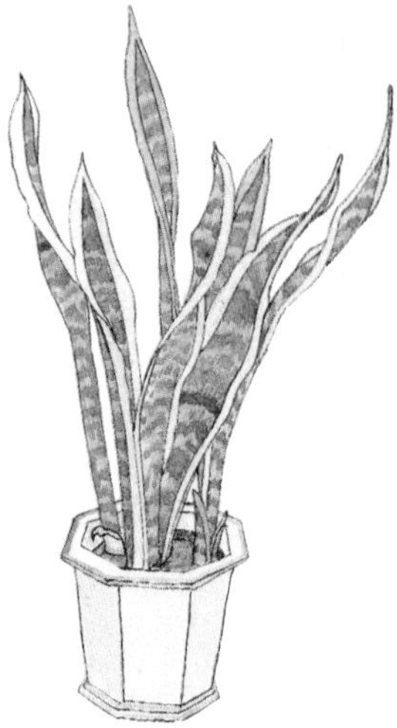

Rhoicissus rhomboidea

Centre: Saxifraga sarmentosa

Sansevieria trifasciata 'Laurentii'

Coleus') but are not as handsome. The leaves of *P. oertendahlii* are white-veined and become purple beneath as they age; and both stems and leaves of *P. tomentosus* are covered in grey down. All will grow in any good soil- or peat-based potting mixture in pots, or the sprawling kind in hanging baskets, in a minimum temperature of 13 °C, with normal watering, though *P. oertendahlii* will be even happier in a warmer place and *P. australis* can be kept a little drier in winter. All can be increased by summer cuttings in a warm propagator and some by division when repotting in spring.

Pteris (Ribbon Fern, Table Fern)
Though most of these ferns come from hot countries, they are not difficult to grow and most will survive where the temperature does not fall below 7 °C though they will be happier and more handsome in a warmer place. They make excellent house plants out of direct sunshine but with good light. Grow in a peat-based mixture or in a soil-based mixture containing about twice the usual quantity of peat. Keep this nicely moist throughout the year, and in summer keep the atmosphere fairly humid. Increase by division when repotting in spring.

P. cretica, which has numerous varieties, is one of the most popular species; *P. biaurita argyraea*, with a silver band down the centre of each frond, one of the most handsome. It is also one of those that most appreciates warmth.

Rhoeo
There is only one species, *R. discolor*, and it is a handsome, low-growing plant spreading by rhizomes (creeping, often underground stems) and forming rosettes of lance-shaped, rather fleshy leaves that are lustrous green above and reddish purple underneath. A variety named *R. discolor* 'Vittatum' has leaves striped with pale yellow.

These are easy plants to grow in rooms or shaded greenhouses provided they can be given a fair amount of warmth. Though they will survive in a minimum of

7 °C they will be much happier if the temperature never falls below 13 °C and is above 15 °C most of the time. They will grow in any good soil- or peat-based potting mixture, which should be kept moist throughout the year. Increase is by division when repotting or by cuttings of rosettes detached in spring or summer and rooted in a warm propagator.

Rhoicissus (Natal Vine)

One species, *R. romboidea*, is popular as a climbing plant for rooms and greenhouses in which it can be shaded from strong sunshine. It is a vigorous plant, clinging like a vine by means of tendrils, and so it needs trellis, canes, wires or something reasonably slender yet strong for support. The leaves are bronze when young but become greenish with age. It will grow in any good soil- or peat-based potting mixture which should be kept moist throughout the year, though watering should be kept to a minimum if the temperature falls below 13 °C. Tips of shoots can be pinched out at any time if they threaten to grow too far and plants can be more severely pruned in spring if this seems necessary. Stems can be layered at any time or cuttings will root in a warm propagator in summer.

Sansevieria (Bow-string Hemp, Mother-in-law's Tongue, Snake Plant)

These are semi-succulent, evergreen plants. By far the most popular kind is *S. trifasciata* 'Laurentii', a highly distinctive foliage plant that will put up with a lot of shade and quite a lot of ill-treatment. Its firm, fleshy, strap-shaped leaves stand erect, corkscrewing a little so that a number of plants, standing together, look rather like a broad-leaved seaweed growing under water. The leaves are deep green, cross-banded and edged with yellow, decidedly handsome and quite unique. *S. hahnii* is a shorter species with dappled, grey-green leaves forming a rosette. Both will grow in any good soil- or peat-based potting mixture in pots in rooms, greenhouses or conservatories in which the temperature does not fall below 7 °C, but will be happier and more attractive if the temperature most of the time can be 16 °C or more. It is not a plant that needs a lot of water though the soil should never be allowed to become quite dry. It is readily increased by division of the rhizomes in spring when it is repotted. Five centimetre, V-shaped cuttings inserted point down in a sand and peat mixture will root during spring and summer, but will require patience.

Saxifraga (Mother of Thousands)

The best saxifrage to grow as a pot plant is *S. sarmentosa*, a ground-hugging perennial which spreads, like a strawberry, by runners bearing plantlets along their length. These will root wherever they touch the soil and can be detached and potted as new plants. The leaves are rounded, marked with grey and purple, but these colourings are much brighter, more extensive and more varied in an excellent variety named *tricolor*.

The small, pale pink flowers, produced freely in sprays, are quite attractive. This saxifrage is virtually hardy and very easy to grow in a light room, greenhouse or conservatory in which it can be shaded from strong sunshine. It will thrive in any good soil- or peat-based mixture and should be watered fairly freely in spring and summer, moderately in autumn and winter, and very sparingly should the temperature drop below 7 °C.

Schefflera (Queensland Umbrella Tree)

There seems to be doubt about the correct name of *S. actinophylla*, since some authorities call it *Brassaia actinophylla*, but there is no doubt that it is a very handsome evergreen plant. In Queensland, where it grows wild, it makes quite a large tree, but it can be grown for several years in a large pot or a tub and its shining green leaves, each composed of several quite big leaflets, are very decorative. It is not one of the easiest plants to grow, being sensitive to cold and to overwatering, but in a warm room or greenhouse, with temperatures of 15 °C or more and with careful watering, it will thrive. It does not even mind quite dense shade which can be a big advantage indoors. It is best grown in a good soil-based potting mixture though it can be grown in a peat mixture if well fed in summer. Increase by seed sown as soon as it is ripe in a warm propagator.

Scindapsus (Ivy Arum)

These evergreen climbers are closely allied to philodendrons and sometimes confused with them. The most popular is *S. aureus* which has green leaves irregularly splashed with yellow. There are several varieties of it, some much more heavily variegated than others. Its use and cultivation are similar to those of *Philodendron scandens* except that it is more sensitive to overwatering and so the soil or peat mixture should be kept just moist in winter, no more.

Scindapsus aureus 'Marble Queen'

Selaginella

Most people seeing selaginellas for the first time would probably mistake them for very large mosses or very small, spreading ferns. They are, in fact, allied to ferns and some of them make delightful small pot plants requiring little heat but a great deal of water and atmospheric moisture. They need to be grown in a very spongy mixture, such as half and half live chopped sphagnum moss and sphagnum peat. They like to be in shade at all times and can be grown beneath taller plants. Many will put up with temperatures as low as 7 °C though some, such as the delicately formed *S. kraussiana* and *S. uncinata*, prefer temperatures of 16 °C or more. All are easily increased by division when repotting in spring.

Setcreasea (Purple Heart)

These are low-growing herbaceous plants, the best of which, *S. purpurea*, has soft, downy purple leaves which are better in colour if grown in good light, though they can be scorched by hot sunshine. Grow in pots in any good soil- or peat-based potting mixture in a light room or a greenhouse that is lightly shaded in summer, and with minimum temperature of 13 °C. Keep the soil nicely moist but avoid overwatering at all times, especially in winter. Increase by cuttings in a warm propagator in spring or summer. If plants become straggly the stems can be shortened to stiffen them and encourage branching.

Syngonium podophyllum

Tradescantia fluminensis 'Quicksilver'

Zebrina pendula

Syngonium (Goosefoot Plant)

This is another genus of climbing or creeping arums allied to philodendron and sometimes confused with them. Syngoniums will stand quite a lot of shade and so make good house plants. Many have the broadly arrow-shaped leaves so typical of the arum family and all like warm, damp conditions. The temperature should not fall below 15 °C. The compost, which can be a good either soil- or peat-based mixture, should be kept moist throughout the year and the air should be as humid as is practicable. Indoor plants may be allowed to climb around columns of wire netting packed with damp moss and in greenhouses plants can be frequently syringed in summer. All can be increased by cuttings in summer in a warm propagator. Among the best to grow are *S. podophyllum* and its numerous varieties, some of which are variegated cream or white.

Tradescantia (Spider Wort, Wandering Jew)

This is a big genus of herbaceous perennials and a very varied one, some species being fully hardy. Most valuable as greenhouse plants are *T. fluminensis* and its varieties. These are sprawling plants which grow so rapidly that they can become a nuisance, but are excellent for hanging baskets, to trail over the edge of staging or even to grow beneath it, since they will put up with a lot of shade and moisture. It is the variegated-leaved varieties that are best, with green leaves striped with white and sometimes also tinged with pink. These are virtually indestructible plants which will grow in any good soil- or peat-based potting mixture, in cool or warm conditions, the one essential being plenty of moisture. They can be increased by cuttings at almost any time of the year. *Zebrina pendula* is similar, as shown below.

Woodwardia (Giant Chain Fern)

These ferns are too large for most greenhouses but where there is room for a plant with a 3 m spread *W. radicans* is worth consideration. It is one of the most impressive ferns and its large fronds are doubly divided. It is nearly hardy and can be grown in any frostproof place in a spongy compost of peat and leaf mould with some soil. It needs shade from strong sunshine and is evergreen, so must be watered throughout the year. It can be raised from spores sown when ripe on the surface of damp peat in a cool greenhouse, also from buds that form towards the ends of the fronds and which will form roots and new plants if pegged to the soil and kept moist.

Zebrina (Wandering Jew)

Z. pendula and its several variegated varieties have exactly the same decorative merits and require identical treatment to *Tradescantia fluminensis*, also popularly known as Wandering Jew. The difference lies in the leaf colours which in zebrina always include some purple on the undersides of the leaves and sometimes above, and the leaves are always striped.

Table of Foliage Plants

ABBREVIATIONS

Type. Sb, shrub. Hb, herbaceous plant. An, annual. Bi, biennial. Cl, climber. Bl, bulb. Cm, corm. T, tuber. Br. bromeliad. Pm, palm. Suc, succulent. F, fern.

Temperature. C, cold, no artificial heat. Cl, cool, minimum 7°C. Int, intermediate, minimum 13 °C. W, warm, minimum 18 °C.

Soil. Av, average, John Innes type or peat based. S, sandy, extra sand or grit. Hm, humussy, extra peat and/or leaf mould.

Atmosphere. B, buoyant r.h. 50 to 60 per cent. H, humid, r.h. 70 to 80 per cent. D, dry, r.h. 30 to 40 per cent.

Light. Sun, no shade required at any time. Sh, shade from all direct sunshine. Semi, shade from strong sunshine in late spring and summer.

Water. N, normal watering, fairly freely in spring and summer, moderately in autumn and winter. W, keep dry in winter, water normally at other times. S, keep dry in summer, water normally at other times. PW, water sparingly in winter. PS, water sparingly in summer.

Name	Type	Temperature	Soil	Atmosphere	Light	Water
Acalypha	Sb	W	Hm	H	Semi	N
Adiantum venustum	F	Cl	Hm	H	Sh	N
A. cuneatum & A. tenerum	F	W	Hm	H	Sh	N
Aechmea	Br	W	Hm	H	Sh	N
Agave	Suc	Cl	S	D	Sun	N
Aglaonema	Hb	W	Hm	H	Sh	N
Aloe	Suc	Cl	S	D	Sun	N
Ananas	Br	Int/W	Hm	H	Sun	N
Aphelandra	Sb	Int	Hm	H	Sh	N
Araucaria	Sb	Cl	Av	B	Sun	N
Asparagus	Hb/Cl	Cl	Av	B	Sh	N
Aspidistra	Hb	Cl	Av	H	Sh	N
Asplenium	F	Cl	Hm	B	Sh	N
Begonia Rex	Hb	Int	Hm	H	Sh	PW
Blechnum	F	Int	Hm	H	Sh	N
Bryophyllum	Suc	Cl	S	D	Sun	N
Caladium	T	W	Hm	H	Sh	N
Calathea	Hb	Int	Hm	H	Sh	N
Chlorophytum	Hb	C	Av	B	Semi	N
Cissus	Cl	C	Av	B	Semi	N
Cocos	Pm	W	Hm	H	Sh	N
Codiaeum	Sb	Int	Av	B	Semi	N
Coleus	Hb	Cl	Av	B	Sun	N
Cordyline	Sb	C	Av	B	Sun	N
Cotyledon	Suc	Cl	S	D	Sun	PW
Cryophytum	An	Cl	S	D	Sun	N
Cycas	Sb	Int/W	Hm	H	Sh	N
Cyrtomium	F	Cl	Hm	B	Sh	N
Cyperus	Hb	C/Int	Av	B	Sun	N
Davallia	F	Int	Hm	H	Sh	N
Dicksonia	F	Cl	Hm	H	Sh	N
Dieffenbachia	Sb	W	Av	B	Semi	N
Dizygotheca	Sb	W	Av	B	Semi	N
Dracaena	Sb	Int/W	Av	H	Semi	N
Echeveria	Suc	Cl	S	D	Sun	PW
Eletaria	Hb	Int	Av	B	Sh	PW
Eucalyptus	Sb	Cl	Av	B	Sun	N
Fatshedera	Sb	C	Av	B	Semi	N
Fatsia	Sb	C	Av	B	Semi	N
Ficus carica	Sb	C	Av	B	Sun	N
F. elastica & F. benjamina	Sb	Int/W	Av	H	Sh	N

Name	Type	Temperature	Soil	Atmosphere	Light	Water
F. radicans	Cl	Cl	Av	B	Sh	N
Fittonia	Hb	W	Av	H	Sh	N
Grevillea	Sb	Cl	Av	B	Sun	N
Gynura	Hb	W	Av	B	Semi	N
Hedera	Cl	C	Av	B	Sh	N
Howeia	Pm	Int	Av	B	Sh	N
Hypoestes	Hb	Int	Av	B	Semi	N
Kleinia	Suc	Int	S	D	Sun	N
Leucadendron	Sb	Cl	Hm	B	Sun	N
Lippia	Sb	C	Av	B	Sun	PW
Lygodium	F	Int	Hm	H	Sh	N
Maranta	Hb	W	Hm	H	Sh	N
Mimosa	An	Int	Av	B	Sun	N
Monstera	Cl	W	Av	H	Sh	N
Musa	Hb	W	Av	H	Sun	N
Neanthe	Pm	Int	Av	H	Sh	N
Neoregelia	Br	W	Hm	H	Sh	N
Nepenthes	Hb	W	Hm	H	Sh	N
Nephrolepis	F	Int	Hm	H	Sh	N
Nidularium	Br	W	Hm	H	Sh	N
Pandanus	Sb	Int	Av	B	Semi	N
Pelargonium	Sb	Int	Av	B	Sun	N
Peperomia	Hb	Int	Av	B	Sh	N
Philodendron	Cl	Int/W	Av	H	Sh	N
Phoenix	Pm	Int	Av	H	Semi	N
Pilea	Hb	Cl	Av	B	Semi	N
Platycerium	F	W	Hm	H	Sh	N
Plectranthus	Hb	Int/W	Av	B	Sh	N
Pteris	F	Cl	Hm	H	Sh	N
Rhoeo	Hb	Int	Av	H	Sh	N
Rhoicissus	Cl	Int	Av	B	Semi	N
Sanseveria	Hb	Int	Av	B	Sh/Sun	N
Saxifraga	Hb	C	Av	B	Semi	N
Schefflera	Sb	Int	Av	H	Sh	N
Scindapsus	Cl	Int	Av	H	Sh	N
Selaginella	Hb	Cl/W	Hm	H	Sh	N
Setcreasea	Hb	Int	Av	B	Semi	N
Syngonium	Cl	W	Av	H	Sh	N
Tradescantia	Hb	Int	Av	H	Sh	N
Woodwardia	F	Cl	Hm	H	Sh	N
Zebrina	Hb	Int	Av	H	Sh	N

6 Cacti

People often talk of cacti and succulents as if they were different things. In fact cacti are succulents, a particular section of them distinguished from others by various botanical characteristics of little importance to gardeners. Still, there is sense in thinking of cacti separately, for they have peculiarities all their own. Most are leafless, unlike succulents, which have fleshy leaves used to store water to sustain them during long periods of drought. Cacti do this in their swollen 'bodies' or stems. However, it is well to remember that deserts which can be blazing infernos by day are often bitterly cold at night. Fortunately there is no need to reproduce such conditions in greenhouses since most cacti will succeed in any sunny place in which the temperature never drops below 6 °C, and for much of the winter remains decidedly cool, for then the plants will remain at rest and require little or no water. Then in early spring the temperature can rise to 13 °C at night and there will be no need to worry if it rises above 20 °C with the sun shining, though by that stage ventilation should be given, for high temperatures under glass can be more damaging than similar temperatures in the open.

However, there are exceptions to this general regime. The epiphytic, tree-living cacti like the epiphyllums and the Christmas and Easter cacti (schlumbergera and rhipsalidopsis), actually like it rather cool and shady in summer and need water all winter, though not a lot.

Most cacti like soil that is gritty and porous, and some like it to be alkaline as well, with added limestone or chalk. Peat-based mixtures are only for the epiphytes, the rest requiring a good soil-based potting mixture with a generous addition of coarse sand, grit or crushed brick. The precise quantity is not important but it would certainly not be overdoing it to use twice as much as for non-succulent plants.

Because the potting mixture is so porous, it does not hold water well and so, in spring and summer, cacti and succulents are likely to need water just as often as and in similar quantity to non-succulent plants. It is in autumn, and even more in winter, that they can be allowed to become rather dry – not completely so but with only a little moisture in the soil except for the epiphytes.

All can be grown in pots or they can be planted in cactus 'gardens', rather like little fragments of desert, with sandy soil and random stones. If in pots they will need to be repotted occasionally, not every year unless they are growing fast but perhaps every second year. Some of the spiny kinds can be painful to handle but a half sheet of newspaper folded several times makes a band that can be slipped around each plant to hold it securely without actually touching it with the hands.

Most kinds can be grown from seed which should be sown as soon as it is available, on the surface of sandy soil or very lightly covered by it. No shading will be necessary as with so many other seeds.

A collection of cacti – an unbelievable variety of colour and form.

Seeds of cacti have learned to germinate in bright sunlight. Some kinds can be divided; some make offsets that can be detached with roots; and some have stems that can be severed and inserted in sandy soil as cuttings.

Cacti are fascinating plants with a variety of form and colour that is quite unbelievable until one has worked with them for a while. Most will put up with so much bad management that they are ideal 'beginner's plants'.

Aporocactus (Rat-Tail Cactus)
A. flagelliformis is a sprawling plant with tail-like stems and small crimson flowers in summer. It is one of the easiest to grow.

Astrophytum (Star Cactus, Bishop's Cap)
The popular names refer to the curious shapes of the bodies of these stemless plants. The flowers are carried on top in summer and are quite showy. They are all small plants which could be grown on a sunny window ledge. They like some crushed limestone or chalk in the soil.

Cephalocereus (Old Man Cactus)
Column-shaped bodies covered in long silky white hairs, hence the popular name. *C. senilis* is the best kind to grow. The rose-pink flowers open at night.

Cereus (Column Cactus) – *see* illustration overleaf
Again the popular name is highly descriptive. The columns are deeply ribbed, often wickedly spined, and can branch to give a massive candelabra effect. With age some plants can become very large but plants in pots will remain manageable for years. *C. forbesii* and *C. peruvianus* are two good kinds but there are many more. Most are tough and easy plants to grow.

Echinocactus (Golden Barrel Cactus, Mother-in-law's Armchair) – *see* illustration overleaf
The bodies of these cacti are almost globular, set close on the ground, and covered with star-shaped clusters of spines. Some can grow very large in time, reaching a diameter of a metre, but in pots they grow slowly, and seldom become unwieldy. *E. grussonii* is a favourite because of its decorative yellow spines.

Echinocactus grussonii

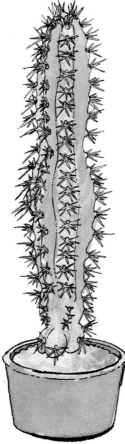

Cereus jamacaru

Ferocactus pilosus

Echinocereus

'Echinos' was the Greek name for a hedgehog and so all cacti with names beginning with 'echino' are very spiny. All species of echinocereus are columnar, like cereus, and most have attractive flowers, which, in some species, are quite freely produced. *E. fitchii* is specially recommended as a flowering plant, the flowers being quite large and glowing pink, and *E. purpureus*, sometimes called the Purple Hedgehog, is also spectacular in flower. Most kinds are sensitive to overwatering, and should be grown in extra gritty soil in the smallest pots that will contain them.

Echinopsis

Like echinocactus these are mainly barrel-shaped plants, but small ones which can be grown in 7.5–10 cm pots or in pans. They have quite showy flowers which, in some species, are very sweetly scented but they are not the easiest of cacti to persuade to flower regularly. They need a long, cool period of rest in winter and even in summer they appear to be best out of direct sunshine, which is unusual for cacti. *E. multiplex*, with pink flowers; *E. tubiflora*, with white flowers and *E. eyriesii*, also white, are among the best species and there are also numerous hybrids.

Epiphyllum

Some of the most spectacular flowers are to be found in this genus; large, elaborately formed blooms in vivid shades of red and pink, also gleaming whites and pale yellows. The stems are flattened and the habit of growth is different from that of most other cacti, except the allied schlumbergera and rhipsalidopsis, since in nature these are tree dwellers existing on an accumulation of humus in bark and enjoying the shade provided by a canopy of branches. In greenhouses they are best grown in hanging baskets, pans or half pots, in peat or leaf mould or a mixture of both, with some chopped sphagnum moss to make it even more spongy. In summer they can be suspended outdoors from the branches of trees or be placed in a shady frame and it is only from late winter throughout spring, when they are flowering, and again in late summer and early autumn, when they are making their growth, that they need much warmth and water. At other times they like to be cool and growing in soil that is just moist and no more. They are best repotted after flowering. Cuttings will root in moist peat or sphagnum moss in spring or summer.

Ferocactus
This is another genus of barrel cacti with more or less globular but much-ribbed bodies, wickedly armed with star-shaped clusters of long spines. Some can grow very large but growth in pots is slow. In general they are easy cacti to grow, responding well to the normal cactus treatment.

Gymnocalycium
Small to medium size plants, with more or less globular bodies on top of which quite large flowers are produced at intervals during spring and summer. They like the ordinary cultural routine recommended for cacti. One species, *G. mihanovichii*, produces sports (mutant forms) with coloured, instead of green, bodies. These cannot live on their own but have to be grafted on to ordinary green plants. Such plants are sold freely in garden centres and other places, red and yellow being the colours usually offered though pink and white sports are available. Once grafted, cultivation is as for normal cacti.

Lobivia
Mostly fairly small cacti with globular or short cylindrical bodies from the sides of which quite showy flowers can be produced if the plants are managed properly. As with some other cacti, it is the rest period in autumn and winter that largely determines the freedom with which the flowers are produced. At this season a temperature around 5 °C is ideal and the plants need very little water. Then in spring the temperature can rise to 13 °C or higher; the plants will resume growth and the buds will be there to produce flowers. *L. haageana*, with yellow flowers, is one of the best. *L. aurea* also has yellow flowers but some experts believe that it is not a true Lobivia and should be called *Pseudolobivia aurea*.

Mammillaria (Pincushion Cactus, Wart Cactus)
This is one of the biggest genera with scores of species. Most have small, rounded bodies (hence the popular name Pincushion Cactus) with small flowers borne in a ring near the top. They make excellent pot plants, small enough to be grown on a sunny window ledge and most respond to the normal cactus regime of cool, rather dry winters, and warm, moderately moist summers. They enjoy some ground chalk or limestone in the otherwise normally gritty soil mixture.

Notocactus (Ball Cactus)
The popular name is a good one since the growth bodies are usually ball-shaped, often much ribbed and

A hybrid Epiphyllum

Mammillaria

very spiny. They are mostly small plants with quite large, starry flowers found on the top of the ball but the flowers are shortlived, each usually opening and fading within one day, though there may be more to follow for weeks on end. They respond to the normal cactus treatment, and need a really good rest period in winter.

Opuntia (Prickly Pear)

These are everyone's idea of cacti with their fleshy, pad-like growths, awkwardly jointed together so that they form large, strangely branched plants, eventually of almost tree-like size. If individual pads are broken off and are pressed into damp sand they will soon form roots and grow into new plants. In some hot countries opuntias have become dangerous weeds and have to be ruthlessly controlled. In greenhouses they are easily grown but are not among the most handsome or desirable of cacti.

Parodia (Tom Thumb Cactus)

Small plants with more or less globular, ribbed or quilted bodies and starry flowers produced in spring

Opuntia

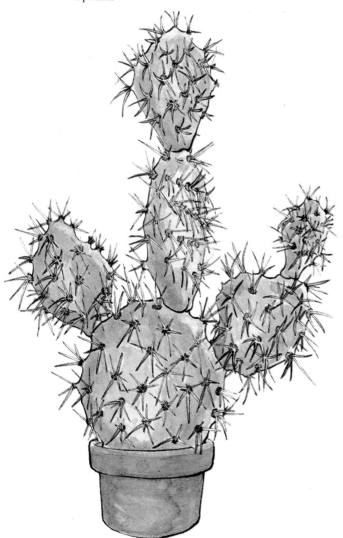

and autumn. There are a great many of them, all quite easy to grow under the normal cactus conditions. *P. aureospina* has yellow spines, and golden-yellow flowers, *P. mairana* is orange, *P. sanguiniflora* is red and *P. massii* is orange-red and there are many more just as good.

Rebutia (Crown Cactus, Pygmy Cactus)

These are all small plants with rounded or cylindrical bodies packed in clusters and producing really effective flowers. Because they are so small (some can be grown in 6 cm pots) and so cheerful in bloom, they are highly popular and a great many varieties, many of them hybrids, are available. They respond to the normal cactus treatment and are particularly satisfactory plants to grow from seed.

Rhipsalidopsis (Easter Cactus)

These are epiphytic cacti requiring similar treatment to the epiphyllums. They closely resemble the Christmas cactus (schlumbergera) in their flattened, jointed, arching growths terminated by brightly coloured flowers; but they flower later, in the spring and early summer rather than in winter and early spring. *R. gaertneri* and *R. rosea*, both with bright pink flowers, are the kinds usually grown.

Schlumbergera (Christmas Cactus, Crab Cactus, Lobster Cactus)

These are so closely related to, and so much like, rhipsalidopsis that the two genera are very often confused with one another – and in both catalogues and gardens the names as frequently exchanged. The true Christmas Cactus, flowering in winter, is *S. buckleyi*, a hybrid between the Crab or Lobster Cactus, *S. truncatus* (often sold as *Zygocactus truncatus*), and another species named *S. russelliana*. Both these species and the hybrid only flower when days are short and nights are long. Indoors, artificial lighting can upset this and prevent plants from flowering; and low temperatures can also delay flowering until the spring. Temperatures of 13 °C or more are desirable in autumn and winter. These are good cacti for moderately heated rooms that are not lighted in the evenings. (*See* illustration p. 10.)

Selenicereus (Night-Flowering Cactus)

Sprawling plants with relatively slender, snake-like stems and astonishing flowers which, in *S. grandiflorus* are white, richly scented and sometimes as large as dinner plates. They open at night. These plants like a richer soil than most cacti with plenty of root room and a fair amount of water. In some ways cultivation is more like that of non-succulent flowering plants than that of other cacti.

7 Orchids

Like cacti, orchids are a race apart, plants with their own peculiar style of living which is only rarely similar to that of other plants. This is a vast race, embracing thousands of species and innumerable hybrids raised by enthusiastic gardeners. For orchids do arouse enthusiasm, so great that many people devote their whole lives to studying and growing them. The literature on the subject is vast and opinions on how this or that species should be grown are varied. Orchid growers tend to be specialists who view the non-specialist intruder with suspicion and some contempt. Yet their very success, especially in improving and speeding methods of propagation, is reducing the price of orchids and making them much more widely available to people who formerly would not have thought it possible to afford orchids, let alone to grow them. Excellent varieties are offered for sale in many places, even in some multiple stores, and increasing numbers of plant lovers are discovering that orchid growing is neither particularly difficult nor expensive.

In fact many orchids can put up with a surprising amount of ill-treatment though clearly this is not the way to get the best out of them. Since they grow wild in many parts of the world, cool as well as hot, dry as well as wet, it is not possible to generalize about their cultivation. A great many grow in soil like other plants and so are known as terrestrial orchids, but most of the very popular tropical or subtropical kinds are epiphytic plants, which means that they grow in trees or on rocks, out of contact with soil, and derive their nourishment from the plant debris that accumulates in such places, from mosses and other lowly plants which like to grow on bark and moist rock, and directly from the air. Some of their roots often hang in the air absorbing moisture from it while other roots cling to bark or whatever else offers them anchorage.

The lesson to be learned from this is that epiphytic orchids do not require normal potting composts. They want something extremely spongy and absorbent yet with enough substance not to decay too rapidly, so leaving the plants unsupported. All kinds of mixtures are recommended, usually based on live sphagnum moss, chopped up or pulled apart, with fibre of some kind added. Years ago this was prepared from the roots of osmunda fern, sold as osmunda fibre, but this has become so scarce and expensive that other materials have had to be sought. Fibre from other ferns' roots is one possibility, another is to use shredded bark or bark chippings, materials that are now freely available at a reasonable price in most places. For some plants peat may be added and some growers like to have a few lumps of charcoal to keep the compost sweet.

Then there are orchids, such as the popular cymbidiums and paphiopedilums (they are still often called cypripedium) which need a firmer compost, mainly of peat with perlite or fragments of expanded polystyrene added to keep it open and well aerated, yet at the same time being themselves absorbent and so retaining the moisture on which all orchids depend so much. A typical mixture of the first type would be 2 parts by bulk osmunda or other fern root fibre and 3 parts sphagnum moss or pine bark chippings with sufficient perlite or polystyrene granules to pepper it white. A mixture of the second type could be 2 parts of peat, 1 of good quality leaf mould, 1 of fibrous loam well broken up but not sieved, plus a little sand or perlite. An intermediate type of compost, which grows cymbidium well, is 2 parts of peat, and 1 of either coarse sand, perlite or polystyrene granules. But the variations are endless and orchids, like other plants, will grow in a considerable range of composts provided they get the right quanities of moisture and food and are grown in a suitable temperature and humidity range.

As for other plants, it is convenient to divide orchids into three temperature regimes: cool, meaning temperatures around 10–13 °C in winter, rising to 13–18 °C in summer; intermediate, 13–16 °C in winter, rising to 16–21 °C in summer; and warm, 18–21 °C in winter, rising to 21–27 °C in summer. Humidity usually needs to be high, especially in the warmer temperatures when dry air can do a great deal of harm. This is one of the things that makes it difficult to grow orchids in rooms, though many thrive in plant cabinets in which the necessary humidity can be maintained.

Most orchids need to be kept moist for much of the year and the high humidity helps to keep down loss of water by evaporation. Many have a marked resting season when they need to be cooler and drier than at other times and most are best repotted just as they are coming out of this period of rest and are making new roots, which can usually be seen creeping over the surface of the compost or the side of the pot or basket in which they are growing.

Many orchids make pseudo-bulbs which are fleshy, often rather bulb-like growths above the roots, and as the plants grow, fresh pseudo-bulbs are added in front of the old ones. After a while the oldest commence to shrivel and eventually wither away, but before this happens old pseudo-bulbs can be detached and repotted on their own, when they will usually start to grow strongly again. This is a simple, if rather slow, way of increasing stock. Orchids that do not make pseudo-bulbs can generally be divided when they are being repotted and this results in a similar slow but easy multiplication.

The necessary humidity is obtained by syringing plants frequently with water and also spraying water on paths and under staging. Orchid houses are often constructed with a solid sub-stage a few centimetres below the slatted stage on which the pots stand. This sub-stage is then covered with sand or pea gravel which can be kept constantly wet, so giving off a lot of water vapour, especially at the higher temperatures. Automatic humidifiers, similar to those used in hospitals and other buildings, can also be installed.

Since most orchids like light shading, orchid houses should be equipped with blinds; or they can have a slatted lath cover fixed about 15 cm above the glass to produce the same kind of dappled shade that is cast by a canopy of leaves.

Aerides (Fox-Tailed Orchid)
Epiphytes with narrow arching sprays of spurred and scented flowers. These are very beautiful plants which do not make pseudo-bulbs. They can be grown in the intermediate or warm house in a fibre and sphagnum moss mixture with abundant moisture in summer but only enough in winter to keep the roots moist. They flower at various times, A. odoratum, white and purple, in summer.

Angraecum
Epiphytes with thick stems, densely packed with a double row of leaves. There are no pseudo-bulbs and they are not easy plants to propagate. The flowers, borne in spikes, are frequently scented. Some kinds have long stems and are semi-climbers. All need a fibre and sphagnum moss mixture and warm house treatment, with abundant moisture in spring and summer but only enough to keep the compost moist in winter. A. sesquipedale has green and white flowers in winter or early spring.

Calanthe
Terrestrial orchids, some of which lose their leaves in winter while others are evergreen. The two most popular kinds, the species C. vestita, with sprays of white and rose flowers and the hybrid C. bella, with white, pink, and crimson flowers, are both deciduous

and flower in late winter or early spring. They need a minimum temperature of 15 °C and more light than many orchids. A peat and sand or polystyrene granule compost will suit them and they should be repotted annually in spring, after flowering. They make large pseudo-bulbs and can be increased by division when repotting. They require no water in winter, when at rest, but should be watered freely in spring and summer, while growing.

Cattleya
These are everyone's idea of an orchid, with large, flamboyant blooms which, when cut, make marvellous floral decorations and corsages. Cattleyas are epiphytes requiring the fibre and sphagnum moss type of mixture. They will grow in intermediate house conditions, need only light shading, and must be watered the year round but much less freely in winter than in summer. Almost all the varieties grown are hybrids with flowers in various shades of mauve, purple, and crimson, with white or yellow, or some all white. They flower at different times according to variety.

Coelogyne
Relatively small epiphytes making clusters of marble-like pseudo-bulbs which can easily be split up when repotting in spring. *C. cristata*, with white flowers in late winter or early spring, is one of the best. It will grow well in intermediate house temperatures or even

A hybrid Cymbidium

a little lower, likes a fibre and sphagnum moss mixture, and should be watered freely while in growth but sparingly when at rest in winter.

Cymbidium
These splendid plants with arching sprays of bird-like flowers have become the most popular of all orchids and there are hundreds of varieties in a wide range of colours including some very beautiful and unique shades. Some species are epiphytic and some terrestrial but the cymbidiums cultivated in greenhouses are almost all complex hybrids which are best grown in a terrestrial mixture of peat and perlite, sand, or polystyrene granules. All thrive in an intermediate house and many will also grow well in a cool house. They flower at various times but mainly in spring and early summer. They need good light, but shade from strong sunshine; and water all the year, but far less in winter, when they are resting, than in summer, when they are growing. They are best repotted in early spring directly new growth of shoots and roots is observed.

Dendrobium
Epiphytes with elongated, cane-like pseudo-bulbs which also act as stems and bear the leaves and flowers. These are often blotched at the throat with some dark colour, such as crimson or maroon, and are very varied both in colour and in the way in which they are produced. Many like warm house conditions but two of the finest species, *D. densiflorum*, yellow and *D. nobile*, rose, white and crimson, will grow well in an intermediate house. All should be grown in a fibre and sphagnum moss type of mixture, should be watered freely while growing and sparingly when at rest, and like good light but shade from strong sunshine.

Dendrochilum (Chain Orchid)
The popular name is appropriate since these small epiphytic orchids have slender, chain-like trails of tiny, scented, usually white or cream flowers. They make charming pot or hanging basket plants for a moderately shaded greenhouse with intermediate house temperatures. They should be grown in a fibre and sphagnum moss type of mixture which should be kept well moistened throughout the year. Increase is by division when repotting in spring.

Epidendrum
Another genus of small epiphytic orchids, the most popular of which is *E. vitelinum*, with slender but erect spikes of small orange-red flowers in autumn or winter. It will succeed in a cool house, minimum temperature 7 °C, in a fibre and sphagnum moss mixture which should be kept just moist in winter but should be watered freely in summer. There are clusters of small globular pseudo-bulbs which can be divided when repotting in spring.

Above: Miltonia spectabilis

Top right: Lycaste deppei

Bottom right: a hybrid Oncidium

Lycaste

The most popular of these are *L. skinneri* and its hybrids or varieties all of which can be grown in a peat and sand, perlite or polystyrene granule mixture in intermediate house temperatures. The flowers are rather like those of cymbidium but carried singly on short, erect stems and are white or various shades of pink, rose and purple. They require very little water while at rest in winter and should be in good light before they come into flower in late winter or spring. While in growth they must be watered freely.

Masdevallia (Tailed Orchid)

Strange little orchids in which the three sepals, which form the most prominent part of the flower, are elongated into slender tails. They are small plants lacking pseudo-bulbs and they can be grown in a cool house, minimum temperature 7 °C, in a fibre and sphagnum moss mixture which should be kept moist throughout the year but less so in winter than in summer when the plants also enjoy a damp atmosphere. *M. chimaera*, with large greenish-yellow flowers heavily spotted with blackish purple, is typical of this fascinating genus.

Maxillaria

Another genus of small epiphytic orchids with unusual flowers, in some species hooded, in others spidery, and often strangely blotched or spotted. They are easy plants to grow in an intermediate house in a fibre and sphagnum moss mixture which should be kept moist all the year, though with some kinds which form pseudo-bulbs only occasional watering is necessary in winter. Others that have no pseudo-bulbs require more frequent watering even when at rest.

Miltonia (Pansy Orchid)

The popular name is a good one, for the flat flowers, with broad often strikingly blotched petals, do look rather like huge pansies. They are epiphytes for intermediate house treatment though temperatures should not be allowed to mount too high in summer. Most of those cultivated are hybrids and will thrive in a fibre and sphagnum moss mixture kept moist in summer. They flower at various times from late spring to autumn and should not be syringed while in bloom as excess moisture can spoil the flowers.

Odontoglossum (Lace Orchid, Tiger Orchid)

This is one of the most popular and highly developed genera of orchids. All are epiphytic and all enjoy the conditions of the intermediate house but in other respects they differ greatly. *O. crispum* and the many hybrids associated with it bear their medium size flowers in long arching sprays and are excellent cut flowers. By contrast *O. grande* has much larger flowers borne in twos and threes on relatively short, branched stems in autumn and winter. Their colour is tawny yellow, banded with chestnut, hence the popular name

Tiger Orchid. The *O. crispum* varieties and hybrids have white flowers splashed with various shades of purple and produced at different times of the year. All can be grown in a fibre and sphagnum moss mixture which should never get quite dry but *O. grande* needs very little water in winter, considerably less than *O. crispum* and its associates which need to be nicely moist even at that season.

Oncidium (Butterfly Orchid)

The popular name really applies to one species only, *O. papilio*, which has large, butterfly-like, yellow and brown flowers carried singly on long slender stems; but all the oncidiums are light and graceful flowers. Many produce their flowers in loose sprays and most are some shade of yellow, with brown or brownish-red spots or blotches. All are epiphytes thriving in the fibre and sphagnum moss type of mixture. Most like the temperatures of the intermediate house but *O. papilio* will do better in the warm house and a few will grow in a cool house. Most need plenty of water while growing in spring and summer but very little when at rest in winter though they must never be allowed to become quite dry. They flower at various times of the year.

Paphiopedilum (Slipper Orchid, Lady's Slipper)

Many gardeners still call these distinctive orchids, with a pouched lower petal and a fan-like upper sepal, by their old name Cypripedium, now used only for some hardy or nearly hardy species. Most of the popular kinds will grow in a fibre and sphagnum moss mixture to which some loam has been added but the genus contains both terrestrial and epiphytic species and most of the garden varieties are complex hybrids so that they show considerable variation in their preferences. Some, including the very tough *P. insigne* with yellowish-green and purplish-brown flowers, will grow in a cool house, others prefer the higher temperatures of the intermediate house and some like warm house conditions. All are evergreen and without pseudo-bulbs so they must be watered throughout the year, though much less in winter than in summer. Most, including *P. insigne*, flower in autumn, winter or early spring and should be repotted every year in spring. (*See* illustration overleaf.)

Phalaenopsis (Moth Orchid) – *See* illustration overleaf.

Exquisitely graceful orchids with quite large, moth-like flowers elegantly arranged along arching stems. Many are all white or white flushed with pink, rose or purple. They are epiphytes so will grow in the fibre and sphagnum moss type of mixture and they have no pseudo-bulbs so they must not be allowed to get dry at any time. They enjoy warm house conditions and can flower for a long period if conditions are right.

Pleione

Small and nearly hardy semi-epiphytic orchids with little pink, rose, white or pale yellow, funnel-shaped

Paphiopedilum fairieanum

flowers borne singly on short stems. They can be grown, almost without artificial heat, in pans filled with a compost of equal parts fibre, sphagnum moss, peat and good fibrous loam. They form pseudo-bulbs and require very little water in winter though they should not become quite dry. Flowers appear in spring and from then until early autumn they should be watered fairly freely. Annual repotting is desirable immediately after flowering when the clusters of pseudo-bulbs can be divided, if desired.

Sophronitis

Small epiphytic orchids, the most popular of which, *S. coccinea*, has vivid orange-red flowers in autumn and winter. It is a species for the cool or intermediate house grown in a fibre and sphagnum moss mixture in shallow pans or on pieces of bark. All species have small pseudo-bulbs but no marked resting season and so must be watered throughout the year, though much more sparingly in winter than in summer.

Stanhopea

Epiphytes which have the curious habit of flowering downwards so that they are usually grown in baskets and suspended from the greenhouse rafters. The flowers are oddly shaped and often unusually coloured, waxen in texture and strongly scented. The plants make pseudo-bulbs, should be grown in the epiphytic type of fibre and sphagnum moss mixture which should be kept moist throughout the year but much more so in summer than in winter. They can be grown in the intermediate house temperatures.

Vanda

Epiphytes, some of which are semi-climbing in habit and make long aerial roots. The flowers are borne in angularly branched sprays and are delicate blue in the most popular species, *V. caerulea*. This will grow well in an intermediate house but another popular kind, *V. sanderiana* with buff-coloured flowers spotted with red, needs warm house treatment. All will grow in a mixture of fibre and sphagnum moss and this must be kept moist all the year but far more water is required in summer than in winter. *V. caerulea* flowers in autumn, *V. sanderiana* earlier, towards the end of summer. There are also spring and early summer flowering species.

Zygopetalum

The kind most commonly grown, *Z. mackayi*, has highly distinctive flowers, the lip speckled purplish blue and white, the upright sepals olive-green and brown. Several of these strangely beautiful flowers are borne in a loose spike in winter and they last for several weeks. It is only semi-epiphytic and likes a mixture containing some good loam or peat as well as fibre and sphagnum moss, which should be well watered in summer, kept just moist in winter. It likes the temperatures of the intermediate house.

Phalaenopsis lueddemanniana

8 Vegetables

For the vegetable grower a greenhouse can have two distinct uses, though neither excludes the other. It can be used for raising seedlings earlier than would be possible out of doors, so that they can be hardened off and planted out as soon as the weather is favourable; and it can also be used for growing some crops throughout, from seed sowing to harvesting. Most of these will be rather tender crops, such as tomatoes, cucumbers, aubergines and capsicums (peppers), which are not too reliable out of doors even when started under glass, but there are also some, including French beans and lettuces, which can be grown perfectly well in the open in summer, but can be obtained out of season in a greenhouse.

Let us first of all look at the possibilities of seed sowing for planting out. Quite a lot of crops can be forwarded in this way. Onions, which are slow growing in the early stages, can be sown in late January or during February for planting out in the latter half of April. Seeds will germinate in any good soil- or peat-based mixture in a temperature of 13–16 °C and this can be maintained very cheaply in a small warmed propagator. If the seeds are sown a couple of centimetres apart there will be no need to prick out the seedlings which can go on growing in their seed pan or tray until planting out time. They should have at least a fortnight in a frame, or at any rate without any artificial heat, before they are planted out.

Leeks can be sown in the same way, and there is some advantage in doing this, even up to the end of March, since germination will be faster and more certain under glass.

Lettuces can also be sown from late January onwards though, since lettuce seeds germinate and grow much faster than either onions or leeks, seedlings from very early sowings will be ready for planting out before the weather is settled and mild enough for them to go completely unprotected; however, polythene tunnel cloches will give all the shelter necessary and an early crop of lettuces can be very profitable.

Brussels sprouts benefit from a long, steady season of growth and there is often considerable advantage to be gained from sowing in February for planting out in April or early May. Exactly the same applies to the very early varieties of sprouting broccoli known as calabrese. Fast-growing cabbages, such as Greyhound or Golden Acre, can be sown under glass from mid-January until early March for June–July use and summer cauliflowers, such as Polar Ice, All the Year Round and Delta, can be given the same treatment for a similar result.

Celery is almost always germinated in a greenhouse since outdoors it is slow and irregular. Early March is the time and the temperature range recommended for onions will suit it well. By mid-March only occasional extra heat, mostly at night, is necessary to maintain a 13 °C minimum. Celeriac is a near relation raised in the same way.

Then there are more tender vegetables such as French and runner beans, tomatoes, outdoor or ridge cucumbers, vegetable marrows and sweet corn. Since these will withstand little or no frost, timing becomes a rather critical matter. One needs to know one's district and the likely date of the last damaging frost, but early June is usually a perfectly safe date to aim for (in many places it could be mid-May). For beans, marrows, and sweet corn, all of which germinate and grow quickly, that means sowing at the end of April or early in May. There is advantage in sowing the seeds in pans or small pots 6–8 cm in diameter as the seedlings can be planted out from the pots with little or no root disturbance.

Tomatoes grow more slowly and require slightly higher temperatures. If one wants well-developed plants in 8–10 cm pots for planting out in late May or early June seed should be sown about mid-March; if one is satisfied with small plants in 6 cm pots planting out one can delay sowing until the second week in April. In either case a temperature of 16–18 °C is desirable and is easier and cheaper to maintain in April than in March. The February plants will almost certainly require a little liquid feeding during the last fortnight or so before they are planted out to keep them growing strongly, especially if they are in a peat-based mixture which contains little reserve food. The temperature should never drop below 10 °C as this will check growth, and seedlings which get severely chilled can take weeks to recover, if indeed, they ever do so completely.

Now let us consider crops to be grown throughout in the greenhouse.

Tomatoes

These are the favourites and they can be highly profitable if well grown. It takes something like three to four months from sowing to first picking, depending on the amount of light (including day length as well as intensity) and the temperature range as well as the variety. Commercial growers may be sowing in December in well-warmed houses, probably with artificial lighting for the seedlings in the early stages, but few home gardeners would be wise to sow before mid-February with the expectation of fruit from June onwards throughout the summer. A temperature of 16–18 °C is necessary for quick germination and the seed can be sown in either a soil- or peat-based seed mixture. Tomato seeds are quite large enough to be spaced out individually, about 1 cm apart and the seedlings can be left undisturbed until they have their first pair of true (indented as opposed to smooth-edged) leaves, when they should be potted singly in 6 cm pots in a good soil- or peat-based potting mixture. They must be moved on into 10 cm pots as soon as the small ones are comfortably filled with roots and before roots commence to grow out of the drainage holes in the bottom of the pots.

After this stage there are several possibilities. Tomatoes can be grown throughout in pots, in which case pots 20–23 cm in diameter will be required for fruiting and the young plants can go directly into these as soon as the 10 cm pots are well filled with roots. The mixture should be a fairly rich one (if soil-based it can be either John Innes No. 2 or 3) since tomatoes are hungry plants. There is not the same flexibility of richness with peat-based mixtures, so if these are used supplementary feeding with a liquid tomato fertilizer

Tomato 'Golden Sunrise'

should start after four or five weeks.

Alternatively the tomatoes can be planted in a bed of good soil which contains some well-rotted manure and a peppering of a compound fertilizer such as National Growmore (about 26 g of fertilizer to 10 l of

Tomato plants in growing bags.

soil). The bed should be at least 20 cm deep and 60 cm wide. In this plants should be spaced at least 40 cm apart, preferably a little more. If there is to be more than one row these should be at least 60 cm apart with a wider alley between each pair of rows so that one can move freely between them. Overcrowding results in drawn plants which crop badly and are more likely to become diseased.

Advantages of growing in beds are that the tomatoes require less frequent watering and feeding and are, on the whole, easier to manage than in pots. Advantages of pot culture are that fruit usually commences to ripen earlier and it is fairly easy to move the plants as they get bigger if they require more room.

Another possibility is to plant the tomatoes in growing bags. These are specially made black plastic bags already filled with a peat-based potting mixture suitable for tomatoes, cucumbers, etc. The bags are rather longer and narrower than those ordinarily used for peat composts. They are laid flat on the ground, several of them end to end if necessary, and are then slit open along the top so that three or four tomato plants can be planted in each. The peat mixture is kept out of contact with the soil of the greenhouse by the plastic bag so it cannot become infected with soil-borne diseases. The bag also holds the moisture in the peat and prevents rapid drying out. Tomatoes grow well in these bags provided they are correctly watered and adequately fed but they do need earlier and more frequent feeding than plants growing in soil. It is usually necessary to start feeding with a liquid tomato fertilizer four or five weeks after planting in the bags and to continue feeding about once a week until the last trusses are fully formed and are commencing to ripen.

Yet another system is known as ring culture. When the tomatoes have filled their first pots they are planted in good soil-based potting compost in rings which are bottomless containers usually made of some sort of waterproofed cardboard – though they can be of any material – and about 23 cm in diameter and depth. These rings must be stood about 45 cm apart on a 15 cm deep bed of clean gravel, washed boiler ashes or any other material that is porous yet highly water absorbent. It is referred to as the aggregate.

After planting, the soil in the ring is well watered so that it is wet right through, after which the water is applied to the aggregate only, which is kept constantly moist. Water is drawn up into the rings by capillary attraction so that the soil in them remains evenly moist. All feeding, which should be done in just the same way as for tomatoes growing in pots, beds, or bags, is applied to the soil in the rings, not to the aggregate. In a week or so the tomato plants will have filled the rings with fine fibrous roots and will be drawing all their chemical requirements from them. They will also be penetrating the aggregate with a much coarser root system which will provide the plants with most of their moisture.

Pot, bag, and ring culture all have the merit that relatively small quantities of growing compost are required and it is both easy and fairly cheap to replace this annually, so avoiding any buildup of soil-borne pests or diseases.

Indoor tomatoes are almost invariably trained as single stem cordons. All side shoots which form where leaf stalks join stems are removed while still very small and only the main stem is allowed to grow upwards. It is tied to a cane or stake or is held up by soft fillis attached in a loose loop near the bottom of the tomato stem and tied at the top to a rafter or to a wire strained the length of the house just below the glass. As the tomato plant grows the main stem is carefully guided around this vertical string so that it is supported. Whatever is used must be quite strong for the weight of a tomato plant in full bearing is quite considerable. When the plant reaches the roof of the house, the growing tip is removed and no further growth is permitted. In commercial houses tomatoes often grow to a height of 2 m or more. In small greenhouses 1.5 m is a more likely height and the plant will have produced five or six trusses of fruit.

Tomatoes need quite a lot of water and the soil or peat mixture must never be allowed to become dry. In summer, when the weather is warm and sunny, tomatoes are likely to need watering every day, in cooler weather every other day or perhaps twice a week but they should be looked at daily to make certain that the compost is moist. It is possible to install automatic systems of watering and this is particularly easy when the ring culture method is used since it is difficult to overwater the aggregate and some kind of slow trickle system can be used to keep it wet.

Tomatoes are also hungry plants. After the first few weeks they will have exhausted much of the readily available chemical food in the soil and what is left will need to be supplemented by either dry or liquid feeding. 'Dry' feeding means scattering a fertilizer very thinly over the surface of the soil or peat and leaving it to be washed in when the plants are watered. 'Liquid' feeding means that the fertilizer is dissolved in (or, if already a liquid, diluted with) water and applied from a watering can or through a diluter attached to a hose. The rule should be 'little and often' and once well established and growing fast, tomatoes will usually respond to weekly feeding. But do not be tempted to use any more fertilizer, or at any greater strength than is recommended by the manufacturers. Excessive feeding can cause severe leaf scorching and even defoliation.

Fruits should be gathered as soon as they are half ripe, salmon or deep pink rather than scarlet or vermilion in colour. They will go on ripening off the plant and their removal helps remaining tomatoes to swell and ripen faster.

Tomatoes like a pleasantly warm temperature between 16 and 26 °C. Higher than that is not so good, though sometimes it cannot be avoided, but everything reasonable should be done, such as opening ventilators and the greenhouse door if necessary to keep it around the optimum level. In some very sunny places shading may be necessary at times but it should be as light as possible since tomatoes grow and ripen best with sunshine.

Sometimes tomatoes flower freely but produce little fruit, the flowers falling off without being properly fertilized. Fertilization is mainly the work of insects, such as bees, but it can also be done by hand with a soft artist's paint brush or a rabbit's tail tied to the end of a cane. This is used to distribute ripe pollen from flower to flower and the most effective time to do this is in warm sunny weather when the golden pollen is dry and readily adheres to the brush. It is brushed off one flower and then dusted back onto the stigma of another flower. If it is ripe it is quite easy to see the pollen grains adhering to the fine hairs of the paint brush.

There are a few pests and diseases that can be really troublesome if permitted to get the upper hand. Leaf mould, also known as cladosporium, is one of these, a fungus that attacks the leaves, especially towards autumn when the air is moist but temperatures are commencing to fall. Some tomato varieties are resistant to this disease and all are less likely to catch it if the temperature never falls below 13 °C and the air is kept on the move. It may help to install a small electrical heater or fan to combat the disease. Spraying occasionally with a good fungicide such as Bordeaux Mixture will also help by killing fungal spores before they have a chance to germinate. This disease appears as yellowed blotches which spread rapidly and produce a khaki-coloured mould on the underside of the leaf. If not checked the whole leaf withers and hangs down or falls off (*see* p. 37).

Greenback is a physiological disorder which causes the fruits to ripen irregularly, remaining green, or yellowish green, around the stalk end. It is associated with potash deficiency in the soil but some varieties are much more subject to it than others.

There are various viruses that attack tomatoes causing yellow blotching of the leaves, but without the distinctive mould on the lower surface which is characteristic of cladosporium: bunching of the shoots at the top of the plants; bronzing of leaves and streaking of stems; leaves divided into threadlike segments; stunting, etc. There is no cure for any of these diseases and affected plants should be destroyed as soon as observed.

Tomatoes are also attacked by various soil-borne diseases which destroy the roots and cause the plants to wilt, but if the soil is changed annually, or tomatoes are planted in growing bags, there is little danger that wilts of this kind will occur.

Blossom-end rot occurs where the soil has been allowed to get very dry but it may be four to six weeks before the highly characteristic symptom shows. This is a flattened black patch on the fruit at the far end from the stalk. Whitefly is the most persistent pest: the tiny, white, moth-like creatures which can breed so fast that in a bad attack they fly out in white clouds when disturbed (*see* pp. 35–6).

There are many tomato varieties, some of them rather expensive, first generation (F1) hybrids which are usually very uniform, others ordinary varieties which may be just as satisfactory for home use. Typical are Ailsa Craig, with very regular, medium sized fruits; Big Boy, very large, rather irregular fruits with solid flesh and excellent flavour, fine for slicing; Carter's Fruit, very even, good flavour, with skin which peels off easily; Craigella, like Ailsa Craig, but resistant to greenback; Davington Epicure, a large, thin-skinned tomato with few seeds; Eurocross A, with well-shaped fruits, resistant to cladosporium, fruits very sweetly flavoured; Golden Sunrise, an old but unsurpassed

Cucumber Pepinex

yellow-fruited tomato; Herald, medium size, well-shaped fruits of first class quality; Moneymaker, a very heavy cropping tomato; MM, like Moneymaker, but resistant to cladosporium and greenback; and Supersonic, large, very solid, well-flavoured fruits.

Cucumbers

This is the second favourite greenhouse crop with most home gardeners but cucumbers are not quite as easy to manage as tomatoes; nor do the two crops mix particularly well, since cucumbers require a much moister atmosphere, the kind of humidity which would encourage cladosporium disease to attack tomatoes. The time between sowing and fruit cropping is about the same and February or March are good times to make a start. Sow seed singly in 6 cm pots in a soil- or peat-based mixture, placing the rather flat elliptically shaped seeds on edge so that water does not collect on them. Germinate in a temperature of 18–21 °C or 22–24 °C for those varieties which produce all female flowers.

When the seedlings appear, the temperature can be lowered slightly to 15 °C at night rising to about 18 °C by day. As soon as the little pots are full of roots, plant the cucumbers, either one in each 23–25 cm pot or on the summit of mounds of soil made on a bed of soil either on the floor of the greenhouse or on solid staging. The bed itself should be about 15 cm deep and about 1 m wide and each mound should be made with about two buckets full of soil. Whether in pots or a bed the mixture should be rather a rich one with well-rotted manure, if available, mixed with twice its bulk of good soil. Failing manure, spent mushroom compost can be used with soil in the same proportion, but with a peppering of a good compound fertilizer. Alternatively cucumbers can be grown in the same kind of growing bags as those used for tomatoes but they will then require even more feeding, as they are, if anything, even hungrier plants than tomatoes.

They also need more moisture, both in the soil and in the air, and can be syringed with clear water several times a day to keep them damp. Water can also be splashed on the floor or paths of the glasshouse or shallow trays of water can be placed over or near the heating apparatus to give off water vapour. However, if the source of heat is an electric stove, make sure that no water drips onto it.

Cucumbers are not restricted to a single stem but are allowed to make side growths which are tied out horizontally to wires or any other convenient supports. The main stem will need to be tied more or less erect to a cane pushed firmly into the soil near the base of the plant and its tip should be pinched out when it reaches the glass. Side shoots should have their tips pinched out at the second leaf beyond the first female flower that forms on each. Normal cucumbers produce both male and female flowers and, since better fruit is produced without fertilization, the male flowers should be picked off as soon as they can be identified. The difference between a male and female flower is that the former has only a slender stem whereas the female has a shorter stem plus a little embryo fruit to which the flower is attached. Some varieties have been bred to produce virtually nothing but female flowers which saves the time taken looking for and removing male flowers, but these varieties require a slightly higher temperature for satisfactory germination.

Unlike tomatoes, which enjoy good light and sunshine, cucumbers grow best with a little shade. The glass on the sunny side can be lightly stippled with one of the greenhouse shading compounds or thin blinds can be pulled down by day when the sun is shining, but the shade must not be too dense.

After a while the soil will become so full of roots that some will appear on the surface. They should be covered with a 1 cm thick layer of rotted manure, mushroom compost or moist peat. This process can be repeated if necessary.

There are numerous varieties. Pepinex (also known as Feminex) is a first generation (F1) hybrid which produces almost all female flowers; Conqueror will grow with less atmospheric moisture and stronger light than most and is a good variety to choose if cucumbers and tomatoes are to be grown in the same greenhouse; Telegraph is a very old variety which produces fine fruits; Topnotch is an extremely heavy cropping F1 hybrid cucumber; Butcher's Disease Resisting is an old and reliable favourite; and Greenspot is a more modern F1 variety which produces similar, rather ribbed fruits.

Aubergines (Eggplants)

These are grown in very much the same way as tomatoes and associate well with them as they also like a warm, fairly dry atmosphere and plenty of sunshine. Seed can be sown from January to April but February and March are usually the best months to choose unless a good deal of heat is available. They can be spaced out in seed trays or sown in twos or threes in 6 cm pots. If the former method is adopted the seedlings are potted singly as soon as they have two rough leaves (do not count the first seed leaves). If sown direct in pots the seedlings are singled to one in each pot. Either way they will need to be moved on to 15 or 18 cm pots in which they will fruit or else they can be planted about 20 cm apart in growing bags.

Aubergines can be grown in any good soil- or peat-based potting compost but it is best to stick to one type throughout, so if they are to fruit in growing bags the seed should be germinated in peat-based seed mixture and the seedlings moved on to peat-based potting mixture. Like tomatoes, they are fairly hungry plants and will require earlier and more frequent feeding if grown in peat than in soil. The feeding can be done as described for tomatoes.

Aubergine 'Slim Jim'

Throughout aubergines like a temperature range of 16–21 °C which can rise on sunny days to 26 °C, above which the freest ventilation should be given, including opening the house door if necessary, to prevent the temperature from rising further.

When each plant is about 15 cm high the tip is pinched out to make it branch. When the flowers have set and the young fruit can be seen these should be reduced to four, or at most five, per plant. Stems will need to be tied to a cane or some other support as the fruits swell and become heavy.

Good varieties are Burpee Hybrid, Early Long Purple, Short Tom and Slim Jim.

Capsicums (Peppers)

A crop similar to aubergines in growth and requirements and, like them, very suitable for cultivation in a sunny greenhouse with a temperature range of 16–21 °C rising a few degrees higher on sunny days. Seed should be sown as described for aubergines and the seedlings potted on into 15 or 18 cm pots or planted about 20 cm apart in growing bags. When the plants are about 15 cm high the tips are pinched out to make them branch but there is no need to limit the number of fruits produced per plant.

As with other greenhouse crops it is wise to use the same type of mixture throughout, a peat-based seed mixture if the plants are to be grown in a peat-based potting mixture or in peat-filled bags, a soil-based seed mixture if a soil-based potting mixture such as John Innes No. 2 is to be used for the final potting. Plants will need free watering throughout and weekly feeding after they have been in their final pots or bags for about six weeks. Fruits can be used as soon as

Capsicum 'Twiggy'

sufficiently large, either green or fully ripe which will be red or yellow according to variety.

Recommended capsicums are: Canape, with large fruits; New Ace, also large; Outdoor, a good variety to raise in the greenhouse and plant outdoors in early June in a warm sunny position; Paprika Wondertop, shaped like a deeply ribbed tomato; and Slim Pim with long thin fruits. All these are red when fully ripe.

Lettuces
Though so easy to grow outdoors or raise early in spring under glass for planting out later, lettuces are not the easiest of crops to bring to maturity under glass, particularly in winter and early spring when they are most valuable. The ordinary varieties need light as well as warmth, and in its absence become weak and drawn and fall easy victims to grey mould disease which can reduce the crop to pulp in a few days. Special varieties have been bred for winter and early spring cropping but even these need care and understanding, a very light greenhouse, sufficient but not too much heat – around 13–18 °C – and careful watering. Lettuces are easiest to manage as an autumn or early winter crop since they can then do most of their growing before the days are really short.

Seed should be sown thinly in trays or pans in peat- or soil-based seed mixture from August to December according to the date at which the crop is required. In good conditions it takes ten to twelve weeks from sowing to first cutting but as the days get shorter growth gets slower, so that lettuces sown in late October would be unlikely to be ready to cut until February and might be as late as March.

Lettuces are best grown in beds of good soil on the floor of the greenhouse or made up on staging, which has the advantage of bringing the plants nearer the glass where the light is better. The soil should not have been used for lettuces for some years and should be mixed with some sand and peat to make it more porous. It will also need some fertilizer. A John Innes No. 1 type of mixture will do or the plants can be grown in a peat-based mixture in growing bags.

The seedlings should be planted as soon as they can be handled easily, spaced 20 cm apart and well watered in. They must be protected from slugs by having slug pellets or methiocarb scattered around them which should be renewed from time to time. The soil must be kept nicely moist but the foliage should be fairly dry, so water should be given from the spout of a watering can directed at the soil not the leaves. Cutting can commence as soon as the plants are of usable size. There is no need to wait for them to form large hearts, which in any case the winter varieties rarely do.

Suitable varieties to grow as autumn or winter crops under glass are Kweek, Kordaat, and Kloek, all Dutch raised especially for this purpose.

French Beans
These can be grown successfully in an unheated or moderately heated house for an early supply in May or June before fresh beans are available from outdoors. For the earliest crop seed should be sown in January in a temperature of 16–18 °C. To economize on heat the seed can be germinated in a seed tray inside a propagator but this will only save about fourteen days' fuel bills as by that time the seedlings will have to be potted singly and will almost certainly have to be brought out into the greenhouse where a minimum temperature of 13 °C will have to be maintained to keep them growing. There will also be a slight check to growth when moving the beans from seed trays to pots.

Uninterrupted growth can be obtained by sowing the seeds singly in 6 cm pots and, as soon as white roots appear at the drainage holes of these small pots, repotting in 13 or 15 cm pots in which they will crop. Other methods are to sow directly in a bed of good soil on the greenhouse floor, spacing seeds 8 cm apart, and, if there is room for more than one row, spacing these at least 30 cm apart, or to sow at similar spacing in peat-filled growing bags.

Beans like fairly rich soil containing some ground limestone or chalk. John Innes potting compost No. 2 or something of the kind will suit them well. They need as much light as possible and temperatures around 15–18 °C, and should be well watered, especially when in flower and when the pods are lengthening. If grown in peat they should be fed once a week with a compound liquid fertilizer from the time they start to flower. Masterpiece is an excellent variety to grow under glass.

Mushrooms

Since mushrooms grow best in the dark, it might seem a waste of greenhouse space to grow them there, but there are occasions when it can be economical. Mushrooms may, for example, be grown under the greenhouse staging in space which can be readily blacked out by hanging sacking or black polythene in front of it. They may also fit in as an early or late crop to be taken fairly quickly when the greenhouse is not required for anything else. They like an air temperature between 10 and 15 °C and this accords well with the temperature requirements of many other greenhouse plants.

Mushrooms can be grown in composted stable manure, which should contain quite a lot of straw used as bedding, or in fresh straw composted with special chemical activator prepared for making mushroom compost. Either way the process of composting is similar. The fresh manure or straw, suitably moistened and treated with activator according to the manufacturer's instructions, is made into a heap about a metre wide and deep and of any length according to the quantity to be made. It should quickly ferment and become quite hot and after a week of this it must be completely turned with a fork, the inside portion being brought to the outside and vice versa. If any of the decaying manure or straw has become dry because of the heat of fermentation, it should be well wetted as the turning proceeds. After about five days the process is repeated, and then, at five-day intervals, at least twice more, until the initial strong heat of fermentation starts to decline and all the straw is rotten and easily broken.

It will take from three to four weeks to prepare the compost. It is then spread in large wooden boxes about 25–30 cm deep or is built into flat-topped beds about 20 cm wide and of any desired length. A thermometer should be plunged into the centre of the bed to record its temperature and as soon as this reaches a steady 21–26 °C the bed is spawned.

The spawn, as purchased, must be broken up into small pieces about 3 cm across and these are pushed into the warm compost about 2 cm deep and 20 cm apart all over the bed or box which is then covered completely with a 15 cm thick layer of clean straw. After ten days or so the spawn should be growing sufficiently freely to be seen as thin white filaments in the compost. This is the time to cover the compost completely with a mixture of equal parts moist peat and well broken up chalk to a depth of 3 cm. The straw is then replaced on top of this peat and chalk 'casing'. About six weeks later the first mushrooms should be ready for picking and the crop should continue for about another six weeks. During this whole time the atmosphere should be kept moist by sprinkling water on paths or surrounding ground and the bed should also be kept moist, though it is unlikely to need large amounts of water which can do far more harm than good.

Crops for Forcing

Several crops can be forced in a moderately heated greenhouse from about November until March. The principal among these are rhubarb, chicory and seakale, all of which should be grown outdoors in the ordinary way until it is time for forcing.

Rhubarb roots are lifted, one or two at a time, as required. They should be the strongest roots available, dug up with as much root as possible. It may hasten subsequent growth if they are left lying outdoors for a night or so before the forcing process commences though this is not essential. This should be done in as nearly complete darkness as possible. The under stage space may be blacked out in some way or the rhubarb can be covered with deep boxes. Whatever method is used, the roots should be planted, or put into tubs or boxes large enough to allow them to be just covered with soil. It need not be particularly good soil since it is only required to keep the roots warm and moist.

In a temperature of 16 °C or more shoots will appear quite quickly and in a few weeks it will be possible to start gathering bright pink or red leaf stalks which can be broken out cleanly close to the crown of the rhubarb plant. Continue to gather until the root has no more growth to offer when it should be discarded.

Chicory is grown from seed sown outdoors in spring or early summer and *seakale* can be grown either from seed or from root cuttings planted outdoors in spring. In late October or early November the plants are dug up, the leaves cut off, and the roots packed together in some cool but sheltered place, such as beneath the north-facing wall of a building, where, if covered with soil, peat, or sand, they will come to no harm for months.

As required, they are potted in boxes of any convenient size, the roots packed almost shoulder to shoulder, the right way up and barely covered. Seakale usually makes branching roots and it is only the thickest central root and its crown that should be forced. Smaller side roots, known as thongs, can be cut off, tied in small bundles, and replaced in the moist sand, peat or soil, to be replanted outdoors as root cuttings in the spring. Since the roots must be planted the right way up and, once severed, it is difficult to tell one end from the other, it is wise to indicate this when severing them. This can be done by making a sloping cut at the bottom end of each root and a square cut at the top.

The roots to be forced, if kept moist in a temperature of 16 °C or more, will soon start to produce shoots and these can be severed close to the crown as soon as they reach reasonable size, say a length of 15–20 cm.

9 Fruits

Many kinds of fruit can be grown in greenhouses but the days when space could be found for plums and cherries or heat provided for pineapples and bananas are gone. For all practical purposes the choice now lies among six kinds: grapes; peaches, and their smooth-skinned allies nectarines; strawberries; melons; and apricots, with figs as a possible seventh option, though the demand for them is small. Oranges can also be grown, though mainly for ornamental purposes.

Vines

In many ways these are the most rewarding of greenhouse fruits and vineries have been a feature of gardens ever since glasshouses were improved sufficiently in construction to make vine cultivation possible. But therein lies the rub. It was 'vineries' that were built, not greenhouses for multitudinous purposes, for the grape vine is not a good mixer and, if it is to be grown successfully, it must be allowed to call the tune in any glasshouse in which it is planted. In winter it must be cold, which will not suit more tender companions, in summer it must be allowed to cover the roof space with its abundant foliage, which will not suit other plants that also enjoy the sun, and it will so fill the greenhouse border with its roots (unless they are channelled outdoors, a solution which only shifts the problem elsewhere) that nothing else can be grown in them. So if you decide to grow grapes be ready to call your greenhouse, however small, a vinery and run it primarily for the benefit of the grapes, using it for other plants only so far as this can be done without detriment to the vines.

It is possible, but not easy, to grow vines in tubs or very large pots. By far the best way is to plant in a specially prepared border either inside or outside the greenhouse. The advantage of having the border inside is that everything is then under control, even the temperature of the soil and the amount of water that falls on to it. The advantage of an outside border is that the need for watering is greatly reduced since most of the vine's requirements will be met by normal rainfall, but the border may be too wet at some periods and there will be no easy way of warming it up to encourage early growth. The border should be the length of the house and about 2 m wide.

Grapes do not require high temperatures at any time. Many varieties can be grown successfully without any heat other than that provided by the sun. Even those choice varieties that do require extra warmth to start them early and/or allow them to go on ripening late will only need this for brief periods in spring and early autumn. At no time is there any advantage to be gained by letting the thermometer run above 26 °C and a range from March to August of 15–21 °C will suit all grapes well.

What they do need far more than extra warmth is abundance of light and air. The vinery must be in the sunniest, most open place possible with plenty of ventilators both at the ridge and in the sides so that air can flow through the house freely in summer when the weather is hot, and again in winter when the vines are resting.

The soil needs to be good, moderately alkaline, with plenty of calcium. Fairly rich fibrous loam is the best base with the addition of well rotted manure and a good sprinkling of ground chalk or limestone. It is not desirable that the vine roots should ramble freely, so if possible they should be contained by a wall around the

border or by a sheet of strong polythene buried vertically to form a barrier at least 60 cm deep.

One vine can be trained to fill a large vinery but many home gardeners will prefer to have several varieties, each restricted to a single main stem or 'rod' with the grapes borne on relatively short annual side growths from it. In this case the vines should be planted about 1 m apart along the side walls of the greenhouse, if it is span-roofed, or along the low front wall if it is a lean-to. Either way a single stem from each vine will be trained straight up to the ridge and will remain throughout the life of the vine, but will not itself ever bear any fruit, which will be restricted to the side growths from it.

Young vines should be purchased in pots or other containers during the autumn or winter, shortened to 1 m, and planted in February or March just as they are starting to grow. Contrary to usual practice when planting from containers, the ball of roots and soil should not be left undisturbed; instead, much of the soil should be carefully shaken off and the coiled roots even more carefully disentangled so that they can be spread out evenly in the new soil. If this precaution is not taken there is danger that the roots will remain in the pot ball, refusing to grow out of it or taking a long time to do so.

Because the roots must be disturbed in this way, the plants must be watered with special care from the outset. Each vine may produce several shoots but only one, the strongest (which is usually the uppermost) is retained, the others being rubbed out. This stem is tied to wires strained horizontally about 25 cm below the glass, the wires themselves spaced 40 cm apart. When this first shoot has grown 2 m its tip is pinched out to check it and give it time to thicken a little and another shoot from it is trained up to the ridge of the house. All side growths have their tips pinched out at the second leaf. In winter this first main stem is shortened to about 2 m and the following spring the uppermost shoot from this is trained to the ridge, where it is pinched to stop further extension. This completes the formation of the main rod, which, in subsequent years, merely gets thicker but never grows any longer.

Meanwhile side growths are being trained along the wires each side of the main rod, and so about 40 cm apart. It is on these that fruits are borne in summer, and each winter each side growth is cut back to two dormant growth buds (about 5 cm). In this way stumps or 'spurs' develop on the main rod, from each of which one new side growth (lateral) is allowed to grow each spring. Once formed, the vine gets no larger and it carries just the same number of new laterals, and, hopefully, bunches of fruit each year.

During spring the young shoots, one from each spur, are tied to the training wires. The tip of each is pinched out either two leaves beyond the first flower truss or when it is 60–90 cm long if no flower truss has

Opposite: Black Hamburg grapes

been produced by then. This prevents the side growths of adjacent vines from overlapping too much and so producing too dense a cover of foliage.

When the flowers are developing the temperature can, with advantage, be a few degrees higher; and the air can be fairly dry so that pollen is easily distributed. This can be helped by tapping the vines or dusting the flowers lightly with a soft camel hair paint brush. Fertilization is essential if berries are to form.

Provided all goes well, there will probably be too many berries per bunch for full development. For some purposes, wine making for example, this matters little, but if the largest possible grapes are required for dessert, the bunches must be thinned. This is done with special sharp-pointed scissors two or three weeks after the berries are formed but while they are still very small. Up to half the berries may be snipped out, especially the inside ones and those towards the end of the bunch. It is a tedious job requiring considerable patience and care.

From spring to autumn the soil must be kept nicely moist. It can become drier in autumn but should be given a very thorough soaking in late winter before the vines start to grow again to make sure that the subsoil, as well as the surface soil, is satisfactorily moist.

Winter pruning, when the laterals are shortened to two buds, is done as soon as the leaves have fallen. To hasten leaf fall once the grapes have been picked, all heating is discontinued and the ventilators are kept wide open. After pruning the vine rods can be partially untied so that their ends hang down and they can be left like this until growth has started from all the spurs in spring. The purpose of this operation is to prevent the rising sap rushing to the top of the rod, so making the upper buds start into growth long before those lower down. Once growth has started evenly all down the rod it can be raised again and tied in its normal position.

Vines are started by closing the ventilators and, if necessary, using artificial heat to raise the temperature to about 13 °C. This can be done as early as January or as late as March according to variety and the time at which it is hoped the grapes will ripen.

Vines require annual feeding. In late winter the bed should have a sprinkling of a compound fertilizer such as National Growmore or a special vine fertilizer, followed by a good mulch of well-rotted manure, decayed garden refuse or spent mushroom compost. A second light application of fertilizer can be given in early June to help summer growth and berry development.

Vines can suffer from mealy bugs, which suck the sap from stems and leaves and protect themselves with a white, mealy covering. This prevents sprays getting to them but they can be removed with a stiff paint brush dipped in an insecticidal solution. It also helps if loose bark is removed in winter by rubbing the hand up and down the main rods.

Mildew can be troublesome, especially if ventilation is poor or growth is too crowded. It can be checked by spraying in summer with dinocap or benomyl.

There are many vine varieties but some are not easy to grow. Black Hamburg, with black grapes, and Buckland Sweetwater, with green berries, are two that are reliable and satisfactory. Gros Colmar has very large black berries but is not top quality. Madresfield Court is one of the best flavoured grapes that is also reasonably easy to grow.

Peaches and Nectarines

These two fruits, though different in appearance, require identical treatment since the nectarine is simply a smooth-skinned sort of mutation from the peach. Both are fairly hardy but they flower early when the weather outdoors is often wet and cold, and the blossom sets badly even if it is not actually destroyed. Another difficulty out of doors is that some of the most delicious varieties ripen slowly and are often not ready for picking by the time autumn brings the season to a close. Under glass, even without any artificial heat, it is possible to protect the blossom adequately, get an excellent set of fruit, and ripen it all by the end of September.

The easiest way to grow peaches and nectarines under glass is to plant them in a bed of good soil. If the house is of the lean-to type the bed can be against the back wall and the trees can be trained to wires on this, but it should be a sunny wall. If the house is of the span-roofed type the trees can be planted close to either wall (or both if preferred) and the branches trained fanwise on wires strained lengthwise about 15 cm below the glass.

The soil should be fertile and reasonably porous, with some manure or garden compost mixed in and a generous dusting of bone meal. Trees are best planted in autumn but, if purchased in containers, can be planted at any time provided this can be done without serious root damage and without the soil falling off the roots. Ideally trees should be spaced 5 m apart but in small greenhouses this is not practicable and a couple of trees can be accommodated in a 4 m house spaced 2.5 m apart, but they will require more restrictive pruning.

If fan-trained trees are purchased choose those that have no central stem except for the short main stem or trunk from which all branches radiate more or less evenly. The reason for this precaution is that a long vertical stem will tend to take a disproportionate share of sap and so will always grow faster and produce more side growths than its less favourably placed competitors.

Peaches and nectarines flower and fruit on young stems which were formed the previous year, so pruning is designed to maintain a constant succession of replacement growth. In the early years some stems are allowed to go on extending and branching to form the main framework of the tree, evenly spread out and spaced 20–30 cm apart. Once the available space has been filled, these foundation branches will remain more or less permanently unless some become so badly damaged or diseased that it is necessary to cut them right out, in which case they should be replaced as quickly as possible with new branches.

Fruit is not borne on these main stems, but on the side growths produced from them. Those retained for the purpose one year will flower the following spring, ripen their fruit that summer and be cut out in the autumn or early winter. Meanwhile other new shoots, known as laterals, will have been retained and trained to take their place, but not too many of them, all surplus shoots being removed at an early stage. It is necessary to allow the young terminal growth to remain to draw sap through the fruiting stem, and maybe a second shoot somewhere near its centre point with the same object, but the really important thing is to look for, and retain, a new growth as near the bottom of each fruiting stem as possible. This is the replacement lateral, the one that will be retained when the fruit-bearing lateral is cut out at the end of the year and will be trained in its place, for that is what must be done with all the new growth. It must be tied in neatly to strained wires or trellis work, keeping as even a spacing as possible so that no growth gets in the way of another or deprives it of light. Well trained peaches and nectarines look most attractive and are splendid examples of the pruner's art.

Apart from this special method of pruning (which is equally applicable to Morello cherries and these will grow in the shade) the cultivation of peaches and nectarines is much the same as that of any other deciduous fruit trees under glass. Trees must be allowed to rest in winter, when ventilators can be opened and all heating discontinued. In late winter borders need to be well soaked to make good the water reserves in the subsoil and as soon after that as is desired, ventilators can be closed and a little artificial heat used, if necessary, to start the trees growing. When the flowers are fully open they are dusted very gently each day with a soft camel hair paint brush to distribute ripe pollen and so ensure that the flowers are well fertilized and plenty of fruit sets. Alternatively the training wires can be tapped or twanged like banjo strings to jar the stems and so shake out the pollen.

It is quite possible that too many fruits will set in which case the surplus can be removed a few weeks later. There is no way to make up a deficiency of fruits and no drawback in starting with too many provided they are reduced adequately in good time. Thinning out starts when the little fruits are of marble size but should not be completed until the stones are well formed, a condition that can be checked by cutting one or two fruits open. The reason for this slight delay is that there is often a fairly heavy natural fall of fruits while the stones are forming. It can be aggravated by too much or too little water and also by sudden and considerable falls in temperature. Aim to keep the soil nicely moist throughout the season of growth, roughly from March to late September, after which it will do no harm to let the border become a good deal drier. Aim also for a temperature range between 13 and 21 °C. Higher temperatures may cause leaf scorching and attacks of red spider mites, and lower temperatures will check growth. Provided these temperatures are assured, ventilation can be free with advantage to the trees.

The final thinning should leave 20–30 fruits per m², rather more for nectarines which are usually smaller than peaches. Picking should commence as soon as fruits are ripe and usually it is possible to spread it over several weeks.

Peaches can also be grown in tubs or very large pots but it is not as easy as in beds since the plants starve or become dry far more easily and require more constant and skilled attention. Pot plants are usually allowed to form small bushes, with the main branches spread evenly all round and not spread out fanwise in a single plane. In other respects pruning is the same as for trained trees, with regular removal of unwanted shoots but retention of sufficient young growth to replace the previous fruiting laterals at the end of the year.

The first indication of attack by red spider mites will be a greyish or bronzy mottling of the leaves. If the undersides are examined with a hand lens the tiny reddish mites will be seen mainly along the angles of the veins. Remedies include spraying with clear water and giving increased ventilation but these may not prove sufficient and if not trees should be sprayed with derris, resmethrin or dimenthoate, but not while fruits are ripening.

Good varieties of peach are Amsden, early; Peregrine and Rochester, mid-season; and Sea Eagle, late. Good nectarines are Early Rivers, early; Elruge and Lord Napier, mid-season; Pineapple and Rivers Orange, late.

Strawberries

In many ways strawberries are the most practical fruit for the home greenhouse. They take up little space, are easily grown in pots, which need not be more than 15 cm in diameter, and they are best renewed annually which, at any rate for a few years, can be done with home-produced plants.

There are two possibilities: the usual one of growing an early ripening summer strawberry such as Cambridge Vigour or Grandee to give a crop a few weeks earlier than could be obtained out of doors even with the aid of cloches; and the other less common one of going for an autumn crop with the aid of a remontant or perpetual-fruiting variety such as Gento. In either case the plants must be produced by rooting strong runners as early as possible the previous summer. Runners should only be selected on sturdy plants that are cropping well; only the first plantlet on each runner should be used and no more than six runners retained on any one plant, however good. The plantlets are pegged into small pots filled with a good soil- or peat-based potting mixture and sunk to their rims in the soil around the parent strawberry plants, where it is convenient to peg the runners into them. Pieces of wire about 8 cm long, bent like hairpins, make suitable 'pegs'. The rest of each runner, beyond the pegged plantlet, is cut off. Runners pegged in June or early July should be sufficiently well rooted by late July or early August to be separated from their parent plants, and removed, in their pots, to a frame or sheltered place. A week or so later the pots will be full of roots and the plants can be repotted directly into the 15 cm pots in which they will fruit. They should have a fairly rich soil-based mixture of the John Innes No. 2 type or, if a peat-based mixture is preferred, they must be fed directly the pots are full of roots.

All through the autumn and winter the strawberries can remain in a frame or sheltered place outdoors, or if no such places are available they can stand in a greenhouse, which is best unheated until January. From then onwards the plants, either in small batches or all together, can be started into growth by maintaining a minimum temperature of 10 °C rising by day to 15 °C or more. If no artificial heat is to be used it is best to wait until March and then raise the necessary temperature by closing the ventilators.

Plants will want sufficient water throughout to keep the soil moist but not sodden. Even those in fairly rich soil composts are likely to require supplementary feeding with liquid fertilizer at weekly intervals from about early May. Plants need good light and are usually happiest standing on a shelf quite close to the glass, but as the summer approaches they can be shaded from strong sunshine. When the flowers are wide open they can be fertilized by dusting them lightly with a soft camel hair paint brush and this should be repeated daily until the flowers commence to fade.

As soon as the fruits commence to swell, the temperature can be raised a few degrees to encourage even further growth. They should be picked as soon as they are nicely coloured, as picking helps to speed the swelling and ripening of later fruits. When all the strawberries are gathered the plants should be destroyed. A slightly different routine is necessary for late-fruiting remontant varieties. These can stand in an open frame outdoors until September when they should be brought into an unheated greenhouse and placed as near the glass as possible. Extra warmth will only be necessary to disperse surplus moisture and keep the temperature above 10 °C.

Every few years it is desirable to purchase entirely new stock from a reliable source as there is danger of virus infections building up in number and severity in any strawberry bed that is not under expert surveillance.

Ogen Melon

Melons

These fit neatly into the greenhouse regime as their cultivation resembles in many respects that of tomatoes and cucumbers. Melons love sunshine, must have their female flowers fertilized, and usually cannot mature more than four large fruits per plant though some of the small-fruited varieties can produce more.

Seed can be sown any time from January to early May but since melons like temperatures between 16 and 20 °C, early plants can be expensive and they are also much more difficult to manage because of the short days. In moderately heated greenhouses mid-March is a good time to start. Sow seeds singly or in pairs in small pots in a good soil- or peat-based seed mixture and germinate in a temperature of 18 °C. Reduce seedlings to one per pot and, as soon as the soil is nicely filled with roots, plant on mounds of rich soil prepared exactly as described for cucumbers.

Training is also similar to that of cucumbers, the main stem being taken up under the rafters towards the ridge of the house, and side stems tied out more or less horizontally on wires strained at least 15 cm below the glass. The main stem should have its tip pinched out when it is about 2 m long and side shoots are similarly stopped when 30 cm long.

If plants commence to flower while still fairly small all female flowers, which are attached to a small embryo fruit in contrast to the thin-stemmed male flowers, are picked off. The objective is to get several female flowers at an almost identical stage of development on a sturdy plant and fertilize them all on the same day with pollen from male flowers. In this way none gets a start over any of the others and it is likely that all will mature. If one fruit does get ahead of all the rest it will monopolize the sap flow and starve out the others. Fertilization should be done around mid-day. The simplest way is to pick a fully developed male flower and invert it over the open female flower so that ripe pollen falls on the sticky stigma. This can be repeated several times on successive days. A few days after fertilization it will be possible to tell whether it has been successful as fertilized fruits will commence to swell quite rapidly while those that are not fertilized will turn yellow and fall off.

Melon plants are watered and fed like cucumbers but they are not shaded at all. As the fruits gain in size they must be supported and special melon nets, like tiny hammocks, can be purchased for the purpose and slung from the training wires.

The ripeness of melons can be judged to some extent by the sweet smell they develop, and also by the softening of the fruit, especially at the flower end. The ripening process can continue after cutting but the best flavour is developed when fruits can ripen fully on the plant.

Good varieties are Charentais and Blenheim Orange, both large-fruited, and Ogen, small-fruited.

Apricots

The best place to grow apricots is trained against the sunny back wall of a south-facing conservatory or lean-to. Here the trees will have space to grow and all the warmth and light they love. Such trees are best fan-trained and should be spaced 5 m apart though it is possible to grow them a little closer than this.

A good and well-drained loam soil, with a liberal quantity of well-rotted manure or decayed compost mixed with it, will suit apricots well. They will also require an annual mulch in spring with manure or a manure substitute as well as feeding with liquid fertilizer or foliar feeding in summer.

Unlike peaches, apricots bear on stems that are in their second year or more. The object of pruning is not to produce a constant succession of new growth for fruiting, as with peaches, but to prevent the older growth from becoming overcrowded.

Much of the work can be done in summer by rubbing out young shoots for which there is clearly no room and shortening others to about six leaves directly the first flush of growth is over. In the winter some of these side shoots can be left at this length, some shortened still more to two or three buds, some cut right out. As these age, a few of the older branches can be removed, but not more than one or two at a time, to be replaced by young growth, so maintaining the vigour of the tree.

Feeding and watering are as advised for peaches and nectarines and trees can be started into growth in the same way; but apricots are usually grown without artificial heat, the greenhouse providing the extra protection and warmth which is all the apricot requires.

Good varieties are Alfred, Hemskerke and Moorpark.

Figs

These can take up too much room to be very popular with the home gardener but their foliage is highly ornamental and a fig tree trained over the back wall of a sunny conservatory can be most attractive, though not necessarily outstandingly profitable. Unlike many fruit trees, figs do not require rich soil, which makes them grow too strongly, and for the same reason it helps to confine their roots by means similar to those described for vines. One fig tree will cover at least a 5 m length of wall, and a border 1 m wide running the length of the wall will be ample. The border should be well drained with a good layer of hard rubble 60–90 cm down to help surplus water to drain away quickly.

Figs like sunshine and warmth. Unlike hardier fruits, there is no need to expose them to cold in the winter by throwing open the ventilators. On the contrary, if the temperature never falls below freezing it is possible that two crops can be ripened in one year:

one by midsummer from fruits that were formed the previous summer and remained on the tree all winter; the second from fruits that were formed the previous autumn, many at the ends of young stems, and which also overwintered but at a smaller size. These fruits should be ready to pick in September.

Trees are trained as fans, the branches tied to wires strained horizontally along the wall. The object is to maintain a constant supply of healthy young, or fairly young, growth and get rid of old branches that are losing their vigour and ability to produce new growth. Most of the work is done in autumn and is a thinning operation but there can be summer pruning as well to get rid of badly placed or overcrowded young stems.

The soil must be kept moist throughout the year but far less water will be required in winter than in summer when the large and abundant foliage makes figs rather thirsty plants.

The favourite variety is Brown Turkey.

Calamondin Orange *(see overleaf)*

Oranges

Oranges are quite large evergreen shrubs with handsome shining green leaves and white, sweetly scented flowers. They are considerably hardier than most people realise, and can be grown outdoors in Britain from about late May until early October, after which they will require protection from frost but little more if it is ornament rather than edible fruit one is after. The difficulty, when little or no artificial heat is used, is that no flowers are likely to open much before the end of June and that is too late for fruits to ripen the same summer. This does not matter if the oranges are being grown primarily for ornament as the immature fruits will hang all winter, green but quite attractive, and will ripen the following year. However, for good eating quality it is necessary to get quicker and uninterrupted ripening and this may involve some extra warmth from February to March to get flowers open in May and then more warmth in autumn to complete the ripening of the fruits. It is unlikely to be economical but it can be interesting.

The simplest way to grow oranges is in very large pots or tubs in a moderately rich soil-based compost such as John Innes No. 2. This enables them to be moved indoors or out as required with a minimum of fuss and no check to growth. At all times oranges require as much sunshine as is available and they should be watered normally, never allowed to become dry at any time but also not kept constantly sodden. From early May until late August a little fertilizer can be added to the water every seven to ten days; for they are fairly hungry plants.

Pruning is mainly a matter of thinning, best done in summer, to get rid of unprofitable growth and keep bushes open so that air can circulate freely and sunshine can reach the leaves and fruits. The pests most likely to be troublesome are mealy bugs and scale insects. Spraying is not always effective against these and it may be necessary to sponge the insects off with soapy water or a solution of diazinon or malathion.

In warm countries where oranges are grown commerciallly there are numerous varieties but in Britain it is seldom that any of these are available. The Calomondin Orange, really a species from the Philippines named *Citrus mitis*, is offered as an ornamental plant. Its fruits are too small to be of much use for eating but they are freely produced and look most attractive on the bushes. The best way to get large edible oranges is probably to raise them from seed which germinates freely in a temperature of 15–18 °C, but it is impossible to be certain that the seedlings will all be alike, or that any of them will really be the most suitable for cultivation in our relatively dull and cool climate.

143

General Index

144

The Conservatory at Syon House, Brentford, built in the 1820s. Far more glass was used then than earlier in designing buildings for plants; and this one was originally heated by air ducts beneath the floor (see Introduction).

Index of Plant Names

Begonia manicata, *one of the numerous different flowering begonias (*see pp. 43–4)

Overleaf: the author's conservatory in full bloom – a model for the ambitious.